The Reivers

The Reivers

The Story of the Border Reivers

ALISTAIR MOFFAT

BIRLINN

This edition first published in 2008 by
Birlinn Limited
West Newington House
10 Newington Road
Edinburgh
EH9 1QS

www.birlinn.co.uk

Reprinted 2010, 2011

ISBN: 978 1 84158 674 8

eBook ISBN: 978 0 85790 115 6

British Library Cataloguing-in-Publication Data
A catalogue record for this book is available from the British Library

Typeset by Hewer Text UK Ltd, Edinburgh
Printed and bound by CPI Cox & Wyman, Reading, RG1 8EX

I have spent many happy months filming in the Borders, making the series on the Border Reivers for Border Television, and this book is for all those who helped me do it and have had such a grand time doing it. I hope that Fiona Armstrong, Terry Black, Annie Buckland, Chris Buckland, Paul Caddick, Livvy Ellis, Valerie Lyon, Louise Maving, Paddy Merrall, Eric Robson, Eric Scott-Parker, Allan Tarn and Ken Wynne all enjoy the book as much as I've enjoyed working with them.

Contents

List of Illustrations

Acknowledgements

First I want to thank Hugh Andrew of Birlinn for asking me to write this. I have greatly enjoyed working with him and his team. Too rare in publishing, they are dynamic, business-like and cheery. Birlinn makes authors feel good, even important, even if they're not particularly. And that's also too rare a trick in publishing. Thanks to Graeme Leonard for a brisk and painless edit, and to all my patient readers. Walter Elliot had something of a family interest in this one. And finally my thanks to lovely Liz Hanson for her superb photographs. They are an adornment – as ever.

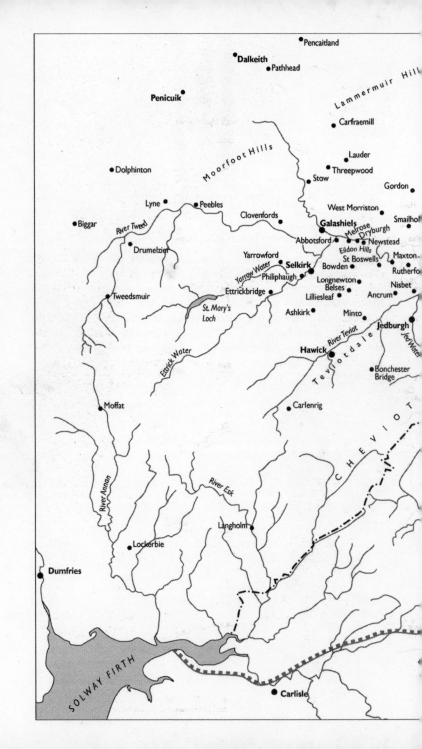

NORTH SEA

St Abbs
Coldingham
Eyemouth
Abbey St. Bathans
Burnmouth
Chirnside
Berwick Upon Tweed
Duns
Tweedmouth
Marchmont
Swinton
Lindisfarne
River Tweed
Eccles
Hume
Coldstream
Farne Islands
Pallinsburn
Ednam
Wark
Carham
Branxton
Iso
Milfield
Bamburgh
Sprouston
River Till
Caverton Mill
Kirk Yetholm
Eckford
Town Yetholm
Yeavering
Linton
Chillingham
Morebattle
Gateshaw

L L S

River Aln
Alnwick
Carter Bar
Alnmouth

River Coquet

River Rede
Redesdale
Otterburn

Wansbeck

Hadrian's Wall

Newcastle
Upon Tyne

River Tyne

0   5   10   15   20   25 kilometres

Part I

1

Moonlight

The night wind whistled out of the west, sudden squalls spattering the ramparts, keeping the sentries moving, stamping their feet against the November chill. When the clouds scudded away into the formless mirk and the sky cleared, the moon lit the pale winter landscape. Bewcastle Waste stretched away to the north of the old fort, and beyond it lay Liddesdale, Teviotdale and trouble.

Leaning on their spears, the sentries peered into the darkness, searching the horizon, scanning the dark heads of the fells. Sometimes a shape seemed to move but another pair of eyes saw it was nothing. The cold and the wet – and the sleepless hour – could numb the senses and make a fool of the most experienced soldier. The Captain had set four troopers on the night watch but allowed only one brazier between them. While two warmed themselves, the others walked the rampart, watching for raiders, for horsemen who might appear out of nowhere, from any direction. But it was a foul night, surely even the most desperate thieves on the Border would stay snug by their fire.

Ten miles to the north, silently snaking through the hills, they were coming. Walter Scott of Buccleuch led 120 riders up over the pass at Whitrope, their ponies looking for the glint of the burn and the narrow path beside it. There was none of the martial jingle of heavily armed cavalry as the column wound its way quietly down through the willow scrub to the mosses of Liddesdale. Sodden now, but much better than nothing, cloaks were wound tight against the midnight chill. Looming out of the darkness, off to their right, Scott and his captains could see the black shape of the castle at Hermitage. No lights showed and if there was a watch, it was only nominal and probably looking the other way. The riders stayed on the east bank of the burn and moved silently on. No patrol would come out of the castle gate but it would not do to embarrass the Keeper by making the presence of a passing raiding party obvious. Only a short way downstream Whithaugh and the tryst with the Armstrongs were waiting.

At the end of September, having left them out on the fells as late as he dared, Willie Routledge and his herd-laddies had ingathered their cattle for the winter. The high summer pastures of the Bewcastle fells had begun to die back and the ground around the sikes and burns had churned to clinging clatch. After cropping for winter hay, Routledge's inbye fields had recovered and his cows would keep their summer condition on through the turn of the year and maybe beyond, if only the incessant rains of last winter would hold off. And his prized ponies were fat and sleek, swinging big grass-bellies in their winter coats.

All four sentries heard it. Each looked up and out to the north. And then at each other. Birdcalls in the dead of a winter's night? Only when their roost is disturbed. Was it a fox – or something more? The sentries waited for clouds to clear the full moon, holding their breath for another shriek from out in the waste, straining to focus in the formless dark. The Captain slept warm in his chamber; who would be bold enough to rattle down the rickety wooden stairs and wake him because a bird had called? Moments passed. No other alarm. Whatever it was had moved on, nothing of any moment. It came on to rain, again.

Sim's Jock Armstrong was in no doubt. Simplest was best, particularly on a filthy night like this. The old reiver wheeled his pony to come alongside Scott's, his eyes were hooded by the dripping rim of his steel bonnet but his rasping voice was clear enough. Scott and his riders should cross the border at Kershopefoot and then strike directly south towards the Bewcastle Fells. And they should come back on exactly the same track. The ponies would find their own scent and their own hoofprints in the dark. And once they had regained the Scottish side, everything should be left to the Armstrongs. They would be waiting, and not even Scott would see them as he passed. It was their ground and they knew its every brake and bush. By early morning all would be done, one way or another, and it would be done well, would it not? Sim's Jock and his riders would earn their cut. Walter Scott smiled and nodded. The board was set – let the game begin.

In the hay barn, the Routledge's dogs dozed in their own body-warmth, cocking an occasional ear as rats scratched and scuttled in the rafters. Bielded from the breeze by the farm steading, most of the ponies were quiet, some sleeping on their feet, all waiting patiently for the night to pass. And the black cattle snuffled in small groups, nosing around the inbye fields, nibbling now and again at the cold and bitter winter grass. One or two splashed across the burn to the farther pasture. The beasts at night somehow seemed peaceful to Willie Routledge, their steaming warmth consoling, their herding instincts a comfort. He and his boys had had a good summer with plenty of calves to sell on at Brampton Market and some to keep through the winter. Up on the shielings, the summertowns, the sun had shone and the good grass grown up through the yellow tussocks of the old. Next year would be even better. If only they could get through the long dark winter stretching out before them.

Towards midnight mist crept over the moonlit landscape, muffling sound, its damp chill seeping through the sentries' warmest cloaks. Beyond the ramparts the world slept, cold and still under a grey blanket. Only wakefulness kept the men warm; it was easy to lean on a spear and nod into a doze. But to allow that was to numb the bones for the rest of the long night. Activity, doing their duty, was what helped and after all Bewcastle Fort had been built and regularly repaired for good reason. It guarded a well-trodden byway into the west marches of England. To its south were vulnerable farmsteads, valuable herds and poorly defended villages.

They were in England now. Nothing could disguise their purpose as Scott's riders kicked their ponies on up the rising ground above the Kershope Burn. They would circle well to the west of Bewcastle Fort. Its new Captain, Steven Ellis, was his name, was reckoned to be more than usually anxious to please his masters in London, old Francis Walsingham and the rest. No courtly fawner or sponger, he was a professional soldier who saw his posting to Elizabeth's northern frontier as an opportunity to distinguish himself in action rather than words, to become part of what the Warden of the East Marches, Robert Carey, called 'a stirring world'. Ellis' troopers were also newcomers to the Border and none had yet compromised their loyalty. Time would surely change that, but for the moment Walter Scott would be cautious, not wishing to alert the Bewcastle garrison and have them clatter out of the fort and after him. Willie Routledge's cows were what he and his men wanted, and anything else they could carry off besides.

Scouts reported back. Dismounting, tying their ponies in the thickets down by the burn, they had crept up a ridge above the farm, seen no light, no watchers, noted that the herd was grazing the inbye fields and noticed some handsome nags in amongst them. Speed and stealth now. Scott's men were well armed, bristling with swords, daggers, pistols and spears. They wore steel caps and thick padded jerkins while their captains and a few others were protected by backs and breasts armour. It was not Willie Routledge and his sons who worried the riders but the long road home and the real possibility that the Bewcastle garrison would give chase and that they might have to cut their way through to the border and beyond.

Despite carrying 18 to 20 stone of kit and man, the ponies moved nimbly over the tussocks towards the farmhouse, keeping it between them and the cattle. Suddenness would unsettle the beasts and raise the house. Scott had split his force. Most waited to round up the cows and oxen and catch the ponies while a dozen dismounted. With Scott leading, they crept towards the thatched farmhouse like foxes.

Too experienced and too wily for needless drama, Scott lifted the latch and tiptoed inside. By the glow of the dying fire his men could see the sleeping family become restive – until their leader woke them by holding his pistol to Willie Routledge's head. A moment's uproar was immediately suppressed by some rough handling. All were quickly dragged and bundled into a corner of the room as Scott went out to supervise the roundup. The men raked around the farmhouse for valuables as Routledge swore and cursed at them. One pulled out a cowering, squealing daughter by the hair, forced her to kneel by the fire and held a dagger to her throat to encourage her father and terrified family to keep quiet.

Out in the fields the raiders caught up the ponies in halters and gathered the cattle into a tight pack. Once they were ready to move off, Scott's men tied up all of the Routledges and doused their fire. Let them shiver and make no signal. Anything to slow down the likely pursuit. Across rough ground and in the winter dark, cows were slow to drive and one or two would slip through the screen of ponies and need to be herded back.

All had been managed quickly and with scarcely a raised voice. No sound carried as far as the ramparts at Bewcastle, its sentries saw nothing amiss in the November night. But news was travelling. Young Edward Routledge had wriggled free of his bonds, untied the others and while his father and his brothers began quickly to build a beacon to blaze and raise the countryside, he ran, stumbling and falling, over the moorland to the soldiers and their fort.

Scott did not delay, riding up and down, hurrying his men. They had lifted about 40 head of cows and oxen and 20 ponies, most of them mares. The Routledge farm had yielded little in the way of valuables and no man was over-encumbered. But goading and whacking the lowing cows into a trot was difficult – and noisy. At this pace the border was perhaps an hour away, the dawn another hour beyond that.

Pinpointed in the distance, Edward saw the sentries' brazier and began breathlessly to holler and whoop. By the time he had scrambled over the old Roman ditches and ramparts and reached the outer gate at Bewcastle Fort, its Captain was awake and buckling on his breast-plate. Over to the west the Routledge's beacon crackled into life and lit the night sky. Within a few minutes 40 troopers were in the saddle and Edward on his way back to the farm with spare mounts. It was Scott they were after. Routledge knew for certain, and he would most likely be on the trail to the Kershope Burn and the Scottish side.

Even though those leading the stolen ponies could make better time, Walter Scott knew that his raiding party needed to keep all its strength together. If caught up, he would turn and fight while some of his riders kept the cattle from stampede. If they scattered into the darkness and the unfenced moorland, what was the point? Scott rode at the rear, often turning and straining to listen, screening out the grunt and low of the beasts as the herd moved northwards, nearer to Scotland and safety. Not that the frontier itself would protect him, government officials on both sides had the right to pursue raiders across it regardless of jurisdiction. Scott wanted to reach the Kershope Burn because the Armstrongs waited there, well hidden.

Captain Ellis and his troopers hurried along the trail, not far behind and not waiting for Routledge and his boys or anyone else. The rain was holding off, the moon glowed pale as it set and the ponies would somehow find good enough ground to trot. Often they could make out the hoofprints of cows and horses in the muddy sikes. They were gaining, closing fast on the raiders.

Willie Routledge and his sons followed on quickly through the half-light, hoping to catch up the Captain's troop before they engaged with Scott and his men. Willie hated the taunt, 'a Routledge – every man's prey', and was determined to show his family was no soft touch.

Against the paler blue of the dawning sky, on the ridge above the Kershope Burn, Ellis could make out the silhouettes of the raiding party and the cattle clearly. And just faintly he could hear them. The captain would catch them all, red-handed, as they stumbled downhill and across the water. His men spurred on.

Scott could hear them coming. Some of the Bewcastle troopers had booted their ponies into a canter. Silly. Could easily break a leg. But they might be lucky and be upon them soon. The leading raiders were skittering down to the burn, and breaking his silence, Scott roared for support to come up to him on the ridge. The cows splashed over the burn, riders whacking them on. It was difficult to know how close Ellis was. When all were across safely and moving into the woods on the Scottish side, Scott turned his men downhill and followed. At that moment the Bewcastle troop burst out of the mirk, only 40 yards away. Now at the banks of the burn, Scott's men scrambled over. But as Ellis' troop found the level ground, scores of riders erupted from nowhere. The Armstrongs had broken cover. Four Bewcastle men were immediately shot out of the saddle. Many others were badly wounded and the troop routed before their Captain had time to rally them to him. Careless of the grey light and the uneven ground, his men scattered in all directions.

Scott turned in the saddle to look back at the melee. The Armstrong ambush had been expertly sprung, the cows and horses were theirs and a good night's work had been done. On the high ground above the Kershope Burn Willie Routledge and his sons sat on their ponies and watched. If only the young Captain had waited, Willie would have told him why the raiders had returned on the same road. He could have warned them what was waiting.

These things happened. In November 1588 Walter Scott of Buccleuch rode out of his stronghold of Branxholme, near Hawick, with 120 reivers. He had made a tryst with the Armstrongs of Whithaugh in Liddesdale. Here is the full text of the complaint later made:

> Captain Ellis and the surname of the Routledges in Bewcastle complain upon the said Laird of Buccleuch, the Laird of Chesame, the Laird of Whithaugh and their accomplices to the number of 120 horsemen arrayed with jacks, steel caps, spears, guns, lances and pistols, swords and daggers purposely mustered by Buccleuch, who broke the house of Willie Routledge, took 40 cows and oxen, 20 horses and mares, and also laid an ambush to slay the soldiers and others who should follow the fray, whereby they cruelly slew and murdered Mr Rowden, Nichol Tweddle, Jeffrey Nartbie and Edward Stainton, soldiers; maimed sundry others and drove 12 horses and mares, whereof they crave redress.

The raid is the core of this story. It is the essence of all the extraordinary events which took place from the fifteenth to the early seventeenth century on either side of the border between England and Scotland. Thousands of raids like Walter Scott's foray to Bewcastle were run, often several on one winter's night. They formed the focus of a unique criminal society. Over an enormous area of Britain, perhaps a twelfth of the landmass of the island, there existed a people who lived beyond the laws of England and Scotland, who ignored the persistent efforts of central government to impose order, who took their social form and norms from the ancient conventions of tribalism, who invented ever more sophisticated variants on theft, cattle rustling, murder and extortion – and gave them names, like 'blackmail'. And they spoke and sang beautiful, sad poetry and told a string of stirring, unforgettable stories.

In the modern historical period, the tale of the Border Reivers is a tale without parallel in all of western Europe.

2

The Lords of the Names

Queens were executed, monasteries swept into oblivion and a Reformation forced upon his people by Henry VIII of England in his desperation to father a male heir and continue the Tudor line. And once Prince Edward had been safely delivered, this most brutal of English kings began to cast around for a bride for his boy. When James V of Scotland died in 1542 leaving his baby daughter, Mary, as queen, negotiations were soon underway. By July 1543 the Treaty of Greenwich had contracted a marriage between Prince Edward and Queen Mary. She was not yet one year old.

Almost immediately it began to unravel. The Scottish Parliament rejected the terms of the treaty and the nobility divided into pro- and anti-English factions. Henry VIII responded with what Walter Scott called 'the rough wooing'. Punitive expeditions rampaged through the Border countryside, burning and killing across a wide swathe, and in September 1547 a powerful English army drew up in battle order at Pinkie near Musselburgh. The Scots were no match; ten thousand were said to have been slaughtered, fifteen hundred taken prisoner and those who wisely fled the field were pursued up to the gates of Edinburgh.

As is often the case, it was a battle which need not have been fought. Although the English had vastly superior numbers, that fact was fast becoming their most pressing problem. Quartermasters were having great difficulty in supplying such a large army in the field and some historians believe that if the Scots had simply skirmished around them, harrying their communications in classic reiver fashion, then the English would have been forced into a humiliating retreat after only a few days. But rashness, and the urging of Scottish priests (who did not wish their national church to come under the control of York or Canterbury), drove the Scots captains into fighting a pitched battle they were odds-on to lose.

Borderers and their heidsmen must have understood all of this and it no doubt informed their actions. They fought on both sides, and it appears that the Scots contingent manoeuvred themselves opposite the English. A sharp-eyed observer noticed that in addition to their crosses of St Andrew and St George, both sets of Borderers wore a great deal of extra identification; kerchiefs tied like armbands and letters embroidered on their hats. Worse, their national badges were sewn on so loosely that 'a puff of wind might have blown them from their breasts'. But most embarrassing was the discovery that, standing within a spear's length of each other, in the midst of a furious battle, Scots and English Borderers were talking to each other. When they realised that they had been observed, both lots made some show of running at each other and 'they strike few strokes but by assent and appointment'.

It must have been a remarkable sight. Amid the din and clatter of battle, as others fought and died around them, two groups of nominally opposing soldiers making a pantomime out of deadly warfare. People who knew each other well had turned up at Pinkie to be seen to do their duty for the opposing sides but were actually determined to get through the battle, whichever way it went. For the truth is that it was not their fight.

Foreign policy, the aspirations of Henry VIII and the ambitions of the anti-English party in Scotland mattered very little to these men. Names were everything, nationality came a long way behind and loyalty to factions within a nation an even more distant third.

HENRY AND THE CLAP

Syphilis made landfall in Europe at Barcelona in 1493, having travelled across the Atlantic as an early import from America on board the *Nina*, one of Christopher Columbus' ships. It spread like wildfire and at some point in his extended amorous adventures, Henry VIII of England almost certainly caught it. The disease made it difficult for him to father an heir (and contributed to his dynasty's barrenness) and propelled Britain into all sorts of political convulsions. Not the least of these were the tremendously destructive punitive raids of the 'rough wooing'. The sixteenth-century epidemic of syphilis made sexual puritanism popular – as a matter of self-preservation. Previously popular in all gender combinations as a form of greeting, kissing on the lips was replaced by the safer handshake, and the fashion for wigs was encouraged. Sufferers from syphilis often lost all their hair.

Names were what made the Border Reivers who they were – in all important senses. Armstrongs, Elliots, Kers and Maxwells gave unhesitating loyalty to their surnames, what was a huge extended family in some cases. On the English side the Carletons, the Fenwicks, the Forsters and the Robsons felt greater affinity with the Scottish riding families than with those who lived to the south of them. And governments in Edinburgh and London may have done as they pleased but where the heidsman of a name led, those who had the same name saddled their ponies and followed.

These were powerful instincts. Few fought fiercer than family bands. When fathers and sons, brothers and cousins rode side by side, none turned aside and many found courage when the names of their blood needed them at their back. Astute commanders understood these bonds and in battles or skirmishes they always set the older and more experienced men in front, believing that honour and valour flowed down the generations to the younger men behind. Pitched battles between surnames were always the cruellest and bloodiest fights. When the Maxwells were cut to pieces by the Johnstones at Dryfe Sands near Lockerbie in 1593, the slaughter was unrelenting. More than 700 Maxwells were killed and Robert Johnstone of Raecleugh bloodied his lance on that terrible day. He was 11 years old.

Robert must have been a big laddie for his years, able to wrap long legs around his pony's belly and direct it, and also to couch the butt of his lance without being knocked out of the saddle on impact. 'If he's big enough, he's auld enough' is a comment still heard in Border rugby dressing rooms when a young player is brought into the team. And on 6th December 1593 the Johnstones needed every young lad, every rider they could muster. In pursuit of a deadly feud between the two names, the Maxwells had summoned a huge force. Two thousand horsemen rode with their heidsman, Lord Maxwell, and they came to lay siege to the Johnstone tower at Lochwood.

When news of the advancing army – for that is what it was – reached James Johnstone, he moved quickly and determined to fight like the reiver he was. He knew no other way to prevent the extermination of his name. Able to put only four hundred men in the saddle, Johnstone could not confront Maxwell in open country. His riders would be outflanked and rolled up and fatally surrounded. Instead, he laid a reiver's ambush. At a narrow place on the road, with plenty of cover on each side, the Johnstones hid themselves. When enough of the Maxwell vanguard had trotted into the trap, it was suddenly sprung. Roaring their war-cries, the Johnstones spurred their ponies and tore into their enemy's flanks. So furious was the charge that it drove the leading Maxwell riders backwards, forcing them to turn into the midst of the main party following them. Ponies reared and kicked, men were bucked off, weapons dropped, tangled and trampled and a murderous scrummage of confusion turned Maxwell's two thousand into a formless, panicking rabble.

As the Johnstones charged again and again, the battle became a rout and riders poured into the streets of Lockerbie, fighting as they went. Maxwells were trapped in narrow places, hacked at, killed and ridden down. Blood ran in the gutters, spattered on the faces of the living and the dying. Men screamed as they were cornered and skewered by lance and sword-thrust or their limbs were cut off and their bodies butchered unrecognisable. The Johnstones fought like furies for more than their lives – the very existence of their name was at stake on that awful December day. Extermination was what they desperately feared – and to visit it upon the Maxwells if they could.

Dryfe Sands was one of the last battles to be joined in the Borders and one of the most ferocious. And it was fought for the sake of a name, the very bedrock of reiver society.

LOCKERBIE LICKS

When horsemen fought each other head-on, troops of cavalry charging straight towards each other, it was a combination of resolve, numbers and heavier horses which usually won the day. The armies of Islam swept through North Africa and up into Spain and southern France in the eighth century. When the Arab cavalry reached the River Loire in AD 732, they came up against a new enemy. Charles Martel, the Mayor of the royal palace, had gathered a squadron of big horses, what became known as heavy cavalry. Bracing themselves in their stirrups, they charged the lighter Arab cavalry and knocked them off their feet. Islam was driven back to the Pyrenees and eventually across the Straits of Gibraltar. The small Arab ponies were tough, fast and nimble but entirely unsuited to pitched battle on good ground. Just like the Border Reivers. They too were light horsemen, what were known as 'prickers', good at harrying, skirmishing and wearing down a more cumbrous enemy, always fighting shy of taking them on upfront. On a broken battlefield Border horsemen were deadly, pouring through gaps in the line, quickly creating a melée of close-quarter fighting. At the Battle of Dryfe Sands the Johnstones got in amongst the Maxwells and inflicted terrible casualties, particularly on those fighting on foot. 'Get in amongst them!' is still shouted from the terracing at Border League rugby matches. Even on small Galloway Nags a horseman was always crucially higher than an infantryman, slashing downwards with a sword or using the pony's momentum to drive a lance forward. Many at Dryfe Sands suffered bad head and facial injuries from what became known as 'Lockerbie Licks', a passing backhanded cut at an opponent on foot – delivered with great venom.

The tribal surnames and their feral power were very old, reaching back across millennia into the mists of prehistory. When pioneer family bands came north after the end of the last ice age, and hunted, trapped and gathered a wild harvest, they probably enjoyed customary rights over wide swathes of the ancient wildwood. As farming pinned growing populations to more defined areas on the early map of the Borders, the beginnings of the surnames slowly began to form. DNA studies show tremendously long lineages, particularly in rural areas and many Border families of the sixteenth century had been on their land since a time out of mind. Of course, new people came, others moved or were removed but the balance of the human landscape stayed much as it was for a hundred generations or more. When men fought hard to keep or protect their land, they fought with all their courage for their history, and their name. They were seen as indivisible, the one impossible without the other.

Very early in the history of the Borders an old fault-line repeatedly divided communities. Hillmen and plainsmen had long led different styles of life. How the shepherd and the ploughman grew their food was shaped by geography and climate, but the distinctions were rarely absolute. Almost all farmers cultivated the ground and husbanded some beasts and the shepherd likewise. It was a question of degree. But the ploughmen of the flat and fertile plains of Berwickshire and the middle Tweed Valley saw themselves as different from the shepherds of Liddesdale in many ways – and they complained about them. In 1569 the lairds of the eastern and middle marches asserted that while they themselves were peaceable, the thieves of the western ranges were not. In a memorandum to the Scottish Privy Council they insisted that they must be controlled and made to behave like civilised men. And in case anyone missed the point, they supplied a *black list* of the surnames of the worst of them. And there were a few – all Armstrongs, Batesons, Bells, Crosiers, Elliots, Glendinnings, Hendersons, Irvines, Johnstones, Nixons, Routledges and Thomsons. In all this there is more than a whiff of superiority, the sense that the men of Liddesdale, Ewesdale, Annandale and Eskdale were little more than savages.

LIONEL AND TONY

Recent research suggests that men who bear the same surname are likely to be relatives. Lionel Blair and Tony Blair? Analyses of DNA testing of pairs of British males with the same surname shows that 25 per cent are direct if distant relatives. The Y chromosome passed from fathers to sons is the genetic link. The rarer the surname the greater the chance of men bearing it being related. Border Reivers knew all this anyway – but probably would have been appalled that the police plan to use the data to track down criminals.

For their part the hillmen found their lives more defined and con-strained by geography. Over the valuable and accessible lands of the eastern plains the winds of social change might more easily blow. But in an upland valley, with one track in and one track out, there was less traffic of every sort and the year was shaped by the movement of flocks and herds, the time-hallowed journeys of transhumance. The communities of the hills were more conservative, perhaps closer-knit and more intimately tribal than those down in the valley bottoms and the broad fields of the east.

The herdsmen who moved their beasts around the flanks of the Cheviots and the hills and moors north of the Hexham Gap had more in common with each other than with the plainsmen who farmed the lower ground. The distinction between English and Scottish mattered much less. This is an important facet of the story of the Border Reivers. Since the earliest records were kept, the tribes of the northern Pennines and of the Cheviots and Southern Uplands allied themselves against the Roman invader. The Brigantes and the Selgovae and their satellites united their warbands in an attempt to keep some independence. Part of the reasoning behind Hadrian's Wall was to drive a firebreak between them, prevent them from reinforcing each other along the hill trails which were so dangerous to patrol. Fifteen hundred years later, when the governments in Edinburgh and London tried to exert control, the instincts of the hillmen were little changed.

FOUR AND TWENTY

Until well into the nineteenth century Cumbrian shepherds counted in Old Welsh: yan, tan, tedderte, medderte, pump (1, 2, 3, 4, 5 in English, or Arabic). When sheep were being accounted for on the high fells, Welsh was still shouted against the wind. Different valleys had slight variations; Coniston shepherds shouted tedderte while Borrowdale used tethera. It is an astonishing survival showing the deep conservatism of hill communities. And it is unlikely to have survived only in Cumbria. Mostly unlettered men, the shepherds of the Border hills probably counted as their ancestors did – and for many centuries after English was spoken in the valleys below. Like all Celtic languages Old Welsh used 20-base arithmetic. It reckons 2 × 20 for 40, 4 × 20 for 80 and so on. Memories of this habit lasted on into the twentieth century when old people used a Celtic word order. Instead of 24, they would say 4 and 20. The origins of 20-base counting are obvious and straightforward – the number of human fingers and toes. With their Vs and Xs Roman numerals look as though they might have a different derivation – but they do not. I is the simple symbol of one finger held up, V is from the notch between thumb and forefinger when a whole hand of five is shown and X is when two forefingers are crossed to signify all ten fingers and thumbs linked.

There are some similarities with the society of the Highland clans to the far north. Heidsmen in the Borders appear to have exercised great authority, not unlike the autocratic rule of clan chiefs. Some surnames, like the Moffats, sometimes had no heidsman, and perhaps for the avoidance of dispute, chose to acknowledge another. At the time of the Battle of Dryfe Sands the Moffats saw James Johnstone as their superior and no doubt horsemen of that surname hacked and killed Maxwells in the lanes of Lockerbie. There were many 'graynes' or branches of the Scott family, but Scott of Buccleuch was their unchallenged leader. And when Lord Maxwell summoned his small army of 2,000 riders in 1593, by no means all bore his name – although they were related. Other graynes, such as the Crichtons and the Douglases, often rode in his forays.

These bonds of the blood were reciprocal. In return for unquestioningly saddling his pony and buckling on his sword at a moment's notice, a man might expect to work his land as a secure tenant and enjoy the protection of his heidsman. In fact men who found themselves outside these interlocking relationships, for whatever good reason, could enter into a contract with a heidsman. Known as *manrent*, this arrangement was not common but it did demonstrate the power of the name. And a name was not something to be without in the hills and valleys of the sixteenth-century Border country.

The sense of belonging, of pride and confidence in being an Elliot, a Turnbull, a Selby or a Bell peeps through the records of the time again and again. The Captain of Berwick, the great Elizabethan fortress-town guarding the east coast road, complained that the local recruits for his garrison were 'mutinous and insubordinate to their constables, who are little above their own rank. Being of great clans and surnames, this encourages their obstinacy'.

When obstinacy shaded into excess, heidsmen could threaten the ultimate sanction. They could condemn men to be disnamed, to be removed from the surname and cast into outlawry. In the Border country disorder became so chronic in the sixteenth century that central government was forced to rely upon heidsmen controlling their people directly. By making solemn promises and sometimes giving up hostages, the lords of the names retained an independent ability to enforce good behaviour amongst their people. And if their people continued to misbehave and promises and pledges (the term most often used for hostages) were repeatedly broken or forfeited, then the heidsmen were compelled to disname the persistent offenders. The process sometimes called 'putting to the horn' involved a public declaration that certain men were no longer who they used to be or might claim to be. They had lost their name and become 'broken men' or outlaws, that is, outside the laws of Scotland and, more importantly, the laws of their heidsman. So great was this loss that many broken men formed gangs, thereby creating a surrogate surname. 'Sandy's Bairns' was one such gang of thugs and they mounted raids on both sides of the border in the 1590s. After he had been cast into outlawry – no mean feat for an already lawless surname, Kinmont Willie Armstrong appeared at the head of a notorious gang known as 'Kinmont's Bairns'.

BALEFIRE

'Bale' in Old English originally meant pain or woe, and a balefire burned at the death of a leading person, a chieftain, even a king. They were lit on hilltops so that the message of an important death could be quickly transmitted. The modern meaning is related to 'ball' and describes a bundle, normally of hay or straw. In an unexpected way these two quite separate meanings combined at the time of the Border Reivers. As early as the fifteenth century there existed a sophisticated warning system for the lighting of balefires. Here is a set of instructions in early Scots. Some of the words sound an echo of fifteenth-century Border dialect:

A baile is warnyng of their cumyng, quhat power whatever thai be of. Twa bailes togedder at anis, thai cumyng in deide. Fower balis, ilk ane besyde uther and all at anys as fower candills sal be suthfast knowledge that thai ar of gret power and menys.

in English:

The [burning] of a bale is warning of their coming, whatever size [the force] might be. Two bales [burnt] together at the same time means that they are certainly coming. Four bales, each beside the other and [burnt] all at once like four candles are a sign of certain knowledge that they are of great power and menace.

It could all go horribly wrong. The balefire system was revived in 1803-4 when Napoleon Bonaparte threatened to invade Britain. At Hume Castle a lookout was certain he could see one blazing near Berwick. In a state of high excitement he fired his bundles, and all over the Borders other balefires crackled into life. As in an episode of 'Dad's Army' volunteers pulled on boots and uniforms and hurried to their muster-points, no doubt grabbing their muskets as they scrambled out the door. The countryside was in uproar and at any moment Napoleon's cuirassiers were expected to come clattering along the Berwick road, tricolours flying. They did not. No one did. It was all a ghastly mistake. What the hapless lookout on Hume Castle had seen was the everyday work of some Northumberland charcoal-burners. One of their mounds had burned out of control, flames licking into the night sky. What happened to the lookout is not recorded, but he will not have been popular and never allowed to forget what happened.

Broken men could be bold. So many regularly met in the streets of Hawick that government troops made their way south from Edinburgh to deal with them. The Earl of Mar's men surrounded the town. A proclamation was cried from the mercat cross pointing out to the inhabitants that it was a capital crime to harbour broken men, and in a short time more than 50 were rounded up. Mar did not delay and while six of the more important prisoners were sent for trial in Edinburgh, 18 were bound hand and foot and dragged down to the banks of the Teviot. There, wriggling and kicking, they were held under the water until drowned. Cheap and quick, and a dire warning.

James VI and I learned the power of disnaming in the Borders. In 1604 he applied it to the Highland clans and in order to cure the MacGregors of their love of cattle stealing, he banned their name entirely. It simply became illegal to be called MacGregor and any man bearing that ancient surname could be hunted and killed. The whole social and military structure of the clan was undermined. Alasdair MacGregor, the chief of the name, and five of his leading men, were hanged at the mercat cross for the crime of refusing to give up their name. Clan Gregor scattered. Some took to outlawry in the mountains, others adopted pseudonyms like Gregory, Grant, even Campbell. It is more than a lexical coincidence that the Gaelic 'clann' for clan translates directly as children or bairns – as in 'Sandy's Bairns' or 'Kinmont's Bairns'.

The year after the disnaming of Clan Gregor, James VI and I applied the same principles in the Borders. One of the most persistently infamous of the reiving families were the Grahams of Eskdale and the Solway mouth. While the royal courts did not ban the name of Graham, the king's officers did their utmost to extirpate it. Wholesale deportations to Ireland were backed by hangings and press-gangings into armies to fight in European wars. These draconian measures broke the power of the name, but did not remove it. Grahams found their way back to their native places – if not their old reiving habits.

Those who kept their names in the Borders were rarely known by them. As in Wales and the Scottish Highlands, Borderers used a relatively small stock of surnames. There existed many Scotts, Armstrongs, Robsons and Ridleys at any one time, most of them living in the same small area. The mists of confusion thickened when little imagination was used in the giving of christian names; the same handful recur down the generations and also sideways to cousins and uncles. It seems that scores of Walter Scotts, Gilbert Elliots,

Robert Kers, Andrew Forsters and Thomas Carletons lived in the sixteenth century, many of them at the same time.

Mistaken identity is more of a danger for historians than it was for the reivers. Scots and English borderers seemed to know exactly who was who, especially when it came to the collection of blackmail (of which more later) and the fact that these men could recognise each other in the smoke and confusion of the Battle of Pinkie is extraordinary.

They had help. Until the recent past Border farmers were often known by the name of their farm rather than what appeared on their birth certificate. The same thing happened in the sixteenth century. When Walter Scott of Buccleuch rode with Walter Scott of Harden to rescue Kinmont Willie Armstrong from Carlisle Castle in 1596, the shorthand ran that Buccleuch and Harden saved Kinmont's skin.

Blood ties bound tight in the Borders, and how people chose to address each other often remembered that closeness. Not only to avoid confusion in the mosaic of similar names but also to remind everyone of the precision of relationships, patronymics and occasionally matronymics were used. As with the Highland clans, a father's name was added to his son's, and men called 'Sim's Jock', 'Dick's Davie' or 'Sandie's Gib' are all to be found in the records. If any unclarity remained names could run to a third generation with the like of 'Gibb's Geordie's Francis' or 'Sandie's Rinyon's Archie'. Where a father was not available, mothers stepped in for 'Kate's Adam', 'Peggie's Wattie', and 'Bessie's Andrew'.

Further refinement could be added by the application of a nickname. These are very colourful and often eloquent. Like 'Nebless Clem Crozier', 'Halflugs Jock Elliot' and 'Fingerless Will Nixon', some had stories to tell and how Clem lost his nose, Jock part of his ears and Will his fingers would add real pungency to the dry recital of dates and places and people. Other nicknames were mercilessly observational. John Armstrong squinted and was 'Gleed John', Will Armstrong had a twitch and was 'Winking Will' and Jerry Charlton had a tuft of hair sticking up and was 'Topping'. A dark nature conferred 'Ill Will Armstrong' and 'Evilwillit Sandie'. Perhaps 'Unhappy Anthone' met them both on a particularly bad day.

Sexual preferences were unblushingly caught in the web of nicknames. 'Dand Oliver the Lover' was bland enough and Dand obviously enjoyed female company. More direct are 'Dog Pyntle Elliot' and 'Wanton Pyntle Willie Hall'. 'Pyntle' is Border Scots for 'penis'.

More surprising is the clear recognition of homosexuality. Gay reivers such as 'Davy the Lady Armstrong', 'Buggerback Elliot' or 'Mistress Kerr' are unexpected even though the image is hard to reconcile. Buggerback and Dog Pyntle were brothers (although scarcely able to compare notes) and Davy the Lady was the younger brother of Sim the Laird Armstrong, one of the most feared heidsmen in the Border hills.

Some nicknames are impossible to parse, their meaning long fled. What prompted 'Sweet Milk' or 'Hen Harrow' or 'As It Looks' to be applied is now mysterious – and very intriguing.

What is so attractive about these nicknames is that they sound a faint echo of how the reivers spoke and dealt with each other. They suggest a boisterous, grimly humorous society where men called a spade a shovel and enjoyed a good laugh at others' quirks and preferences.

Boisterousness often shaded into something darker. And a rare documented example of a Border Reiver talking is dark indeed, the testament of a cruel, ruthless but ultimately honest man. The surname of Burn (sometimes rendered Bourne) held land to the south of the Teviot, in the old Jedforest which grew on part of the Scottish slopes of the Cheviots. They were a hard-bitten, violent bunch, acknowledging Robert Kerr of Cessford as their leader, and even though he was a government official, the Warden of the Scottish Middle March, they enjoyed his open patronage and protection.

On a September night in 1596 Jock and Geordie Burn were returning from a routine raid across the Cheviot tops. Driving cattle before them, the Scots reivers were very unlucky. Riding through the gloaming they were intercepted by Sir Robert Carey, the Warden of the English East March, who was out on patrol with 20 troopers at his back. Hopelessly outnumbered, Geordie Burn, his uncle and their two henchmen fought ferociously. One escaped, two were killed, and Geordie was overpowered and taken prisoner.

Probably at Harbottle Castle, Carey had Burn quickly tried, convicted and condemned to death. But sentence was delayed while the news of the reiver's capture was allowed to reach the ears of his patron, Sir Robert Kerr of Cessford. Perhaps there would be an advantageous negotiation, perhaps an attempted reprisal which might deliver more prisoners to Carey. In the event there was silence. No word came over the hill trails and Geordie Burn realised that he had been abandoned and was likely to hang.

Sir Robert Carey's curiosity was stirred. It is said that the warden disguised himself and with two companions went to Burn's cell to talk with the condemned man. The swagger had gone, and in his resignation, the reiver reviewed the life he had led. Carey later wrote down what he remembered. It amounts to the only authentic testament left by a Border Reiver:

> He voluntarily of himself said that he had lived long enough to do so many villanies as he had done; and told us that he had lain with about 40 men's wives, some in England, some in Scotland, and that he had killed seven Englishmen with his own hands, cruelly murdering them; that he had spent his whole time in whoring, drinking, stealing, and taking deep revenge for slight offences. He seemed to be very penitent, and much desired a minister for the comfort of his soul.

This is fascinating, a catalogue of thuggery, rape, murder, larceny and excess freely confessed – and regretted. Faced with the hangman's rope, Burn was anxious to bargain with his maker as he owned up to all his sins and asked for a minister to advise him. The transaction has an old-fashioned ring, the medieval arithmetic of damnation. Perhaps like their patrons, the Kerrs of Ferniehurst, Burn's family had kept their catholic faith, such as it was, for a generation after the establishment of Reformation Scotland. The enumeration of 40 rapes (it is hard to believe that Burn was referring to extra-marital affairs) and the murder of seven Englishmen sounds like a request for other offences to be taken into consideration. He had been taken by Carey for cattle stealing and having been condemned to die had no need to confess to anything else. It sounds as though the reiver was asking to see a minister to enquire after the tariff operating for the fires of hell. What could he expect for 40 rapes and seven murders? Geordie offers no mitigation except penitence, he just wants to know how bad it will be.

The listing of all these crimes and the tone in which Carey records them also has a routine ring. The Burns were not especially notorious and no more than normally active as reivers. The likelihood is that each Border district had a quota of gangsters doing much the same thing. If that is so, then these were grim times. Observers noted that even in pursuit of their daily duties – working the land, herding beasts – many Borderers went about armed, or with a weapon of some sort close at hand. No wonder.

THE PENRITH PLAGUE

In 1598 God's Punishment tore through Cumberland and West-morland. An inscription on the wall of the parish church at Penrith records an astonishing figure. Apparently 2,260 perished in an outbreak of the plague. Around 640 died in the town, half the population, and a further 1,800 from the farms and villages of the Eden Valley. At almost exactly the same time in Carlisle 1,196 died in unspeakable agony from the same disease. It is a forgotten epidemic. In their 'Return of the Black Death', Susan Scott and Christopher Duncan show that no such thing happened. The epidemic was not a return of the Black Death. What ripped through these horrified communities was in fact a lethal virus not unlike ebola, and it was transmitted not by infected fleas living in the fur of rats but directly from person to person. All they had to do was breath. For this reason the disease spread like lightning, and with their housing huddled close and overcrowded, towns were perfect vectors. Entering Britain through the port of Newcastle, this version of ebola travelled west across Stainmore to Penrith and then made its deadly way north to Carlisle before crossing the border to reach Dumfries. It was an appalling illness, its victims vomiting blood and tissue, haemorrhaging internally and burning with fever. Mercifully many died quickly and their bodies were flung in plague-pits without any ceremony. They also died alone because it became too risky for a minister to give them the last rites and families fled for fear of becoming infected. Curiously this phenomenal outbreak is noted by few historians or many contemporary commentators – even though it presented a much greater threat than any Border Reiver.

Just as Geordie Burn's confession offers a momentary glimpse of a life of reiving, so the following tells how the law-abiding majority saw these thugs. The Bishop of Carlisle wrote to Cardinal Wolsey in London in the 1520s. He was even-handed:

there is more theft, more extortion by English thieves than there is by all the Scots of Scotland . . . for in Hexham . . . every market day there is four score or a hundred strong thieves; and the poor men and gentlemen also see those who did rob them and their goods, and dare neither complain of them by name, nor say one word to them. They take all their cattle and horse, their corn as they carry it to sow, or to the mill to grind, and at their houses bid them deliver what they have or they shall be fired and burnt.

Defiant, confident in the numbers and fearsome reputation, the outlaws regularly rode into town – all over the Borders. Like Tombstone, Dodge City and other notorious locations in the Wild West, the law-abiding folks of Hexham, Carlisle, Hawick and Berwick had much to abide. Those gangsters who lifted their cattle during the week could glare shamelessly on market days at the farmers they had impoverished – and in turn the farmers were compelled to scuttle about their business, heads down, avoiding eye contact, mouths shut. On the wild frontier the rule of law had fled.

THE TIME OF OUR LIVES

In the sixteenth century few knew what time it was, at least in the sense that we mean it now. No one owned timepieces and the only institution which cared enough about the time of day to mark it was the church. In order to summon monks to say the offices of the day – vespers, compline and so on – bells tolled the canonical hours and the day began to divide into more than simply dark and light. To Americans the term 'fortnight' is meaningless. It is a relict of the way in which ordinary people used to count the days – or rather the nights. Fortnight is short for fourteen nights and the obsolete 'sennight' for a week was in common use in the sixteenth century. Except for Sunday most normal weekdays merged into each other. People did not work hours, they did tasks which finished when they finished. Turning points of the seasons were prominent – like Michaelmas, Lammas, Whitsun and so on, as were saints' days. The names of these days often survive in the calendar but the meaning has been lost. Christianity used to have many dietary laws (fish on Friday and abstinence in Lent are the only popular survivals) and periods of restriction were usually preceded by a 'carnival'. It literally means 'farewell to meat' and Shrove Tuesday was when Christians ought to have been shriven – or confessed their sins to a priest. Few Border Reivers will have bothered.

Jedburgh may have been an exception, at least for part of the sixteenth century. The town government was thrawn, assertive, independent and willing to fight for its rights, sometimes against unwise odds. In the early 1570s Scotland was riven with dissension between catholics and protestants, between the influence of France and England, and the focus of the former was Mary, Queen of Scots and of the latter, Elizabeth I of England. These alignments were further complicated by the increasingly complex position of Mary's son and heir, James, and his claims to the throne of England.

Jedburgh stood firm and sure for the protestant cause while the loyalties of Border heidsmen were split. Scott of Buccleuch and Kerr of Ferniehurst were catholic supporters of Mary and Kerr of Cessford had fallen in with Elizabeth and protestantism. When Queen Mary's party sent a royal herald to read out a proclamation at the old mercat cross at Jedburgh, matters quickly became explosive – and somewhat theatrical, even farcical.

When the herald had dismounted to climb up the steps to the base of the cross, the provost, his bailies and no doubt a substantial crowd had gathered around. Proclamations were of prime importance and the means by which government directives were popularly transmitted. But when the herald unrolled his parchment and read in a loud voice that all men should obey Queen Mary only and ignore all others, the provost stepped forward to call a halt. The herald was taken hold of and forced to eat his parchment. Piece by indigestible piece, it was stuffed into his mouth. That was bad enough, but things were about to get much worse for the poor man.

A hurdle was found and the Queen's herald was 'caused to loose down his points'. In modern parlance, his trousers were pulled down around his ankles. The Jedburgh men then forced him to bend over the hurdle and with a horse's bridle, they spanked his bare backside.

It was an appalling humiliation for a royal officer and when the man sat carefully on his horse to take the road back to Edinburgh, no one doubted that retribution would quickly come the other way. Scott of Buccleuch and Kerr of Ferniehurst (whose tower lies only a little over a mile south of Jedburgh) mustered more than 3,000 riders and descended on the town. But the provost and the townspeople were ready, having laid in six days of provisions and sent urgent messages for aid from Robert Kerr of Cessford. Immediately he rode to the rescue and reinforcements of musketeers and cavalry hurried south. Buccleuch and Kerr of Ferniehurst were compelled to abandon the siege but the latter continued to burn with indignation and he pursued the feud against Jedburgh energetically. The Kerrs tormented the town with 'riots and murders', and the close proximity of Ferniehurst hung like a constant black cloud.

KERRY MITTS

There is a persistent Border tradition that the family of Kerr were left-handed. The example always cited is the spiral staircase in their towers. Other surnames built theirs turning clockwise so that if they had to fight a retreat up the stair (always a strong possibility in the second half of the sixteenth century), they could keep their un-guarded left side to the outside wall and swing a sword blade downwards with their right hands. With the left-handed Kerrs the stair ran anti-clockwise, confusing everyone except them. In the Borders lefties are still called 'kerry-mitted', or 'kerr-handed' or 'corry-fisted'. Interestingly, but probably coincidentally, the Scots Gaelic word for 'left' is 'cearr' with a hard 'c'. It also means 'wrong' or 'a wrong un' and derives from an ancient Celtic root word 'kerso'. Perhaps it is all true. The Kerrs were certainly aggressive and recent sociological research had shown a high correlation between left-handedness and skill in combat, or at least a liking for a fight. In tribal societies in Africa and Polynesia statistics suggest strongly that those with a high proportion of lefties also have a high proportion of violent crime. This research solved a conundrum for the principles of natural selection. Generally speak-ing left-handedness is a disadvantage and yet the number who are is not diminishing. The reason may be that lefties are good at combat – possibly because of the element of surprise and awkwardness. This translates into modern versions of single combat – such as tennis. The proportion of successful tennis players who are left-handed is much higher than the incidence in the general population.

Feud between a surname and an entire town was unusual, but blood-spattered, long-running vendettas between families were not. Throughout the sixteenth century the Border country was disfigured by serial, often interlocking feuds and as momentum built there were more and more raids, assassinations and even full-scale battles such as Dryfe Sands. By 1596 25 English surnames and ten Scottish were at feud in some way or other. The effect was to render the Borders even more lawless. Redress or legal retribution was paralysed because of the high risk of sparking yet another feud, and as a consequence reivers could ignore the law with increasing impunity. Robert Carey's execution of Geordie Burn was a brave exception.

The Maxwells and the Johnstones sustained what was probably the longest and bloodiest feud in British history. It began in the early sixteenth century and like many arguments, large and small, its origins were soon forgotten.

More important were the dynamics of local politics. At stake between the Maxwells and the Johnstones was control of the Scottish west march. It stretched from the watershed between Langholm and Hawick at Mosspaul, north to the Tweedsmuir Hills and away west to the River Cree in Galloway. A huge domain, it was the jurisdiction of its warden, and both the Maxwells and the Johnstones coveted the office.

Although it is likely to have smouldered for a long time beforehand, the feud first comes on record in 1528. As often an English government official reported on events on the Scottish side of the border (this is a recurrent theme – the English records are much better than the Scots, and the effect is to make Scots reiving appear more frequent and widespread, whereas in fact, population statistics suggest the opposite to have been the case). Given what was going on, it is hardly surprising that the Scottish records are more scant than usual. By 1528 the feud had crackled and sparked over much of eastern Dumfriesshire, so much so that the Warden of the English West March, Lord Dacre, was moved to write to the London government. He told Cardinal Wolsey that burnings, killings and swift reprisals had been very destructive, almost to the point where farmers and herdsmen saw little point in working their land.

REFORM TIME

By the middle of the sixteenth century, the calendar compiled by Julius Caesar's Roman clerks had got badly out of phase. So that Easter could be held at the traditional time and the Christian festivals which dated from it could fall back into a sensible sequence of dates, Pope Gregory XIII decided to reform the Julian calendar drastically. Catholic countries adopted it immediately but it took Britain nearly 200 years to have the same date as most of Europe.

The problem was that the Gregorian reform involved losing 11 days, something many people found deeply suspicious and worrying. By 1752, the British government decided to fall into line with Europe at last, and 3rd September became, magically, 14th September. There were riots. In several cities crowds called 'Give us back our eleven days!' The problem was that leap years had been throwing the calendar out, and at the turn of the century they had to be divided by 400 otherwise they could not have their extra day. Other drastic changes followed. Until 1752 Britain had celebrated New Year's Day on 25th March, but after that year, it fell on 1st January. Some communities still celebrate Christmas and New Year old style, that is, 11 days after the rest of us. And at the crying of the fair at Langholm Common Riding (when a man stands on the hind quarters of a horse so that he can be both seen and heard) the date is still counted 'auld style', i.e. as it would have been before 1752.

Nevertheless, it often suited English foreign policy to foment the Maxwell/Johnstone feud. It kept the Scottish west march weak and protracted internecine warfare presented no threat to England or English Borderers. In fact Lord Wharton, Warden of the English West March, took a hand in occasional policing in Dumfriesshire, imprisoning either Maxwells or Johnstones or both whenever his government's interests could be served by altering the balance of power.

The Johnstones suffered from a simple and perennial disadvantage. Holding lands primarily in Annandale (the Maxwells' power base lay further west, in Nithsdale and beyond) and allied to smaller surnames such as the Irvines and the Moffats, their fighting strength was always outweighed. The Maxwells were usually able to put many more men in the saddle – in fact it is a tribute to the Johnstones' tenacity that such an unequal feud lasted so long. Because of this weakness, they keenly sought the office of March Warden. As a government appointee a Johnstone warden could call for reinforcements from Edinburgh to keep order, which often meant little more than defeating the Maxwells. As a result the wardenship of the west march was always manipulated in either surname's interest, and the office changed hands with dizzying frequency. Between 1577 and 1588 there was a different warden almost every year, some incumbents lasting only a few months.

This was the period when the feud intensified. Each time a Johnstone was appointed as warden, the Maxwells and all their followers refused to recognise his authority. This made it easier for them to attract outlaws and chronically lawless surnames like the Armstrongs to their cause. Dumfriesshire was descending into anarchy.

In 1584 a Johnstone was made provost of Dumfries. The town lying in the midst of Maxwell lands, the office had traditionally been in their gift, and when the new provost attempted to have himself installed, he was barred from the town. Between July and October that year John Johnstone was unable to enter Dumfries. How the affairs of the burgh were conducted without a provost is not recorded. It was harvest-time and in retribution for his exclusion, Johnstone peruaded the English surname of Graham to come raiding and they burned the crops standing in the Maxwell fields. Dumfries was therefore neither fed nor governed.

National politics sometimes played in what had degenerated into a near-seamless cycle of raid and reprisal. The Maxwells suffered an Achilles' heel. They were a steadfastly catholic family (famously refusing to expel the old abbot and monks of Sweetheart Abbey until well into the seventeenth century) and as the supporters of King James VI grew more and more convinced that he might one day become the I, blatant catholicism needed to be suppressed. As his son and grandson were to discover to their immense cost, England expected a protestant prince and a well-known catholic family doing as it wished in the Borders was not an encouraging advertisement for James' credentials.

In 1585 John Maxwell, the heidsman of the name, was outlawed and as March Warden, John Johnstone was instructed to make an arrest. It appears that he failed, dismally. Maxwell and his allied surnames attacked Johnstone villages and burned Lochwood Tower, killing six of its defenders. Despite some retaliation the momentum of destruction wreaked by Maxwell built relentlessly. With a huge force, 1,700 riders, he raided Moffatdale and upper Annandale, stealing 3,000 head of cattle and burning everything in his path. By the end of the summer of 1585 the Maxwells were in complete control of the west march, every tower and castle was in their hands and John Johnstone was their prisoner. James VI and his advisers had been outplayed by sheer military muscle and aggression. They were forced to accept the unacceptable. Realpolitik allowed John Maxwell to assume the wardenship and do as he pleased in south-west Scotland.

John Johnstone died in 1587, and although consistently compromised by his catholicism, Maxwell held onto power. Raids on both sides stuttered on into the 1590s. It seemed as though the old feud might just fizzle out. But a minor event began a succession of escalating events which led to the battle at Dryfe Sands. Over a stolen horse, the Johnstones attacked the Crichtons, Maxwell allies, and killed 15 of them. It seems an extreme reaction but the slow-burning resentments of 70 years of feuding were easily fanned into flames. Maxwell demanded that the Johnstones surrender to him. He was of course rebuffed and the bloody road to the slaughter in the streets of Lockerbie began.

The battle was certainly vicious, but not decisive. The feud continued on into 1608, even after the March Wardenries had been abolished. James Johnstone agreed to a meeting with Lord Maxwell. There was only one item on the agenda – how to bring to an honourable end almost a century of appalling suffering and destruction. Maxwell had an answer. After tempers flared he shot James Johnstone twice in the back.

Strangely enough it was an answer of sorts. Maxwell fled to France and to exile. On his return, four years later, he was betrayed, arrested and executed. And with that last death, the feud ended.

ST GEORGE

A Roman soldier originally from Cappadocia in Asia Minor, St George was martyred in Palestine in the early 300s. Apparently he tore down the edicts of the Emperor Diocletian because they insisted that the pagan gods of Rome be worshipped. George may have been a cavalry officer for he quickly came to be identified with horsemen, and was also seen as the protector of flocks and herds. In Greece, 6th May, St George's Day (23rd April in England), was the traditional date for the journey to the high summer pastures. He was the ideal saint for the Border Reivers, had they been that way inclined, but after the middle of the fourteenth century, George became England's patron saint. Because of his popularity in Palestine (and Greece where he is also patron saint), it is thought that his cult was spread to England by returning crusaders. The cross of St George, England's flag and now increasingly in evidence on sporting occasions, certainly supports that notion. A red cross on a white field, it was the crusaders' symbol.

At the same time as the Johnstones and Maxwells were attempting to assure each other's mutual destruction, the Scotts were at feud with the Kerrs of Cessford (a dispute which touched on events at Jedburgh), and with the Elliots, who in turn were sworn against the Pringles and also the English surname of Fenwick. Cross-border feuds were less common, perhaps because it was usually the local control of land and political favour which were at stake. The Selbys conducted a vicious war with the Collingwoods after Sir Cuthbert accused Sir John Selby of treason. In 1586 an ambush was sprung on the Newcastle road near Morpeth. Sir Cuthbert and Lady Collingwood were travelling with their son-in-law, Robert Clavering, when the Selbys surprised them and held them at pistol-point. Despite Lady Collingwood falling to her knees and begging for mercy, Clavering's brother was killed and Sir Cuthbert badly wounded. The ground was laid for the beginning of a long and vicious feud, but for once matters played out somewhat differently. Three of the Selbys were arrested and convicted of murder and the Claverings accepted cash compensation for their loss, an old-fashioned blood-price. In this way feud was avoided and the affair quickly and cleanly resolved. But the enmity between the Selbys and the Collingwoods festered on and did flare into intermittent feud.

James Hepburn, Earl of Bothwell, later to be husband of Mary Queen of Scots, Keeper of Liddesdale and master of Hermitage Castle discovered a good reason to fear the visceral power of Border surnames. In 1566 he held high hopes to become the King Consort, the most powerful man in Scotland. Bothwell's ambition was unbounded, he rode to Liddesdale in his pomp, planning to bring order to that nest of feuding thieves. And then he ran into Little Jock Elliot.

Bothwell's troopers swept into Liddesdale and his captains rounded up a few of the more available Elliots, the usual suspects. They were taken to Hermitage Castle and locked up. An aggressive, even head-strong, man, Bothwell was determined to stamp his imperious author-ity, show that he was worthy to be a warrior-king. When he encountered Little Jock Elliot of the Park, a leading Liddesdale reiver, he challenged him to single combat. Shooting Elliot out of the saddle, Bothwell seemed to have quickly settled matters. But then he made a bad mistake. Having dismounted to deliver the coup de grace, the Earl failed to notice that Elliot was not quite done for, and that he had a drawn dagger concealed under his body. In an instant the reiver sprang up and stabbed Bothwell in the face, chest and his hands, as he tried to protect himself. Badly hurt, pride dented, the Earl was laid out in a cart and trundled back to Hermitage Castle. Where the Elliot prisoners had overpowered their captors and taken control. After some negotiation, the bleeding Bothwell managed to regain the sanctuary of his castle. None of this was what he had in mind when he rose that morning.

The incident became famous, not least because of a famous Border ballad and a phrase which has entered the Scottish psyche. The following verse sums up something at the essence of the extraordinary story of the Border Reivers – the power of the name. To inspire fear, respect, and a sense of history, all Little Jock Elliot has to do is state it:

> 'I've vanquished the Queen's Lieutenant,
> And garr'd her troopers to flee:
> My name is Little Jock Elliot,
> And wha daur meddle wi' me?'

3

The Landscape of Larceny

The see of John Leslie, the Bishop of Ross, lay almost as far from the Borders as it was possible to be in mainland Scotland, and yet he understood perfectly how the reivers executed their longer-range raids. Leslie must have spent time in the Cheviot Hills for the description he included in his *History of Scotland* (1572–6) is difficult to better. Here is part of it:

> They sally out of their own borders, in the night, in troops, through unfrequented by-ways, and many intricate windings. All the day time, they refresh themselves and their horses, in lurking holes they had pitched upon before, till they arrive at the dark in those places they have a design upon. As soon as they have seized upon the booty, they, in like manner, return home in the night, through blind ways, and fetching many a compass [taking circuitous routes]. The more skillful any captain is[,] to pass through these wild deserts, crooked turnings and deep precipices, in the thickest mists and darkness, his reputation is the greater, and he is looked upon as a man of an excellent head.

The landscape of the Borders was superbly suited to the dark needs of horse-riding thieves. And it is perhaps appropriate that all those lurking-holes and intricate windings first came about through violence, as a result of an ancient geological collision. Unimaginably long ago, about 450 million years BC, the crust of the Earth was still forming, massive continents were moving, vast oceans filled and drained. What was to become southern Scotland lay on the leading edge of a huge landmass while northern England was on the rim of another. Between them stretched the Iapetus Ocean. When the two super-continents collided, they shoved up the bed of the ocean,

corrugating and buckling it as the harder rocks of Scotland ground
and scraped up over the softer stones of northern England. Geologists
can see the deposit of all that prehistoric drama when they compare
the granite rocks of Galloway with the coal and iron-bearing seams of
West Cumbria. They are very different and what ultimately became
the political frontier between England and Scotland was something
much more profound, the most fundamental geological division in the
British Isles.

This is no mere scientific curiosity. Geology shapes the landscape
and determines its nature. And the landscape forms the character of
the people. Perhaps more obviously the old collision affected the
direction of history because of the angle at which southern Scotland
and northern England met. It was not head-on but more glancing and
it made our geography run from north-east to south-west. Most of the
hill ranges – the Southern Uplands, the Cheviots – are set on that
compass bearing, strung out on parallel lines with the Midland Valley
of Forth and Clyde, the Highland Line and the Great Glen. The
Tweed, the Teviot, the Tyne, the Liddel, the Esk and the important
little River Irthing run their courses in broadly the same way, while the
shorter rivers of Galloway, Cumbria, Northumberland and the Borders flow down from the watershed ridges.

A journey from the banks of the Tweed to the Tyne is instructive.
All that ancient geology had a surprising, counter-intuitive effect. A
traveller takes the road winding up out of the fertile and green Tweed
Basin, through the woodland by the banks of the Jed and up to the
border at the Carter Bar. Those who take the time to park and get out
of the car to look at the long vistas to the north and south see
something unexpected. The valleys they left behind are patterned
with the homely geometry of farming. Green fields and edging shelter
belts lead the eye into the distance, as far as the Eildon Hills on a clear,
crisp day. To the south there are twenty miles and more of moorland
to be crossed before the road descends at Kirkwhelpington and goes
on through a gentler landscape to Belsay and the beginnings of the
western Northumberland plain. In the east and middle marches, much
of the English side of the border is bleaker, more windblown and
desolate.

The western ranges of the Cheviots merge with the hills of the
Southern Uplands. The old road from Hawick to Langholm and
Carlisle beyond it threads through one of the very few passes in these
steep-sided hills, the narrow cleft below Mosspaul. Bleakness and

hard living extended equally on both sides in the west march. And all of this geology had its effects as history flowed back and forth over the hills and what would become a frontier zone.

SIKES, DEANS AND BUCHTS

The names of places can be very old, often the oldest words in common speech. That they originally meant something has often been lost. Few now talk of sikes or deans even though they are generic words. The Border landscape is full of ancient descriptions now masquerading as proper names. Here are a few;

Bucht: a sheepfold
Cleuch: a deep, wooded valley, sometimes a cliff
Cote: a house or cottage
Dean: a small valley or defile, sometimes shortened to 'den' as in Dryden or Frogden
Gill: a ravine with a stream running at its bottom
Haugh: an open, often flattish parcel of land, sometimes by a river or stream
Hope: a hollow found amongst the hills
Knowe: a knoll or hummock
Mains: from the French 'demesne' (originally from the Latin 'mansio'), meaning home or central farm
Rig: a ridge, but also used for old-style cultivation areas and often found in farm names
Shaw: a flat piece of ground at the foot of a hill
Sheils: a permanently occupied hill farm or holding
Sheilings: temporary huts for shepherds
Swire: a steep pass between two hills, as in Redeswire
Sike: a marshy bottom where several small streams rise

After these valleys had been scoured and bulldozed into their modern form by the glaciers of the last ice age which flowed east and south from the ice-dome over Broad Law, the land began to green. Tundra gave way to grassland and as the climate continued to improve a vast wildwood carpeted the landscape, stunted trees and scrub even reaching up to the windy summits of Cheviot and the Carter Ridge.

As the first pioneers paddled up the rivers and made this temperate

jungle their home, they began to make clearings, often using fire.
When these peoples adopted farming as a staple way of life, forest
clearance gathered pace and the optimum temperatures of the later
prehistoric period allowed settlement up in the Border hills. Towards
the end of the first millennium BC there appears to have an organised
migration into the eastern ranges of the Cheviots. In the Bowmont
Valley, south of Kelso, archaeologists have recognised the contours of
terraces created for hillside cultivation and even a degree of soil
erosion as a result. Some long forgotten central power based in the
Tweed Valley probably forced communities to move upcountry, almost certainly as a consequence of overpopulation. But the weather
was better then, the growing season longer and warmer and corn
would ripen at those altitudes. Perhaps the wind was also less relentless.

The ancient wildwood survived in memory for a long time. As late
as 1538, only five centuries ago, the antiquarian John Leland remembered it when he complained that 'the great wood of Cheviot' was
'spoyled now and crokyd old trees and scrubs remayne'. The reality
was that the clearance had continued into the historic period and
evidence of high altitude cultivation, particularly in the Lammermuirs,
is not hard to find. On the beautiful, winding road between Duns and
Gifford an evening sun will often show up a pattern of folded rigs on
the flanks of the bare hills.

The uplands were attractive not only because of the kinder climate,
they were dry in another sense. Before the agricultural improvements
of the eighteenth and nineteenth centuries the Borders landscape was
much more boggy. Valley bottoms were often very difficult to negotiate after the rains of winter. Many old roads preferred the dry and
draining ground of the hills and the network of medieval and early
modern drovers' tracks through the Moorfoots and the Cheviots
remember that. In lower lying ground mosses could be dangerous,
sometimes bottomless, and it was important to know exactly which
way the track turned. Badly herded beasts sometimes blundered into
bogs to be sucked under, thrashing and bellowing in wide-eyed panic.

In short, there existed a vigorous prehistoric and medieval upland
community in the Borders. These were people who cultivated crops on
the high plateaux, who reared animals on good grassland and who
animated places we now think of as bleak and remote, places where
almost no one now lives. In many important ways the hill country of
the middle ages was a good place to live – but it was not to remain so.

In the early fourteenth century the climate began to change radically. The year after the battle at Bannockburn, 1315, saw a dreadful
summer. From the end of June it seemed to rain incessantly (King
Robert I was forced to abandon the siege of Carlisle because his
engines stuck fast in the mud) and the harvest failed. There was
another failure in 1316. This was a prelude to what scientists call 'the
little ice age'. For approximately five hundred years, up to *c.*1850, the
Earth's climate grew harsher. Average mean temperatures fell and a
cycle of 30-year periods of bad weather began. Severe winters were
followed by wet summers. In Europe the paintings of Dutch and
Flemish masters recorded the long, icebound months. Particularly
memorable is Pieter Breughel's *Hunters in the Snow*. Two periods of
poor weather appear to have occured in the sixteenth century, one
prompting reports of extreme, extended spells of rain in the 1570s, the
other producing cold, sunless summers into the 1590s.

SLIPSHOD

Animals undertaking a long journey, usually to market, needed to
be shod. Hooves used to grass and particularly to damp or soft
ground were themselves soft, and since some travelling would be
over hard, firm tracks, protection was necessary. Sharp stones could
cut an animal's foot and make it lame, slow and doomed. There are
many phrases and expressions deriving from the ancient craft of
farriery or blacksmithing, but 'slipshod'is apposite here. It originally referred to a loosely nailed shoe. Other animals, apart from
ponies, were shoed. Geese were made to waddle through hot pitch
or tar, then into a patch of grit and sand, and finally into a mill pond
to cool and fix the mixture. Tough grass and straw socks were
knitted for pigs and their tender trotters, while halved pony shoes
were nailed onto the harder cloven hooves of cows. It was impossible to get cattle to cooperate in the same way as ponies, and so
they were upended and roped to keep them still. When the reivers
lifted cattle, sheep or horses, they had to make a long journey
whatever the condition of their feet, and more than a few must have
gone lame and been left hobbling by the wayside.

Bad weather was rarely reported directly, as something noteworthy in
itself. Periods or incidents influenced, often decisively, by storms or

floods are what helps build a pattern. The terrible raids into Roxburgh-shire led by Henry VIII's generals, the Earl of Surrey and Lord Dacre, were much inhibited by a series of sustained rainstorms. Even though it had not been designed to resist the sort of artillery trundled up by the English bombardiers, Cessford Castle held out against Surrey's siege – because of the weather. The defenders had dug an earthwork, a 'vaw-mure', around the central stone tower, the donjon of the castle. This was likely a deep ditch topped by a massive earthen bank formed from the upcast, so thick that gunstones or cannonballs could not breach it. And the ditch probably presented attackers with, literally, insurmountable problems. The pouring rain must have turned it into a slithering quagmire, its sides too treacherous to be scaled.

When Sir Andrew Kerr, the lord of Cessford, at last came to negotiate, he offered to give up the stronghold if he and his men could leave unmolested with 'bag and baggage'. The Earl of Surrey was much relieved, believing that in the dreadful weather, he could not have hoped to take the castle.

It rained for much of the summer of 1523 and on into the autumn. By October the Scots were retaliating by attacking Wark Castle, an ancient fortress on a height above the south bank of the Tweed. Positioning his guns on the north bank, the Scottish Regent, the Duke of Albany, hoped to bring down the new polygonal artillery block-house built at Wark by the master mason at Berwick. Again the rain intervened. Whether it made ranging and aiming the cannon difficult or the setting of them in a sound footing in a battery impossible is unclear. What is certain is that in 1523 the heavens opened often and for days on end.

When the Earl of Sussex mustered his forces to pursue rebel catholic noblemen into Scotland in August of 1570, it rained so heavily and for so long that the expedition had to be seriously delayed. In 1573 a *tempest* of rain raged for eight days and nights without abating until a long stretch of Berwick-upon-Tweed's medieval walls was washed away and the bridge across the river badly damaged. They had stood since Edward I's time, built in the early 1300s.

Snow fell often in the sixteenth century and heavily, cutting com-munications for long periods. And when the thaws came, streams roared into torrents and the fords across the Tweed became impass-able for many days. In November 1570 a ferocious winter set in and storms blew regularly until the following February. The historian, William Camden, wrote that it was not only frequent periods of warfare which had made Borderers tough, the cruel weather had also 'hardened their carcasses'.

Many of the government officials appointed by Elizabeth I to posts in the Borders came from the south of England, and while complaints about the rain and the cold might have been expected, their comments are not routine grumblings. Some were vehement. The wonderfully named Peregrine Bertie, Baron Willoughby d'Eresby, was a reluctant Warden of the English East March. He hated the Border weather with a passion:

> If I were further from the tempestuousness of the Cheviot Hills, and were once retired from this accursed country, whence the sun is so removed, I would not change my homeliest hermitage for the highest palace there.

Appropriately he died of a heavy cold in 1601.

Notwithstanding Peregrine Bertie's exceptional unhappiness, there is a persistent note of misery at the worsening climate in the 1570s and the 1590s. And it can be no coincidence that this was the time when reiving wound up to its most extreme pitch, when theft was probably less a matter of greed and more a question of survival. In the weeks and months of rain, grass at least grew and hardy cattle, sheep and goats could feed and put on condition, and present themselves as coveted targets for thievery.

Poetry is a risky source of historical evidence, but despite the licence, it can supply atmosphere and make a basic point effectively. Walter Scott of Satchells wrote a famous verse which understands an essential fact of sixteenth-century life in the Border hills:

> I would have none think that I call them thieves.
>
> The freebooter ventures both life and limb
> Good wife and bairn, and every other thing;
> He must do so, or else must starve and die,
> For all his livelihood comes of the enemy.

Leaving aside the rights, wrongs, truths and half truths, Scott's verse does state the economic circumstances bluntly. The consistently bad weather of the second half of the sixteenth century and its sustained effect on the hill peoples of southern Scotland and northern England must have greatly fostered the creation of a criminal society.

AYE IN COMMON!

To people who depended utterly on what it can produce, the question of the ownership of land and the right to it were of the first importance. And yet in the sixteenth-century Border hills, it can be unclear to a historian. To contemporaries it could not have been vague. Around the Border towns and larger villages, there were common lands where the indwellers had customary rights. They could graze their beasts, and cut turf, peat and bracken. Some of the commons were huge – at its zenith Selkirk had 22,000 acres. But what happened in the hills? Where religious houses had been landowners, there was usually great precision. For example, the monks of Kelso Abbey owned much of the beautiful Bowmont Valley which leads close to the foot of Cheviot itself. In a series of documents they set down their boundaries and rights very clearly. It must be assumed that the windblown wastes of the watershed ridges were similarly precisely apportioned. But the historical documentation is hard to come by. The upland society of the Borders remained Celtic in many ways and the old practice of 'gavelkind' (which almost destroyed the medieval economy of Wales) still held, especially in Tynedale and Redesdale. A landowner divided his property equally amongst all his sons – until the individual legacies became so small as to be unviable. (Some historians believe that the poverty created by generations of gavelkind let directly to reiving.) In important ways the surnames of the Borders behaved like Highland clans – did their people have a similar relationship to the land owned by those names and their chiefs, or heidsmen? Sir Robert Bowes, at one time Warden of the English Middle March, seems to have seen the ownership of the valley of the North Tyne as surname-based:

> The country of North Tynedale which is more plenished with wild and misdemeaned people, may make of men upon horseback and upon foot about six hundred. They stand most by four surnames, whereof the Charltons be the chief. And in all services or charge impressed upon that country the Charltons and such as be under their rule, be rated for one half of that country, the Robsons for a quarter, and the Dodds and Milburns for another quarter.

The upcountry was never heavily populated; the quality of the land simply could not support dense settlement. But in the sixteenth century many more people lived in the likes of Liddesdale than do now. Aside from Carlisle, Berwick and Dumfries, towns were really villages and villages hamlets. Borderers lived overwhelmingly on the land, close to what they sowed and reared.

Working in the 1580s and 1590s, a well-known cartographer called Timothy Pont drew a detailed map of Liddesdale. When set beside even the largest scale modern Ordnance Survey for the same area, the differences are striking. Pont's map is closely speckled with place-names, most of them farm-steadings, some of them two or three variations on a single name, many lining the banks of streams and rivers. By comparison the modern map is sparse, the place-names have faded from history, the old cottages and barns reclaimed by the grass. Around Hermitage Castle a dozen farms clustered when Pont plotted his map at the end of the sixteenth century. Graistonhaugh Tofts, Ginglenwells, Rispeylaw, Faskenn, Byresteads and Reddadenn have all disappeared, leaving only shadowy contours in the grass only visible when they are lit by a late evening sun.

EATS AND SHOOTS

Grass is a remarkable plant. Not only is it an excellent coloniser, able to take over large areas very quickly, it also thrives on being cropped or cut. Unusually it grows from the bottom upwards and so when it regularly grazed, it becomes more dense and grows ever more abundantly. What farmers call 'sheep lawns' can be seen over the Border hills. These are places where constant cropping has produced a green, carpet-like effect, the sort of thing suburban gardeners dream of. They should consider renting some sheep – because it appears that most grazing animals like very short grass and bite it close to the roots. Perhaps it tastes better, is more juicy. Two general sorts of grass grow in Britain. Most sheep graze hill pasture, which is entirely natural and full of herbs and other beneficial nutrients. The other kind is sown grass. Its use came about when crop rotation began to demand that fields previously sown with corn or a root crop be returned periodically to grass. It was also a good way of moving animals around to fertilise the ground with their droppings. Most hay is taken from sown grasses such as cocksfoot, timothy or ryegrass, but where a farmer can cut a

crop from high summer pasture or a meadow which has never been
ploughed, he can command a hefty premium for it.

That relative density of settlement meant a landscape much more
intimately detailed, its every resource used and given a name. Small,
dyked inbye fields clustered around low-built farmhouses made from
material close to hand and which blended so seamlessly with the
native colours of the landscape that they could easily be missed by a
modern eye. Outbye was likely more casually wooded than it is now
(leaving aside the massive modern forest planting which has seen
many hillsides disappear under a blanket of sitka green) with copses
and thickets left standing to bield (shelter) beasts and supply a source
of windfall firewood. Peat was cut from dark brown banks which are
now mistaken for erosion, and of course no roads existed. People and
ponies walked along tracks little more than a foot or two wide and
which followed the grain of the land closely. More like sheepwalks on
a hillside than anything we might now call a road.

There were ancient exceptions. Well into the medieval period the
old Roman roads through the Borders were regularly travelled. Wide,
able to take wheeled vehicles and with hard bottoming in place, they
had weathered the rains of more than a thousand winters. At the
beginning of the fourteenth century Edward II led his invading armies
north on Dere Street and the tramping soldiers and their baggage train
were strung out for 20 miles as the old road snaked up through the
Cheviot Hills, passing the tumbled-down ramparts and ditches of the
marching camps dug by the legionaries at Chew Green. The Roman
road then aimed arrow-straight at the ancient army depot of Trimon-
tium, the three Eildon Hills clearly visible to the north, rising up out of
the Tweed Valley. Sometimes called the *Gamelspath* (an early Anglian
personal name, perhaps a powerful landowner), Dere Street was used
by drovers and their great herds making the long trek to southern
markets in the eighteenth and nineteenth centuries, and in the sixteenth century by large and confident bands of Border Reivers driving
herds which rarely belonged to them.

Further east, towards the huge, grey-green hump of Cheviot itself,
runs an even older road also frequently used by reivers running forays.
Clennel Street originally led from Kelso up to the head of the lovely
Bowmont Valley, south of Yetholm, up over the Windy Gyle and
down the English side to Harbottle and the winding River Coquet. It

was certainly busy and important enough for Henry II of England to order the building of a substantial castle to guard its southern terminal. Possibly another personal name, or a description whose meaning is lost, Clennel Street was sometimes marked on maps as 'The Ermspeth', and that means 'The Eagles' Road'. The more usual name first comes on record as 'Clenhill' in 1242 but it may have been trodden in prehistoric times, perhaps when better weather and longer growing seasons allowed cultivation in the valleys on either flank of the Windy Gyle. Clennel Street was certainly used by large raiding parties whose strength made stealth irrelevant. Still, their ponies would have glad of the sure and solid footing. Wheeled traffic could also use Clennel Street and up in the hills stands a lonely eighteenth-century milestone with 'Kelso 15' on one side and 'H11' on the other for the distance to Harbottle. On the latest Ordnance Survey the name has been half-forgotten and the old thief road is now simply marked as 'The Street'.

Mosses could be very dangerous. Not patches of puddled, soft ground spiked by clumps of marsh grass and dotted with willow scrub, but places where a stumble or lost footing would at best result in a bad soaking or at worst a drowning in deep, black pools and their cloying, sucking mud. Fords rather than bridges were where rivers and streams were crossed and if heavy rain made a spate then that was that – until the level dropped. The difficulty – to say nothing of the dangers – of travel kept most peaceable people snug at home in the winter and willing to go only as far as they had to in the summer.

COUNTRY ROADS

While farm workers tended to stay put, travelling only to local markets and little further, medieval roads could nevertheless be busy. Merchants, itinerant craftsmen, pilgrims, nobility and royalty were often on the move. Roman roads such as Dere Street and prehistoric tracks like Clennel Street remained in use well into the eighteenth century. In England, where the Roman province lasted for nearly four centuries, the road network was much more extensive and in the twelfth century, Watling Street, Ermine Street, the Fosse Way and the prehistoric Icknield Way (which travelled along the tops of the watershed ridges) were all named as royal roads and brought into the king's protection. They were metalled, or paved, and had to be wide enough to allow two carts to pass each other, or sixteen armoured knights to ride abreast. This last sounds more like a formula than anything practical. The ancient roads lasted a long time. In the Borders the documents relating to Kelso Abbey talk of a 'via regis' between Roxburgh and Berwick, but despite the royal label, it was likely little more than a track by the banks of the Tweed. The 'Military Road' running to the south of Hadrian's Wall must have been well used. However, water routes were always prefered where possible and if rivers were deep enough, rafts and barges were towed down them. And in the west the Solway was busy.

The Cheviot landscape was changing. Because growing seasons were shortening in the second half of the sixteenth century and the weather generally deteriorating, farmers were abandoning cultivation, what contemporaries called 'tillage'. They were turning over more and more land to pasture. When the Earl of Hertford led a large army through the Borders in 1544 on a tremendously destructive and punitive raid, he remarked that the Borderers in his ranks (for there were plenty) 'will not willingly burn their neighbours' [corn]'. They knew how precious it was and what misery would follow the ruin of a subsistence crop. Stealing cows and sheep was one thing – they might be replaced or retrieved – but burnt corn was a disaster for which there was no remedy.

The gradual movement away from cultivation to pastoralism in turn led to depopulation and impoverishment, trends which showed up in the formal musters of men obliged to render military service which were occasionally held in the English marches. In 1580 and 1584 men who turned up complained that too much land was being given over to the grazing of beasts, and in 1597 the Dean of Durham Cathedral was anxious that the church's holdings in the Borders were too little cultivated. Although no one could be aware of it at the time, it looks very much as though climate deterioration was driving these changes.

BRIGANTIUM

When the Roman invaders pushed north into Yorkshire, they fought King Venutius and the nation of the Brigantes. In AD71 the legions won an important victory at Stanwick and their historian, Tacitus, hinted that they had been up against a confederacy of hill peoples and that Venutius 'had help from outside'. He meant warriors from the northern Pennines, the Cheviots and possibly the Southern Uplands. The Selgovae and the Brigantes were of the same stock as well as on the same side. The most famous Brigantian queen was Cartimandua and her name means 'Sleek Pony'. Letters written from the Roman fort of Vindolanda, near Haltwhistle, confirm a horse-riding society, noting that the natives 'had very many cavalry'. The Brigantian confederacy was a frequent source of trouble, rebelling several times, notably in 138. One of the reasons for Hadrian's Wall was that it cut through their territory, dividing a disruptive people. A horse-riding culture, a persistent threat to central authority – sounds familiar.

Liddesdale still looks like a reiver valley – despite the power lines, the abandoned railway and the tarmac road up to Whitrope and Hawick. A hard place that used to breed hard-bitten people and still a bleak place to live through a bad winter. In the sixteenth century there were likely as many people living in the valley (some historians believe more) as do now. Newcastleton is much bigger, an expanded, planned village which absorbed the old Armstrong place at Whithaugh. But by comparison the modern hinterland is empty, nothing like as densely settled as it was in the time of the reivers.

The Armstrongs rode out of Liddesdale and were a constant cause of trouble, particularly in the English middle marches. The royal officer appointed as warden to protect Elizabeth I's English subjects from Scottish raids (and each other) was Robert Carey and he left a memoir. It is eloquent about how Borderers understood and used the countryside they knew so well.

In June 1601 the Armstrongs mounted a destructive, punitive raid on the little English town of Haltwhistle, near Hadrian's Wall. They attempted to burn it down, 'running up and down the streets with lights in their hands'. But only ten houses were set on fire and after being driven off, the Armstrongs swore they would be back in greater strength to finish the job.

Robert Carey was forced to take decisive action and he laid his plans carefully. So that he could strike quickly against Liddesdale, his men built a stockade on the frontier above Bewcastle and it was garrisoned with 150 troopers. The Armstrongs immediately countered by abandoning their strongholds and farms in Liddesdale and melting away into the landscape. Taking their valuables (and presumably their herds and flocks), the reivers entered the wilderness of Tarras Moss. It lay to the west of Liddesdale in the high valley between Tinnis Hill and Whita Hill. There is a single track road from Newcastleton to Langholm which winds around the edges of what was Tarras Moss and it is a stern, wild and windswept waste. In 1601 it was an impenetrable maze and a place of impregnable refuge for those who knew its tracks. 'It was', wrote Robert Carey in his memoir, 'of that strength and so surrounded by bogs and marshy ground, with thick bushes and shrubs, that they fear no force nor power of England or Scotland.'

On the islands in this inland sea of treacherous mire the Armstrongs believed they could outlast the garrison in Carey's 'pretty fort' on Bewcastle Waste, and all they had to do was wait for the winter to chase away the soft southerners. Carey recorded a message from the defiant reivers:

> They sent me word that I was like the first puff of a haggis, hottest at the first, and bade me stay there as long as weather would give me leave; they would stay in Tarras-Wood 'till I was weary of lying in the Waste, and when I had had my time, and they no whit the worse, they would play their parts, which should keep me waking the next winter.

It was an insolent, cocky but broadly correct analysis, and Carey too knew that winter was no time for large-scale operations in Liddesdale, to say nothing of Tarras Moss. In early July his plan began to unfold. Under cover of darkness the warden sent ahead 150 troopers to circle the moss and bottle up the three safe exits to the west and the Scottish side. His captains were guided by an anonymous traitor, 'a moffled man not known to any of the company, no doubt someone with a grudge'.

The Armstrongs had set lookouts on the high ridges above Tarras but none of them saw the government troopers moving through the half-dark. Once his men had set their ambushes at the exit-paths, Carey moved quickly. With 300 troopers and 1,000 footmen, he attacked the moss. Just as dawn crept over Tinnis Hill, his men surprised the Armstrong camps and with much clang and clamour drove them towards the western exits. Where the ambushes were sprung. Important prisoners were taken but when others saw what was happening, they turned back into the wilderness and disappeared. And none of Carey's men made the mistake of following them.

Robert Carey was an outstanding officer, probably the most effective March Warden appointed by Queen Elizabeth, and the flushing of Tarras Moss was a superbly planned and executed operation. But it was also an exception. Border reivers knew their country intimately and almost always used it to advantage. Agricultural improvement, widespread (and very ugly) forestry planting and effective drainage have combined to change the character of this ancient wilderness almost beyond recognition, making the Armstrongs' use of Tarras Moss and other inaccessible places difficult to visualise. But it was true, there were trackless, uncharted wastes where only natives dared venture, and the reivers really were kings of a wild frontier.

PECORINO

One of the most delicious European cheeses is made from ewes' milk and sold in Italy. Pecorino comes in delicate flavours, from sweet to salty, and can be fearsomely expensive. Border reivers liked it. In their buchts the ewe-milkers of the hills made a variety of very hard, white cheese which they called 'whitemeats'. It kept for a long time without spoiling but was so hard that it had to be soaked and sometimes beaten with a hammer before it could be safely chewed and digested. On long-range raids, riders would take a hunk with them, and also a small amount of oatmeal. This habit was noticed by a French diplomat, Jean Froissart, who visited the Borders in the 1360s: 'Under the flaps of his saddle, each man carries a broad plate of metal, behind the saddle a little bag of oatmeal . . . they place the plate over the fire, mix with water their oatmeal, and when the plate is heated, they put a little of the paste upon it and make a thin cake like a cracknell or biscuit, which they eat to warm their stomachs.' An oatcake remains the best accompaniment to cheese.

Since a time out of mind, back into the deep prehistoric past when the land was even less tamed, the farmers of the Border uplands had in fact been herdsmen who only cultivated crops where they could. They drove cattle and sheep and also lived off a wild harvest of roots, fruits and berries as well as what game they could trap and catch. The earliest name attached to these people was 'Selgovae', meaning 'the Hunters', and in the medieval period the hunting dogs bred and trained by their descendants were famous throughout Europe. It was a persistent tradition. When Border reivers disappeared into their maze of hill valleys, mosses and byways, their pursuers sometimes used hunting dogs, what were called 'slewdogs', or scent-hounds to find their trails. Working on a leash with a handler urging them on, the slewdogs were also known as 'rauchs' in the Borders. They were trained not to bark or become excited when they closed in on their quarries. These animals were very valuable and raiders stole them whenever they could.

BEST FRIENDS

Dogs were domesticated very early in the prehistoric period, possibly from stray wolves who joined a human 'pack'. At first they appear to have been used as guard-dogs, warning of dangerous or unknown approaches by barking or perhaps howling. When wolves still prowled the Border hills looking to take lambs or old and weaker ewes, pastoral dogs warned the shepherds who would try to beat off an attack. When that threat receded in the middle ages (when Border sheep-rearing was radically commercialised by the abbeys of Kelso, Melrose, Dryburgh and Jedburgh), the dogs developed other skills, particularly in herding, what is known as 'the gather'. Border collies (the name seems to derive from 'coaly' or black) were first bred in the late nineteenth century by a Northumbrian farmer, Adam Telfer. Small, compact and very quick over short distances, collies have a keen intelligence and an expressive eye. Their owners of course claim that they are the smartest dogs to be found anywhere. Most ewes would reluctantly agree.

The beasts reared in the sixteenth century, their breeds of cattle and sheep, were much smaller and more hardy than the animals grazing on modern farms. They lived out, watered by streams running down hillsides and sheltered by the natural contours of the land. Mostly black in colour and also dark in nature, cattle were much less domesticated than the big bullocks we see now. In winter their coats grew shaggy and the animals sometimes deliberately rolled in mud to make them matted and therefore better able to keep out the biting wind. This must have made them difficult to see on the hillside on a grey day. When it was stormy, cows could be good indicators of the direction of the prevailing wind. They turn their backsides towards it and drop their heads to use their own bodies as a windbreak. The reivers' cattle will have seemed wild to us, the bulls very dangerous, and difficult to manage with their sharp horns and an instinct for open country.

NOWT, OUSEN AND KYNE

Even the fatter editions of the Oxford English Dictionary make no mention of these words, though they are liberally sprinkled through sixteenth-century reports of reiving. They are all words for cattle and were still in use in the Borders at the end of the twentieth century. 'Ousen' is a variant on oxen (which is an older word for a castrated bull-calf or bullock) as is 'nowt', sometimes written as 'nolte'. The latter can also mean specifically black cattle. 'Kyne' or 'kye' is a general term for cows, but can also mean a milker. All appear to derive from Anglian words first introduced into Scotland in the seventh and eighth centuries. 'Stirk' is used to mean a yearling – either a bullock or a heifer, it appears in no dictionary and yet is still in general use in the Borders. Sheep also had a nomenclature. Wedders were castrated lambs, bred for meat. Gimmers were barren or infertile ewes and a 'tup' is a Border word for a ram, and when fertile ewes had been 'tupped' lambs were expected to follow. Entertainingly 'tup-heidit' means 'a stupid, obstinate man'. Many Border shepherds pronounce it 'tip', and no doubt have come across a few tip-heids. Out on the hills sheep breeding is difficult to control and some farmers in the high valleys above Liddesdale still use an ancient method of contraception. 'Breeking' the ewes involves shepherds sewing a square of stout cloth over the animal's rear end to prevent the tups from mounting them successfully.

Pastoral dogs were slowly losing their prime function as defenders against the wolf-packs which roamed the Cheviots until the middle ages and becoming handy as sheep and cattle herders. More timorous, less aggressive and much smaller than cows, sheep were also more useful, giving both milk and wool. But cattle retained their ancient status as the prime measure of a man's wealth and the herds seem to have been the principal object of most reiver raids.

In springtime herdsmen drove their beasts up to the high summer pastures. As the weather improved and new grass poked through, cattle and sheep were rounded up and the herd-laddies whacked, pushed and roared them onto the old hill-trails. Many pastures were distant from what was known as the wintertown, the home farm, and often sheilings were built at the summertown. These were flimsy structures designed to keep out little more than light rain and wind. Most herd-laddies expected to sleep out through the long, light nights of the summer. No upstanding shielings are to be found nowadays in the Border hills but survivors can still be seen on the Hebridean island of Lewis. On the Barvas Moor, near Stornoway, corrugated iron, wood and sometimes brick huts dot the horizon.

Memories of warm summer nights flit through some of the Border ballads and even in the place-names found in the hills. Up from the wintertown, lassies came to the 'buchts' to milk the ewes, perhaps to make cheese. There was plenty of 'laughin' an daffin' at the yow-milkin'' and probably much else besides. And around the evening crackle of firelight, stories were told. The great tradition – unparalleled elsewhere – of the Border ballads was fostered on these summer nights up on the high grazing. Their written form (for all were held only in memory for many generations), collected by Sir Walter Scott just as they were waning, reflects something of where and how they were recited. Some ballads had dozens of verses, telling long and dramatic stories, and both to involve the listeners (who most likely knew the words anyway) and give the reciter time to remember what came next, the use of the chorus developed. Repeated between each verse, in the same metre, it jogged recollection and kept the tale moving along.

BALLADRY

Following a widespread European tradition, the Border ballads had a standard form of four line stanzas driven by a strong narrative. What distinguishes them is their antiquity. The subject of one of the oldest is the Battle of Otterburn and it was fought in 1388. The opening is classic – and stirring;

> It fell about the Lammas tide
> When muir-men win their hay
> The doughty Douglas bound him to ride
> Into England to drive a prey.

Memorable and with a driving metre, a spoken recital can keep an audience spell-bound. But what is often forgotten is the music. These ballads were originally sung and in his 'Minstrelsy of the Scottish Border', Walter Scott set many of the melodies alongside the text. American musicologists have argued that the ballad tradition transfered to the black communities of the south and they used the form to pass on stories. These often took a blues form, like 'Frankie and Johnny'. But the tradition is not yet dead in the Borders. It appears to be thriving. Collecting ballads and poems composed after Scott published in the early nineteenth century, the historian and poet, Walter Elliot, has compiled a New Minstrelsy of the Scottish Border.

Herds stayed out for as long as possible on the summer pasture. Their absence allowed the inbye fields around the wintertown to recover and be cropped for hay. Those left behind, the women and usually the older men, could use the break to clear up after the clatch and dark of the winter in what Borderers still call 'the redd'. Dykes were repaired, turf cut for roofing and what arable crops there were could grow, safe from beasts breaking in to devour them.

Fattened, glossy with good autumn condition, the herds came down off the hills when the weather began to close down and the year turned around the solstice. These weeks also saw the beginning of the raiding season. Dispersed over the hill pasture (and needing to feed and improve their condition in any case), the cattle and sheep were not a feasible target for reivers in the summer. Far better to come for them where they were handily corralled in the inbye fields and fat and fit enough to make a long journey when they had been lifted. The reivers did not choose to run forays in the winter. The going and the weather was much more difficult (although hard frost could make solid and passable ground out of normally boggy areas), it was the ancient cycle of transhumance which forced them out on rain-swept November nights.

What delivered a party of reivers to their quarry, what indeed made their entire way of life possible was an animal too little remarked upon by historians, the remarkable pony known as the Galloway Nag.

JOCK AND JACK

In sixteenth-century England the more than faintly derogatory term for 'a man of the common people', what we might more kindly term 'a bloke', or 'a fella', was a Jack. The phrase 'Jack of all trades' is a relict. In Scotland the accepted version was 'Jock' and by the seventeenth century, the diminutive 'Jockie' came to be applied to grooms working in aristocratic stables. Later it was also used to describe horse-dealers. By the time horse racing began to organise and enjoy widespread popularity, 'jockeys' had become the name for professional riders hired by owners to sit on their horses. The horses were valuable and had names and well-researched breeding, but their riders were all lumped under one category – wee Jocks.

Also known as 'hobblers' or 'hobbys', they were small, and at only 13 or 14 hands high, would now be thought much too small to carry adults comfortably and suitable only for children learning to ride. But these little ponies were powerfully made, their musculature compact and outline foursquare. In Galashiels, rearing up outside the old town hall, there is a beautifully made bronze sculpture of a fully armed reiver on his Galloway Nag. The rider's feet dangle well below the pony's belly and with his rig-out and weapons, he looks far too heavy, likely to exhaust his mount quickly. Sadly there is now no way to discover if indeed these neat little horses could have managed to bear such a burden. The Galloway Nag became extinct in the nineteenth century – but not before their famous prowess had been noticed by both William Shakespeare and Sir Walter Scott. Here is a second-hand description of the last of them, written in 1858 by William Youatt, an authority on horses and horse-breeding:

> A horse between thirteen and fourteen hands in height is called a Galloway, from a beautiful breed of little horses once found in the south of Scotland, on the shore of the Solway Firth, but now sadly degenerated, and almost lost.

The pure Galloway was said to be nearly fourteen hands high, and sometimes more; of a bright bay or brown, with black legs, small head and neck, and peculiarly deep and clean legs. Its qualities were speed, stoutness, and surefootedness over a very rugged and mountainous country.

Professor Edward Low understood something of the historical role and origins of the Galloways and was also at some pains to point out that nag was not a pejorative term, it simply denoted a small riding horse:

> They exceeded the pony size and were greatly valued for their activity and bottom . . . Besides this part of Scotland [the south] was a country of forays during the rude border wars of the times, when a more agile race than the ordinary pack-horse was naturally sought for; and all along the borders of the two kingdoms, a class [breed] of similar properties existed. Many of the true Galloways of the western counties were handsome, and their general characteristic was activity, and the power of enduring fatigue. Some raids were run over immensely long and difficult distances. Round trips of 100 miles were not uncommon and one daring and celebrated Scottish raid penetrated as far south as Blaydon, across the River Tyne, only a mile or two west of Newcastle. As well as furious, the owners of the stolen cattle must have been amazed. And the ability of the Galloways to deliver their riders to a destination – and then be used to cut out and round up cattle, and after that perhaps expect to be ridden as a cavalry pony in a skirmish or something worse – this was astonishing. They were unique little horses and it is sad that none now live to show how the reivers rode and how they sustained their way of life.

MY LITTLE PONY

The Celtic people of the Borders valued their horses. Calling them 'snow-maned', 'galloping, high-stepping', the seventh-century cavalry warriors of the Gododdin rode out from their fortress on Edinburgh's Castle Rock to challenge the invading Angles in AD 600. On their way south, they stopped at Kelso to be reinforced by Border riders and their prince, Catrawt of Calchvyndd. At Catterick in North Yorkshire, 'the retinue of Gododdin on rough-maned horses like swans, with their harness drawn tight' charged into the ranks of the Germanic invaders and their allies. And were decisively defeated. Their culture and language faded into half-forgotten stories but they did leave intriguing legacies. The Celts of Britain and Europe worshipped a complex and highly localised pantheon of gods. But one fertility goddess was widely revered. She was 'Epona', a mare, and from her the word 'pony' probably derives. Less attractive but equally possible is a Scots-French origin. 'Powny' may come from an obscure French word, 'poulonet' for a little foal, which in turn came from the Latin 'pullus' meaning the same. Eighteenth-century dictionaries defined ponies as 'little Scotch horses' and as the word travelled south it was rubbed smooth into 'pony'. Border Reivers used several names for their riding horses and they may just have coined this one.

Picking their way down steep and slippery hillsides, finding steady footing amongst tussocky bogs, winding their way between boulders and across stoney fords, one of the Nag's greatest qualities was its surefootedness. Much of this was done in darkness, often pursued or pursuing, and although horses have good night vision, the degree of sheer athleticism – to say nothing of trust – between pony and rider is to be marvelled at. Perhaps because the Galloways were small and a man could wrap his legs around its belly to squeeze and thereby give many signals, or shift his seat in subtle ways to change direction, the partnership may have been very close, almost intuitive. One Galloway was celebrated in verse;

> Wat Tinlinn from the Liddelside
> Led a small and shaggy nag
> That, through a bog, from hag to hag,
> Could bound like any Billhope stag.

Often carrying a weapon in one hand and holding the reins in the other, it would have taken no more than a touch on the neck from a good rider to wheel the pony. And in a skirmish where positioning was everything, speed of reaction and nimble footwork of a horse could mean life or death for its rider. A pony able to fiddle its feet to recoil from a blow or launch forward to deliver one was a valuable animal.

Stamina was as prized as agility and although no recent examples exist to confirm that the Galloways could carry a raiding party up over the Cheviot ranges and a long way down the other side – and back – there is an attractive and affectionate memoir from an eighteenth-century Scottish doctor called Anderson which recalls their great depth of staying power:

> In point of elegance of shape, it was a perfect picture; and in disposition was gentle and compliant. It moved almost with a wish, and never tired. I rode this little creature for twenty-five years, and twice in that time I rode a hundred and fifty miles at a stretch, without stopping except to bait [eat], and that not for above an hour at a time. It came in at the last stage with as much ease and alacrity as it travelled the first. I could have undertaken to have performed on this beast, when it was in its prime, sixty miles a day for a twelvemonth, running without any extraordinary exertion.

JOCKS AND GEORDIES

Uncomfortably for some, there is no question that Scots is a dialect of English. To distinguish it from Gaelic and Norn, Scots was known as 'Inglis' in the middle ages. Did the reivers on either side of the border speak in the same way, in the same dialect? Probably. When the Anglian warbands overran the Tweed Basin in the seventh and eighth centuries, their version of Old English gradually came to be spoken across what is now North Yorkshire, Durham, Northumberland and right up to the foothills of the Lammermuirs – and beyond. The Battle of Otterburn was fought in fading light and then under a full moon. The late fourteenth-century Westminster Chronicle records 'the darkness played such tricks on the English that when they aimed a careless blow at a Scotsman, owing to the chorus of voices speaking a single language, it was an Englishman that they cut down'. Shared dialect words between Geordies and Jocks (which are of course much more Geordie than Jock in origin, the direction of linguistic spread being from south to north) remember that common language – the likes of 'bairn', 'canny', 'hoose' and 'bonnie'. On the western side of the border the dialect map is less clear but likely to have been similar. The language of the ballads shows some differences between Scots and English, but they are not striking. Andrew Boorde, an English doctor who practised in Scotland in the 1540s, reckoned that 'English and Scots doth follow together in speech' and in a late sixteenth-century play a dramatic device requires a Redesdale man to be mistaken for a Scot.

It was the Reformation which began to divide the dialect. In the second half of the sixteenth century independent and reformed English and Scottish churches were created and as a result different education systems began to divide the community and polarise the way in which Borderers spoke. Which, bonnie lad and lasses, is a shame.

In an age of motor transport we easily forget that in the centuries before cars and buses, most people could ride, probably as many as can drive nowadays. In the upland communities of the Borders, ponies were central to their lives. They carried herdsmen out into the hills behind their beasts and took them on all sorts of peaceful errands. Young herd-laddies probably threw a cloth and a bridle onto a long-suffering old pony and learned to ride the hard way, no stirrups and roaring and yelling across the heather.

A LOAD OF BOLLS

Units of measurement have changed regularly throughout history. Since around the 1960s we have moved gradually from imperial weights and quantities to metric. The process began officially with the creation of a decimal coinage in 1970 and will end when we talk of kilometres rather than miles.

a boll: 140 pounds
2 bolls: 1 sack
a hand: 4 inches
a cubitt: 18 inches
a military pace: 2 feet, 6 inches
a rod, *pole or perch*: 5 feet
a truss of straw: 36 pounds
a truss of old hay: 56 pounds
a bushel: 8 gallons.

Turned out to graze when not in use, the Galloways grew shaggy in winter, their thick coats protecting them against the worst of the weather. Good ponies were much prized and while out on a raid, reivers always stole them when they could. English legislators went so far as to control the sale of horses into Scotland very strictly. As much as weapons, they were regarded as instruments of war and criminality. English bloodstock and their taller stallions were wanted because, as one observer noted 'the Scots ponies were full of spirit and patient of labour but very little'. Race-meetings were popular along the border, and they provided very plausible cover for illicit horse dealing. A notorious reiver, Kinmont Willie Armstrong, is thought to have come regularly to Langholm Races for much more than sport and he often bought up big English horses for resale in Scotland.

It was a tribute to their central role that when the era of reiving came to an end at the beginning of the seventeenth century, it was specifically forbidden to own a pony over a certain value – in other words a good Galloway Nag.

What this rapid historical sketch – racing back and forth across millennia – serves to show is only that the landscape looked different in the time when the reivers rode and that the hills and upland valleys where they lived were not the windblown wastes they are now. They could be infinitely more dangerous and intimately better known. But much of that ancient knowledge has passed into memory and the community of the hills has almost entirely fled. It is difficult now to believe that only four centuries ago more than 2,000 horsemen could ride out of Liddesdale. But they did.

4

The Condition of Men

Officially Sir Thomas Carleton was Deputy Warden of the English West March, a royal official charged to ensure good order and the rule of law, but by nature he was an expert cattle thief, a talented, well-organised reiver. Under the unconvincing guise of furthering government policy, he plundered deep into Dumfriesshire in the winter of 1547. Needing a base for operations, he led his riders up Annandale to the Johnstone stronghold of Lochwood Tower. One of the reiving freelances in his party, Sandie Armstrong, had told him that although it was immensely well built and appointed, the tower was garrisoned by only a handful of men and some female servants. It was too good an opportunity to miss, and Carleton determined to take it. And very unusually he left a record of what happened.

Lochwood's first line of defence was the treacherous moss which surrounded it. Carleton chose a party of his best men, had them dismount and follow him carefully and silently through the boggy ground. It was late on a dull March afternoon, enough light in the sky to find the path but too little for Lochwood's defenders to pick out the shapes of the reivers creeping closer and closer to the barnekin, the outer wall. When darkness fell Carleton and a dozen men slipped over and into the outer courtyard. They 'stole into the house within the barnekin and took the wenches and kept them secure in the house till daylight'. The serving girls must have been terrified as they were gagged, bound and perhaps worse. Without doubt information was speedily extracted. Locked in the tower were only two men and one kitchen maid. They slept sound, oblivious of the danger waiting below.

As first light crept over the Moffatdale Hills the reivers hid quietly in the courtyard house, squinting out of the windows for signs of life in the tower. They knew that if a sudden alarm was raised and the doors were not opened from the inside that even against only two defenders and a servant, they would not take Lochwood easily. Eventually the reivers saw a man appear on the wall-walk up at roof level. Dressed only in his shirt, no doubt yawning and stretching in the cold morning air, he could see nothing amiss and called inside for the serving lass to go down and open the outer doors. There were two: an iron grill inside to keep out attackers and a wooden one on the outside of the door passage to keep out the weather. When the maid rattled back the bolts 'our men within the barnekin broke a little too soon'. She saw them running towards the doorway and very nearly got the wooden door shut and bolted before the first reiver slammed into it. Shouldering it ajar and with others forcing it open, they clattered inside and raced up the spiral stairs before any more internal defences could be closed against them.

It was a close-run thing and as soon as the stronghold was taken Carleton manned it with a substantial garrison. While they raided the countryside around, Lochwood Tower remained in English hands for three years.

Often called 'peel' towers, many of them patterned the Border landscape. In times of near-anarchy they were focal points of refuge for those heidsmen and local lords who could afford to have one built. Lochwood is ruined now but a very well preserved example of a peel tower occupies a commanding site near Kelso. Perched on a rocky outcrop and looking over wide vistas on every side, Smailholm Tower belonged to the surname of Pringle, and it was well made and very strong.

The term 'peel' tower comes from the barnekin wall described by Thomas Carleton. Many were rebuilt in stone but the original peels or 'pales' were wooden stockades. Inside them animals could be safely corralled and servants housed, as at Lochwood. Often ditches had been dug around the barnekin and the stakes of the stockade driven into the upcast – an ancient practice stretching back millennia to the prehistoric hillforts of the Borders. Thick thorn hedges were sometimes planted around to make an approach more awkward and slow down an assault.

PALUS

Each Roman legionary carried a 'palus', a cut and sharpened stake, in his backpack. It must have been an awkward burden on occasion, but a necessary one. When the Romans tramped into the Cheviots in

AD 79, they built marching camps right on the watershed at Chew
Green. When Border reivers walked their ponies that way, they will
have been able to make out the clear rectangular lines of ditches and
ramparts. And around the sixteenth-century fort at Bewcastle, the
wide encirclement of the Roman camp was obvious. As a matter of
routine, legionaries always dug a camp each time they stopped
overnight for they had learned through bitter experience always to
defend themselves in hostile country. In only a couple of hours they
will have dug a ditch (to a standard plan) and piled the upcast on the
inside. Into the banked up earth they drove their sharpened stakes to
create an instant stockade. Archaeologists have debated how this
worked. A paling fence style with the stakes driven in vertically
might have been easily pushed over by charging attackers. Perhaps
they made caltrops, tying the sharp stakes together in spikey star-
shapes and setting them on top of the upcast. The 'palus' has hung
around in English. Not only has it supplied the derivation of paling,-
as in paling fencing, it has also given us the phrase 'beyond the pale'.
This originated in Ireland. When the Elizabethans were attempting
to colonise the country, they built a long stockade around Dublin –
to keep the natives beyond it.

At Smailholm the view from the short wall-walk at the foot of the
roof-pitch is sweeping. Watchers could see far to the south, away to
the foothills of the Cheviots and the valley-mouths out of which many
raiding parties rode. If English reivers came in strength or a government raid such as Sussex' invasion of 1544 came from the east, on the
road up the Tweed from Berwick, Smailholm could see the approach
from a long way off. This gave the Pringles precious time to make a
decision – to stay and negotiate or gather up valuables and flee into the
hill country and moorland to the north.

At the end of the wall-walk there is a stone seat for the lookout. It
nestles against the chimney breast and on the long winter nights of the
reiving season, whoever was on watch will have shivered and been
grateful to whoever thought of that. Beside is a recess for a small
lantern. It was useful for light, but even more as a means to set fire to
the bundled balefire that lay close at hand in an iron crucible. When it
blazed on Smailholm's top, half the Tweed Valley will have seen it.

Like Lochwood, there are two doors. The inner iron grill was
known as a *yett* and in Border Scots the phrase 'steek the yett!!'

for close the door is still roared on a windy winter's night. Lintels were also often set low, forcing even smaller people to stoop under them, and designed to check anyone rushing to force a way in. Above Smailholm's outer door a slit is cut through the thick wall. Far too narrow to be breached or even easily fired on, it was used to rain arrows, crossbow bolts, and later, bullets on those trying to batter down the door or set fire to it.

The walls of peel towers were very thick, sometimes more than two metres. This was as much an architectural necessity for these tall buildings as for any defensive purpose. Solid and wide founds were needed for what were often the highest buildings for miles around. Certainly thick masonry helped to discourage attackers who might attempt to mine their way in (a tried and favoured method, used to get into Carlisle Castle when Kinmont Willie was rescued, was to remove those stones into which a bolt was slid at a doorway) but it would not have detained an artillery battery for long. That was not their purpose. Border towers aimed to repel fast-moving raiders and not armies trundling cannon around the countryside.

Windows were small and always set high up in the walls, never at ground level. Even on bright days it was very dark inside. The ground floor was lit only by a door, and frequently barrel-vaulted; it was used as a store and occasionally to house beasts rather than human beings. In emergencies milking cows and the best ponies would be quickly led into these 'pends' and tethered with some hay shoved in a handy rack. Measuring an average of 10 by 13 metres, they could accommodate many animals. In the sixteenth century farmers packed their cows and horses together tightly and perhaps as many as 40 might be squeezed into a pend and the yett and outer door secured behind them. It will have been a dark, steaming, smelly and noisy place as the animals sensed the danger outside. Neighing and lowing, they will have splattered the floor in their fear. Ventilation holes were cut in the barrel vault and often a trapdoor led to the first floor.

GUNNERY

Guns, gunpowder, canon and pistols were a feature of European military history for a long time before they became influential. Well into the sixteenth century generals prefered the simple and effective technology of archery to the chancy but spectacular power of artillery. At the siege of Roxburgh Castle James II of Scotland stood too close to a huge canon which 'flew in flinders and a part of it struck him in the thigh', and he bled to death. Experienced bombardiers stood well behind and, for some unknown reason, to the left of their pieces after they had lit the fuse. Reivers carried 'daggs', a pair of single-shot pistols, but many prefered a cheaper and very effective crossbow called a 'latch'. It could be fired with one hand while the other clutched the reins of a pony. It also had a more rapid rate of fire, was just as deadly and not likely to go off by accident. Also, raiding parties much preferred the quiet whoosh of bows and arrows to the loud crack of gunfire – which announced their presence for a mile or two in all directions. But in contrast, the great attraction of set-piece artillery was the noise and the explosive flash. It scared defenders of castles and towns in particular, and huge gunstones (canonballs were expensive) could inflict damage at long range. As fortification developed to keep pace with the technology of artillery, three degrees of defensive capability were recognised. The most formidable could withstand 'a siege royal', that is, the whole power of a king or queen's army to bombard a target. There was a more limited medium-sized fortress, and then at the bottom of the scale, a tower able to withstand 'an insult'.

Towers were essentially a stack of single rooms. Above the pend was a 'chaumer' or chamber with a fireplace set into one of the thick walls. The most accessible (and not least for the daily chore of carting up peats, logs and firewood), this room was where a lord or heidsman ate and transacted his business. And because it was warm in the winter, the place where people slept. These were not the houses of the wealthy, as we might imagine them, and there were few comforts. Benches and long settles rather than chairs, boards and trestles rather than tables and when the weather turned bad all was plunged into near-darkness as wooden shutters were closed over the open windows. Most of these had iron grills and very few contained glass. In fact it was considered such a luxury that there are records of noblemen taking their glass panes with them when they moved on to another tower or castle. Sometimes cattle skins were scraped thin, treated with linseed oil and used as windows. They were translucent and kept out the worst of the wind and cold. On the floor of the upper chamber serving lasses strewed heather and rushes on the floor along with some aromatic herbs – meadowsweet was popular – to keep the smell manageable.

Very little different from earlier medieval castles, Border towers were built for security (and for prestige – these buildings were what historians used to call 'a statement in the landscape') and not comfort, and we are inclined to forget that most people used to pass their lives out of doors, using their houses only for shelter, storage and as places to sleep. Indoors was in any case too dark for many domestic tasks. Darning, weaving, spinning and whatever needed precision and dexterity was brought outside if the weather allowed.

Rooms in these towers seem small to us, as do many in historic buildings. And in these days of hygiene, anxieties about body odour and general prurience, we also forget that until very recently people lived cheek by jowl, were concerned above all to keep warm and dry and cared much less than we do about washing. What would turn up our sensitive noses will scarcely have been noticed in a sixteenth-century Border tower.

Above the first floor chamber was another room, and then sometimes another on top of that, tucked under the eaves (and no doubt draughty). These were privy chambers, or private rooms, and they afforded a heidsman or a lord and his lady the occasional comforts of marriage. Many had beds and in the wills of the period a good bed was considered a valuable item. Downstairs, huddled close to the dying embers of the fire, the lesser people curled up on straw palliasses.

There was little privacy. All sorts of hints and unspoken understandings surround sexual relations at this time and in this setting. With so many people sleeping in a communal space, it took a mixture of brazenness and urgency for a man and a woman to make love so close to others. Perhaps mores were very different, so different as not to be worthy of contemporary comment. Certainly the habit of removing all clothing in order to have sex is very recent. Most people used to remain, almost, fully clothed. But even when all that is born in mind it is difficult to imagine a society where sex was routinely listened to and even observed by others (some of them young), especially when the prudishness of the Scottish reformation began to take a strong hold after 1560. Couples certainly walked down lovers' lanes on a summer evening and records talk of children 'begotten in brake and bush'. Perhaps sex was something opportunistic, to be snatched at in passionate moments rather than a matter of routine. And in the chilly Border country, something of an outdoor pursuit.

Border society in the sixteenth century was ready to recognise illegitimacy as a fact of life, and there appears to have been little prejudice against bastard children. Allowances for them were made in wills and half-brothers and sisters were unquestioningly accepted into large families.

The old practice of handfasting persisted for a long time in the Borders, well into the nineteenth century. This was a form of conditional engagement. Couples could contract to live together for a period before being married by a priest or a minister, and if any children were born, they were provided for as part of the contract. Handfasted couples usually lived together for a year. Men and women kept the tradition going because it was sensible, both for the purpose of testing compatibility and also fertility. This last was very important. Farmers and farm labourers needed children to help with intensive agricultural work and right on into the modern period, men with large families found it easier to find a hire on a farm than bachelors. Handfasting was frowned upon by the kirk, but it lasted until the 1880s and 1890s in farm places in the Borders.

READING, WRITING AND REIVING

In Scotland one of the central tenets of the new protestant faith was literacy. More than cleanliness, it was next to Godliness. Believers had to be able to read the Bible, the sacred word of God, and understand it for themselves and shake loose the ancient and corrupting need for a priest to read and interpret it for them. All that mumbo-jumbo had to go. The 'priesthood of all believers' was how the congregations of the reformed church saw themselves. That meant a completely new education system was needed virtually overnight, especially after the removal of all of Scotland's monasteries and nunneries. Up to the middle of the sixteenth century such schooling as there was had been done by monks and nuns. Instead, there would be a school in every parish open to all. It was a hugely expensive undertaking for an impoverished economy but by the early seventeenth century more than 700 schools had been set up and by around 1700 universal coverage had been achieved. To meet a sudden and urgent need for schoolbooks, psalmodies and Bibles the Edinburgh publishing industry clacked into life.

Border towers and their barnekins were also farmhouses and upper rooms were often used for storage, and a simple toilet was placed on an outer wall of the topmost room. This was only used during a siege or when the nightime weather was so bad and the chamber pot so full that there was no option. At Naworth Castle, originally a tower, Lord Dacre organised the primitive plumbing to supply some grim amusement. The toilets drained into the dungeons.

Tower rooms were connected by a spiral staircase both for economy and for defence. Many had a 'trip-step', a riser which was higher than the others and designed to catch out an unwary attacker. When a large raiding party threatened a Border tower, the occupants often fled before them with pack-horses carrying their meagre goods. If they believed that their stronghold might be blown up with gunpowder, they filled the pend and sometimes the upper floors with smouldering peat. As it burned over a long period (it would have needed a great deal of water to put it out) it discouraged the use of gunpowder, which was much more volatile in the sixteenth century. Blackened with peat reek and in a terrible mess it might be, a tower was at least left intact by this tactic and quickly rehabitable.

When occupants chose to stay or were the victims of a surprise attack, they defended the barnekin wall first. This could be 5 or 6 metres high and a metre thick. Some had wooden platforms on the inside and these allowed missiles to be fired at the attackers. Beasts were corralled inside the barnekin and since they were usually the prize at issue, it was vital to protect them.

If defenders were driven back into a tower and they managed to get the doors locked, raiders sometimes used scaling ladders to fight their way up onto the wall-walk. Roofs were often made from split stone slabs, making them virtually fire-proof. But if attackers could reach the wall-walk, the game was up. Sir Robert Carey wrote that his preferred method of gaining entry to a tower was by lifting off the roof slabs and his men dropping down into the top chamber. Down on the ground, others would have tried to fire the door, and if they could gain access to the bottom of the spiral staircase, it allowed them a strangely named tactic. Scumfishing was what smoking out defenders was called and it appears to have been very effective. In 1545 Sir Ralph Eure's horsemen laid siege to Scott of Buccleuch's tower at Mosshouses on the moors north of Melrose. They hacked down the gate into the barnekin 'and got many nags and nolte and smoked very sore the tower and took thirty prisoners'.

Better than scumfishing or scaling ladders was surprise, and when Sir Thomas Carleton won Lochwood Tower, his diary could not hide his satisfaction at a job well done and a prize cheaply won.

Expense forced less wealthy farmers to seek alternative shelter against the frequent storms of anarchy, larceny and warfare. In Tynedale and Redesdale in particular the 'bastle house' was popular and more affordable than a tower. The name is probably from the French 'bastille' for a fort (although bastide seems more likely with its meaning of 'blockhouse') and examples are to be found mainly on the English side of the border. Some are virtually intact like those at West Woodburn and Tarset in Tynedale. Others have been adapted for use as snug modern houses like the one built inside the perimeter of the Roman fort at High Rochester in Redesdale. Better contructed than most, it benefited from a plentiful supply of squared-off Roman masonary readily to hand.

Bastles appear to have developed from wooden prototypes. In 1541 very strong houses constructed out of squared-off oak tree trunks were recorded. Closely bound together and roofed with turf and earth, they looked like the stout log cabins built in the woods of the eastern United States by early pioneers. Attackers found them very difficult to force or burn.

Stone-built bastles were intended to be equally fire-proof, designed to confound a small band of raiders with only their weapons and ingenuity to hand. Like towers they had a ground floor pend for beasts, probably most of what a smaller farmer owned might fit in, the remaining sheep or cattle driven off to safety. A ladder led to a door at first floor height and when trouble rode into view, the farmer and his family scrambled up and pulled it in behind them. Windows were again tiny. The concept of the bastle house was blunt and simple – it was designed to frustrate attackers into giving up and going home.

For most ordinary reivers home was even more basic, little more than shelters able to keep out the wind and most of the rain. It is often said that it took only a few hours to build one of these primitive houses and that those who had lived in them were not much inconvenienced if they were burned or cast down. Bishop Leslie asserted that they were only 'sheephouses and lodges . . . of whose burning they are not sore solaced'. This does not bear much examination. The destruction of a home, however mean and meagre, is never simply an inconvenience, particularly if the surrounding countryside has suffered the same fate, and the winter storms are blowing hard and children need to be fed and kept warm. Moreover the description of these farmhouses and cottages is familiar. Better documented sources suggest that they were little different from what was built elsewhere in Scotland, where regular burning and destruction was not a sad feature of life.

Even when they had been totally razed to the ground, sixteenth-century houses were usually rebuilt on the same footprint. Most were rectangular and about the same size, 8 or 9 metres long and 4 to 5 metres wide. This relative uniformity was dictated by the weakness of the construction methods, the need to keep warm in the winter and the habit of bringing beasts inside in bad weather. An A-frame was made from trimmed tree-trunks and the footing of the gables packed into postholes. A strong ridge-pole was slung between them. To make the walls, stakes were were driven into the ground, spaced at regular intervals. This was to allow freshly cut willow withies to be woven between them in what must have looked like a large set of hurdle-fences. So that they were supple and manageable, the withies had to be green and a good length. Once the walls had reached a height of at least a metre, they were slathered with mud, clay and even cow-dung, and then allowed to dry and harden. This covering gave the walls solidity and helped to keep out the wind and the rain. Sometimes a few courses of stone provided a more secure anchor for the wall-stakes. For more insulation turfs or peats were banked up against the wicker walls and to mitigate dampness a drainage ditch was dug around the house and filled with small stones. The faint outline of these ditches is sometimes the only trace of a long-disappeared house.

Adzed tree boughs were laid against the ridge-pole with a beam running along the wall-head. Tied with flexible pine roots (these are very strong, but home-made ropes were also used), they supported a roof of heather thatch or turf. This was usually weighted with boulders suspended on either end of long ropes slung over the pitch of the roof. Often, a scatter of these large boulders are all that remains for archaeologists to find. The doorway was generally set in one of the long walls and was often the only source of light, windows being awkward to fit into stakes and withies.

In the middle of a beaten earth floor (clay was best) lay the down-hearth. This was little more than a jigsaw of flat stones encircled by a sill of edgers, some with raised flat surfaces for a simmering pot to sit on. The fire was indeed the heart of the house, used for cooking, heat and light, the smoke curling up into the roof and seeping out through the thatch or turf. Because there was no chimney and sometimes not even a smoke-hole, the upper section of the house was constantly smokey (fires were lit at all seasons of the year) and everything smelled of it. Peat was often burned and at night smoored over to ensure that it could be nursed back into life in the morning. Kindling could be hard to come by and moreover it was bad luck to let a fire die. In the hills wood was scarce but peat-banks usually available on the moorlands. In the common land around towns and villages in the Borders the right to cut peat was well protected.

Most people ate potage – every day. What we might call thick soup bubbled at the side of every down-hearth, constantly being replenished by whatever was available; cereal certainly, water, bones, a wild harvest of roots and fungi, and occasional catches of small animals and fish. Nothing remotely nourishing was ever thrown away, it went straight into the pot. Hedgehogs, squirrels, and small birds made for some variety and wet clay was slapped around them and baked in a hot part of the fire. Sheep which had died from disease or drowned were also a welcome addition to the daily diet. The meat was known as 'braxie'. And while the body flesh was considered very acceptable, the head was not wasted either. Singed in the fire, it was added to the pot to make 'sheep's heid kail'. This was tasty and nutritional and still eaten in the borders up until the mid-twentieth century. Flat stones around the down-hearth and the hot sides of a potage skillet were handy for making unleavened bread, something like modern Greek pitta bread or Asian nan bread. Better-off families owned an iron girdle and oatcakes were well made on those, and some had a cauldron suspended from the ridge-pole by a chain.

THE LANGUAGE OF SOUP

When an older generation of Borderers used to make potage or the thick vegetable and meat stock soup known as 'kail' (after the fibrous plant introduced by the agricultural improvers in the eighteenth century), they always talked of it in the plural, even occasionally addressing it directly. 'They're guid efter the secint day, better on the third, ir ee no?' Kail did not do anything as posh as simmer, it 'seethit', and a 'spurtle' was used to stop it sticking to the bottom of the pan. Eaten with a 'boney spin', they, the soup, was often made with 'ket' mutton, certainly cheap and probably from an old ewe past her lambing days. The meat was not eaten with the spin but lifted out from them, the soup, and cut up and set over boiled tatties. At that point it became singular, and it was guid. When all was done, the spin and the bowl ('bowel') had to be 'sained oot' at the sink. Kail stuck to the utensils as well as the ribs.

Inside the house, but not directly over the fire, awnings were sometime hung when the weather was wild. They caught the sooty drips from a leaking thatch and kept the earth floor from becoming sticky under its covering of rushes, grasses and herbs. These houses might be described as vermin-infested hovels but if they were properly built and had a few three-legged stools, a settle and some decent bedding, they could be snug enough.

On a long winter's night, undisturbed by raiders, and with a warming bowl of potage inside them, Borderers sat in the circle of firelight and listened to stories. And they were wonderful stories, magical, unexpected and utterly memorable.

At the end of the eighteenth century, just as they were beginning to fade from history, Walter Scott listened to these stories and wrote them down. They were the *Border Ballads*, and they have much to say about the lives of the people who made them.

Since they existed only in the memories of older people, many of them women, the ballads had to be discovered and collected. One rendition led to another and with the help of John Leyden, James Hogg, Robert Shortreed and others, Scott made seven 'raids' into the likes of Liddesdale, Teviotdale and Annandale. As these old Borderers sat by their fires and sang the verses to him, Scott wrote down an immense tradition, stretching back into the fourteenth century and perhaps even earlier. Some ballads were very long, and 80 verses was not unusual. Others carried long sections of dialogue, many had crucial variations.

The old songs (all the ballads were originally sung or chanted and *The Minstrelsy of the Scottish Border* reproduces many tunes) often have big, dramatic themes. Warfare, cattle raids, tragic love all animate the action. But there is an overwhelming sense of melancholy, of bad and sad ends. Here are some verses from 'The Dowie Dens o' Yarrow':

> At Dryhope lived a lady fair,
> The fairest flower in Yarrow,
> And she refused nine noble men
> For a servan' lad in Gala.

> Her father said that he should fight
> The nine lords all tomorrow,
> And that he that should the victor be
> Would get the Rose of Yarrow.

The servant-lad was killed and his body flung into the Yarrow Water. His lover rode the hills looking for him:

> But she wandered east, so did she wast,
> And searched the forest thorough,
> Until she spied her ain true love,
> Lyin' deeply drowned in Yarrow

She pulled him from the water and took his body back to Dryhope. Her father was not sympathetic and assured her that she would wed well:

> Haud your ain tongue, my faither dear,
> I canna help my sorrow;
> A fairer flower ne'er sprang in May
> Than I hae lost in Yarrow.

> I meant to make my bed fu' wide,
> But you may make it narrow,
> For now I've nane to be my guide
> But a deid man drowned in Yarrow.

> And aye she screighed, and cried, Alas!
> Till her heart did break wi' sorrow,
> And sank into her faither's arms
> 'Mang the dowie dens o' Yarrow.

Walter Scott's motives for compiling his collection were unabashed. Prompted, inspired and embarrassed by the popularity of Thomas Percy's *Reliques of Ancient English Poetry*, published in 1765, he wrote in the introduction of *The Minstrelsy of the Scottish Border*: 'By such efforts, feeble as they are, I may contribute somewhat to the history of my native country; the peculiar features of whose manner and character are daily melting and dissolving into those of her sister and ally.'

This laudable patriotism was harmless enough, but it did skew the ballads slightly and the history of the Border Reivers a great deal. Nationalism intruded where all that really mattered was surname and the advantage of one surname against another. For example, in historical reality Johnnie Armstrong of Gilnockie was a vicious thug but Scott's instincts and ability to reshape a traditional ballad turned him into a Scottish hero who only raided in England, and was good to his people in his own way. Rough and tough, but just.

THE STRANGER-GAELS

In 1500 more than half the landmass of Britain and Ireland did not speak English or any of its dialects, such as the Scots of the Border ballads. They spoke Celtic languages; Irish Gaelic and Scots Gaelic, Manx, Welsh and Cornish. By 1100 the aristocracy and people of Galloway had become thoroughly Celtic in nature, and west of the Nith, a dialect of Gaelic was spoken. It seems that new immigrants from Ireland and the Hebrides brought a new language and Galloway itself gets its name from them. They were called 'the Stranger-Gaels', or the 'Gall-Gaidheil'. Across the Solway Firth, Cumbria is also a Celtic name and it derives from 'Combrogi' which was rubbed smooth into 'Cymru', the Welsh word for Wales. It means something like 'Land of the Fellow Citizens' and it is a memory of the Roman Empire. Galloway Gaelic was still spoken in the sixteenth century and many of the Dumfriesshire surnames were bilingual. When pilgrims travelling to the shrine of St Ninian at Whithorn crossed the Nith at Dumfries, they were entering the wild realm of the Stranger Gaels.

Walter Scott also had personal, romantic reasons for wishing to collect the ballads before they were lost to memory. As a boy, he had heard them sung by his grandfather, Robert Scott, his Auntie Janet and an old farm-hand, Sandy Ormiston. When very young, Scott had contracted a wasting disease, probably a strain of poliomyelitis, which had left him lame in his left leg. To recuperate, the 'wee sick laddie' was sent from Edinburgh into the fresh air of the Border countryside, to Sandyknowe Farm. The farmhouse lies near the crag which carries the ruins of Smailholm Tower. It was not the present tidy, two-storeyed house with long views to the Cheviots, but a small stone cottage now built into the old farm steading lying a little to the west. Scott never forgot his time by the hearthside at Sandyknowe and his young imagination was fired by the ballads and the tales of his grandfather, his auntie and the old cow-bailie, Sandy Ormiston. He whispered stories of raids and reivers to the wee laddie as they sat at the foot of the old stronghold:

> And still I thought that shatter'd tower
> The mightiest work of human power;
> And marvell'd as the aged hind
> With some strange tale bewitch'd my mind,
> Of forayers, who, with headlong force,
> Down from that strength had spurr'd their horse,
> Their southern rapine to renew
> Far in the distant Cheviot blue,
> And, home returning, fill'd the hall
> With revel, wassel-rout, and brawl.
> Methought that still with trump and clang,
> The gateway's broken arches rang;
> Methought grim features, seam'd with scars,
> Glared through the window's rusty bars,
> And ever, by the winter hearth,
> Old tales I heard of woe or mirth,
> Of lovers' slights, of ladies' charms,
> Of witches' spells, of warriors' arms;
> Of patriot battles, won of old
> By Wallace wight and Bruce the bold;
> Of later fields of feud and fight,
> When, pouring from their Highland height,
> The Scottish clans, in headlong sway,
> Had swept the scarlet ranks away.

That passage from *Marmion*, published in 1808 and phenomenally successful, recalls the power of the old ballads as they worked on the imagination of the wee sick laddie. And as he sat in the warmth of the farmhouse kitchen at Sandyknowe entranced by his Auntie Janet's voice, he was only doing what generations of Borderers had done before him. The ballads are best when simplest, when the four line stanzas sound out the steady rhythm of hoofbeats, of soldiers riding down to England to drive a prey, of drums beating as the gallows rope swings, of hearts beating as widows weep and lovers drown their tragic losses.

Many of the most famous ballads, 'The Battle of Otterburn' or 'The Outlaw Murray' and others take the grand themes and some span long stretches of historical time – and at 80 verses or so, take their time in telling it. Others fly in the faery realm, the supernatural world which lay beyond the flicker of the down-hearth, out into the fell night air and black-darkness where witches, warlocks and elven queens work their spells. Some of these are very old, 'Thomas the Rhymer' was probably composed before 1400 and was added to and changed over the centuries. Here are the first five verses:

> True Thomas lay on Huntlie bank;
> A ferlie he spied wi' his e'e;
> And there he saw a lady bright
> Come riding down by the Eildon Tree
>
> Her skirt was o' the grass-green silk
> Her mantle o' the velvet fine;
> At ilka tett o' her horse's mane,
> Hung fifty siller bells and nine.
>
> True Thomas he pu'd off his cap
> And louted low down on his knee
> 'Hail to thee Mary, Queen of Heaven!
> For thy peer on earth could never be.'
>
> 'O no, O no, Thomas' she said,
> 'That name does not belong to me;
> I'm but the Queen o' fair Elfland,
> That am hither come to visit thee.
>
> 'Harp and carp, Thomas' she said,
> 'Harp and carp along wi' me;
> And if ye dare to kiss my lips,
> Sure of your bodie I will be.'

With their grand martial themes and fey prophesies, the Border ballads were ripe for the further manufacture of romance. And Scott's rendition of them, some improved, others changed, was meat and drink for the romancing of the Border reivers. It began with a patriotic wish to memorialise their stunning musical and poetic culture, grew into a nationalistic urge to see them as Scotland's bulwark against anglicisation and ended with the historical suppression of the overwhelmingly dark side of what happened along the frontier in the sixteenth century. Accounts of the rescue of Kinmont Willie remember its daring and elan, but forget what a deeply unsavoury criminal he was. But then history is often untidy, the loose ends of paradox and contradiction hang everywhere. And if we have Sir Walter to thank for romancing the reivers we must also be grateful that he saved their wonderful ballads.

RIGHT HAND MEN

Most men are right-handed and most battles were fought by men who stood and fought next to each other in a tight line, at least at the outset. This combination of factors has led to persistent and interesting traditions. Because right-handed men carry a weapon in that hand and a shield in the other, they leave themselves vulnerable when they raise their weapon to strike a blow. They cannot cover their own body with their shield and therefore depend on the man standing to their right to protect them with his shield. When the Highlanders charged at Culloden in 1746, the government troops were instructed to bayonet whoever was running at the man on their left. His weapon would be raised and in a disordered charge, his right side was unlikely to be protected by a man running to his right. Right? Right. This was both risky and counter-instinctive. Perhaps some disciplined redcoats did it. The life-or-death importance of a right hand man in battle has led to the use of the phrase for a trusted lieutenant and is also the reason why a best man stands to the right of a bridegroom at a wedding service. He is trying to protect him.

Poetic licence has seeped into other parts of Border history. Those partial observers who reported martial victories, skirmishes won, and raids punishingly executed, are wont to exaggerate the numbers involved. It is almost a tradition to overestimate the opposition army and their enormous losses at the hands of the smaller and braver force who defeated them with surprisingly few casualties. But when English sources claim huge Scottish raiding parties clattering over the border, the numbers simply do not add up.

Reliable historians have compared twentieth-century census figures with estimates of the population in the sixteenth-century Border country and come up with consistent and credible figures. On the English side of the border, in the three marches under the control of wardens, 120,000 people lived. And in the three marches in Scotland there were about 50,000. That imbalance, almost two and a half to one, was weighted by the fact that the only two genuine sixteenth-century towns in the Borders, Berwick and Carlisle, were both English.

What these overall figures show is something stark. On the Scottish side there can have been only 15,000 fighting men at the very most. Discounting half the population because women did not turn out to fight, at least not in a raiding party or an army, and a further 10,000 who were too old, too young, too infirm or disqualified for some other reason, that leaves 15,000. Even if riders as young as Robert Johnstone of Raecleuch are counted, it still feels like an overestimate.

So, when Walter Scott of Buccleuch counted 3,000 lances when he mounted a huge raid into England in 1532, 20 per cent of the total fighting capability of the *whole* of the Border country rode with him. And more, when he called on these men to follow him, Teviotdale must have all but emptied. It seems unlikely.

A comparison between the English and Scottish numbers is also instructive. With the odds so heavily stacked against them, Scottish raiders did well to maintain a balance of power. Even bearing in mind that the amount of Scottish raiding appears exaggerated because it was recorded by English sources (the traffic in the opposite direction was not necessarily less, just under-reported in scanty Scottish sources), it is surprising that Annandale, Teviotdale and the Tweed Valley were not constantly overrun and impoverished more than they were. Geology had also made the northern valleys broader and more fertile – and attractive to raiders – than the long miles of moorland to the south.

Perhaps the Scottish surnames were tighter bound, better organised and more motivated by need and greed. This was not often a national stand-off, with the size of opposing armies set relative to population. Raids and raiding were usually conducted by much smaller groups and this had the effect of rendering this discrepancy redundant. It simply did not matter to a party of 20 reivers picking their way down off the Cheviot tops to lift cows in Coquetdale.

Carlisle was the largest town, and by some distance. The population is estimated at 5,000 for the period between 1584 and 1600. Since the Roman period Carlisle had been an urban centre, its size fluctuating with the tides of history. When Hadrian's Wall was built after 122, a fort was built on the site of the castle and it became a command centre for the whole wall garrison. Parts of the city walls were originally Roman and they survived well into the sixteenth century and beyond. Medieval historians noted the ancient paved streets laid down a thousand years before and William of Malmesbury wrote of an arched building which carried an inscription to Mars and Venus. Carlisle had the history and feel of an ancient city. It still does.

The castle was the headquarters of the Warden of the English West March and the place where justice was dispensed. For Border reivers this could be summary and after sentence had been handed down, their hands were tied behind their backs and they were carted a mile down the London road. At Harraby Hill many had a first and last encounter with the Christian church when they *sang neck-verse* at the busy gallows south of the city. There the condemned tottered on a stool while they listened to a priest or a minister recite the Miserere or the 51st Psalm. As the hangman pushed them, a view of Carlisle was the last thing many reivers saw.

CRUEL JOKES

In the sixteenth century cruelty was thought to be amusing, even hilarious. At the midsummer fair in Paris cat-burning was very popular. The organisers set up a grandstand so that a large crowd could have a good laugh as they watched a net full of screaming cats lowered slowly into a large bonfire. In the Borders smaller-scale cruelties were routinely featured on saints' days and at festivals. Cock-fighting was enjoyed and if a bird was insufficiently aggressive, it would be tied to a stick and people had fun stoning it to death. When St James' Fair was held near Kelso each August, cats were tortured for amusement, set on fire and knocked about in a barrel. The fair has been revived, but not with all its original sideshows. Public cruelty to people was of course common with regular and well advertised executions at Harraby Hill in Carlisle and elsewhere. Best attended were the executions of those found guilty of treachery. Lengthy and horrific affairs, they involved the appalling fate of being hung, drawn and quartered. So that all dignity was removed and the crowd could delight in his involuntary defecation, a victim was usually stripped, his hands bound behind his back and a rope tightened around his neck. It was then slung over a beam and the hangman and his helpers pulled hard to lift the choking, wriggling, retching man in the air. It was then that he pissed and shat himself. Hangmen were expert judges and just as the victim was about to lose consciousness and choke to death, they suddenly let go of the rope and he crashed down onto the wooden scaffold. Revived by buckets of water, the man was dragged to a butcher's table and tied to it. Then he was slit from neck to groin and his intestines pulled out. If he had not died of shock, the victim could watch as his insides were thrown onto a sizzling brazier. And then, mercifully, he was dragged to a block and with the executioner's foot on his back, beheaded. The four quarters of his butchered body were set on display as a grim reminder. Simple hanging was also more sadistic. The knot in a rope was not designed to break the neck and there was no long drop to provide fatal momentum. The condemned were expected to choke to death slowly and noisily, supplying amusement as they did so. 'Dancing a jig' was a common euphemism. It is said that friends were allowed to bribe the hangman who then let them pull on the victim's legs in order to bring his agony to a merciful end. This is said to be the origin of the phrase 'hangers-on'. Sixteenth-century society could be almost unimaginably cruel, but what is striking is the public's delight and perverted fascination with extreme and long drawn-out rituals of cruelty. It speaks of a very different view of the world.

Berwick-upon-Tweed was smaller, but unusually there exists a sixteenth-century census. In June 1565 it was reckoned that 3,511 people were living in the town. Of these more than 2,000 were soldiers, labourers or tradesmen. The focus of their work still exists – a spectacular circuit of sixteenth-century walls.

Berwick was seen as a bastion of English foreign policy and the notoriously mean Queen Elizabeth I finally spent a staggering £128,648 on the construction of impregnable walls. Terrified at the thought of Mary, Queen of Scots as the linchpin of a strategic catholic alliance between Scotland and France (and with Spain to worry about after her sister's marriage to King Philip), she was determined to hold on to Berwick. In 1558 Calais had fallen and with it England's last foothold in continental Europe. With its new and mighty walls, Berwick would be a Border Calais – except that it would not be taken. The town could be easily supplied by sea, and as her father had shown in the terrible raids of the 1540s, it was a handy base for military action against southern Scotland.

Work on the fortification of Berwick had begun in the reign of Mary I but it was accelerated in 1558 for another reason. That year Mary of Guise, the Queen Regent of Scotland, had dispatched French soldiers and engineers to rebuild the promontary fort at Eyemouth, only a few miles up the North Sea coast from Berwick. An unmistakable, threatening gesture, the fort was erected quickly and using the latest Italian techniques to counter artillery attacks. The Berwick garrison tried to halt the work but were beaten back.

More permanent retaliation came with the arrival of Sir Richard Lee in Berwick. A notable military engineer, he immediately set to work. Town walls were very vulnerable to artillery and in Berwick's case from guns at sea as well as on land. The old medieval walls were crumbling and in any case enclosed too great an area. New plans circled the town with massive walls, in some places nine metres across. Stout stone retaining walls were built and infilled with rubble and earth. Artillery fire could certainly hope to damage such a wall but never breach it. Five arrowhead bastions were constructed along the land walls and the guns placed on them had a wide field of fire over the ditching dug in front of them. One of the many problems with sixteenth-century artillery was its lack of manoeuvrability. When attackers managed to advance inside its range and get close to the walls, it was difficult to depress the angle at which cannon fired or move them quickly to cover another area. With the help of an Italian military architect, Giovanni Portinari, Sir Richard Lee solved this by creating artillery positions which fired parallel with and along the length of his massive walls, raking any who tried to lever up scaling ladders or rush through a damaged section. And so that Berwick's guns did not shoot at each other in these places, he angled the retaining walls slightly. The ground in front of them was cleared of housing (some of it has remained open parkland) and these flankers completed total coverage of any attack.

By 1570 Berwick's walls were complete, and despite complaints from the garrison commanders about maintenance, they made the town virtually impregnable. The ingenious design was never put to the test. And in 1603 when James VI became the I, the new walls became politically irrelevant.

DAEMONOLOGIE

The Scottish Reformation brought many social as well as religious changes, but it also engendered a horrific habit of mind which gathered momentum towards the end of the sixteenth century over much of northern Europe. John Knox and his followers wished to create a 'godly commonwealth' of believers, a commonwealth which required to be continually purged of all pollutants. Witches began to be hunted – and with great enthusiasm in the Borders. (Although it must be said that in Germany it became a hysterical epidemic – in 1585 in Trier 118 women and two men were burnt at the stake because 'the prolongation of winter was the work of their incantations'. A grisly example of cultural and climate change coinciding.) In Scotland this vicious obsession was much encouraged by the king's personal interest. In 1597 James VI had published a treatise on witches called 'Daemonologie', and he himself was sometimes present at the interrogation of hapless victims. It was a terrible, disfiguring and lengthy episode, something of which succeeding generations of Borderers ought to be profoundly ashamed.

Houses in Berwick and Carlisle were nothing like as solidly built. Their construction differed little from the wall-stakes and withies of the countryside. Stone was more in evidence and space at a much greater premium. Most houses were built gable end-on to a street and with a narrow lane leading down to the door and the backlands beyond. These alleyways were still in evidence in the centre of Carlisle until a new shopping centre was built in 1984, and some can still be seen in Berwick.

In their long backlands town householders usually kept a milker cow and perhaps some chickens. Like the other Border burghs, Berwick and Carlisle had common grazings and most people led their animals out in the morning and back at night to be milked. Excavations in Perth have turned up the remains of drains and their noisome contents show where animals were kept overnight. Cross-contamination of their droppings and human sewage with a town's water supply often led to a rapid spread of diseases such as typhoid. Because of rising damp in their insubstantial walls, most townhouses had a limited life, perhaps only twenty years. Fires were frequent and sometimes devastating as dry thatch was set alight by little more than sparks from a vigorous cooking fire, and because people in towns lived cheek by jowl, fire always spread quickly. Infectious diseases did the same and when the ebola-like epidemic burst into Carlisle in 1597 it carried off more than a fifth of the population.

TYPHOID TEA

Water-borne diseases and poor sanitation combined to keep urban populations small in the sixteenth century. Frequent visitations of typhoid and other scourges carried off many and it seemed that there was an upper limit beyond which cities were unable to grow. More people, more sewage, more disease. In the eighteenth century improved water supply and better plumbing helped the great industrial cities of the north to expand, but tea also played an important role. At the same time as the fires of the Industrial Revolution began to roar into life, tea became a popular drink and cheap enough to be drunk by many. And the incidence of water-borne disease began to decline markedly. It used to be thought that the business of boiling water to brew tea was responsible for this, but the effect was much aided by the nature of tea itself. In the Far East it was seen as a tonic drink with many health-giving properties of its own. Tea turned out to be good for you.

Modern towns like Hawick, Galashiels, Duns, Kelso, Melrose, Jedburgh, Selkirk and Peebles were little more than villages, their houses clustered around the road that led to an abbey or important castle. Like Carlisle and Berwick most had weekly markets where the necessities of life could be bartered or bought. In the middle ages the Border economy had been energised by the wool trade and the entrepreneurial acumen of the great abbeys and their business-like monks. But with the Wars of Independence, the deterioration of the climate and the depredations of the Border reivers, wool growing and trading had declined dramatically. When the natural port for export and import at Berwick was detached from its hinterland in the Tweed Valley and briskly incorporated into England, further and lasting damage was inflicted. The Reformation finished off the declining and half-ruined abbeys and the great monastic sheep-ranches were broken up and shared out amongst aristocratic families. By the late sixteenth century Borderers lived in a subsistence economy – in a good year.

TRUNK ROADS

Wagga, a man who could fairly claim to have been Carlisle's first mayor, was very proud of the town's water supply. He was the 'reeve' (related to sheriff or 'shire-reeve'), the royal official sent by the Northumbrian kings to rule over the old Roman city and when Bishop Cuthbert visited in 685, Wagga showed him a gushing water fountain. Then he took the saintly bishop on a tour of Carlisle's Roman walls. Nearly 300 years after the end of Roman rule in Britain, a municipal water supply was evidently still in working order. That implies plumbing and the continuing ability to bring water into the city from a distance, and from higher ground. Perhaps there was an upstanding aqueduct somewhere. Clean water of course remained important but when the old Roman plumbing broke down, native tradesmen no longer had the skills to make replacement lead and ceramic piping. To keep the water flowing, they used wood, hollowed-out sections of tree trunks. These often ran by the side of a main road – which is where the phrase 'trunk road' originated.

Market days and saints' days (these took a long time to fade, despite the preachings of the protestant church) supplied welcome variety in the long months of day-in, day-out labour. These were often enlivened by sporting events. 'Baw' or 'handbaw' (pronounced 'baw' but spelt 'ba') was played in most Border towns and villages for centuries, and up until the 1930s games were held in Hawick, Ancrum, Selkirk and St Boswells. Reivers reckoned themselves good players: Willie Armstrong 'the best at thievecraft and the ba, and the Earl of Bothwell was a robust player. Six-a-side matches were organised and Mary, Queen of Scots is said to have watched one played on the river-meadow below Carlisle Castle. The style of play and the rules are blurred but the ba of the sixteenth century does have a lineal descendant, a match played in the old style twice a year. And it does have rules, apparently.

At Candlemas on 2 February and Fastern's E'en (Shrove Tuesday in England – 40 days before Holy Saturday, usually the end of February or the beginning of March, depending on when Easter is that year), the men of Jedburgh play at the ba, what they call handba. Players gather at the mercat cross and divide into two teams. The

'Uppies' team consists of men born in the town south of a line drawn from the car park at the end of the Friars in Exchange Street to the mercat cross and on the Deans Close in the Canongate, as well as those born outside of Jedburgh who first entered the town by a southern road, from Newcastle, the Dunion, Oxnam or Lanton. The same precision applies to the 'Doonies' who must have been born north of the line or first entered Jedburgh by the Edinburgh road, the Monklaw road, or the Ulston road. The size of the teams is limited only by the male population of the town and hundreds have been known to take part.

Aside from common sense on safety, to the outsider there appear to be no rules. At least none are published and everyone taking part seems to know what they are, which suggests that none actually exist. To start the game a leather ba, slightly bigger than a tennis ball and decorated with ribbons, is thrown high in the air. Then it disappears into an immense scrummage. Bodies heave and squeeze, the occasional expletive rising above the melée. Sometimes a runner squirts out of the pack and hares off with the ba. Occasionally someone hares off without the ba to set up a decoy chase while a team member slinks off in another direction with it stuffed up their jumper.

Scoring is a little less opaque. Goals or 'hails' are the object of the game and for the Uppies these are won when the ba is thrown over the railings surrounding Jedburgh Castle grounds. The railings to the left of the main gates, that is, before they turn into a stone wall. Where hails were scored before there were railings is lost in the mists of ancient games. Doonies' hails are more mysterious. They are won when the ba is rolled across an invisible stream. Under one of Jedburgh's streets, the Skiprunning Burn makes its hidden way towards the Jed and if a ba crosses it, on the ground, a hail goes to the Doonies. There is no time limit to the game but darkness late on a February afternoon usually sees the welcoming lights of Jedburgh's public houses twinkle in the gloaming.

FITBA AND HANDBA

On the front page of 'The Southern Reporter' for Thursday 2 March 2006 there is a photograph of a man making a football. He is stuffing it with moss. Rodger Hart is a saddler to trade and he has been hand-sewing and stuffing these little leather footballs for 25 years. He makes ten at a time (they are larger than tennis balls but smaller than normal footballs) for use in the old Handba game played at Jedburgh twice a year. The Earl of Bothwell was evidently a keen footballer – and robust. There are reports of rough play, disputes and a suspected broken leg. And the tale runs that after a particularly vigorous match, the score was two dead and thirty taken prisoner. The rules are hazy and the distinction between handba and fitba blurred. That unclarity remains. When Border rugby teams kick a ball over the crossbar, the crowds shout 'Goal!' and rugby is often called fitba. All of that mythic nonsense about a boy called William Webb Ellis having a brainstorm at Rugby School when it suddenly came into his head to pick up the ball and run with it obscures a much more interesting evolution from the games of handba and fitba played by the Border Reivers and their contemporaries all over Britain.

Jethart handba is very old – and magnificent to watch. It has been played with undimmed passion since the days of the reivers and probably long before. And that passion continues. After the Fastern's E'en game of 2006, a ba legend retired. At the age of 70, after 61 years as a player, Ian Aitchison announced that in future he would become a spectator. After an (accidentally) grazed chin and a cut wrist, the veteran said: 'I'll not be doing this next year. I'll just watch instead.' However, some time later, he went on to qualify his remarks: 'In 2007 I might be tempted to jump in now and then. I'll just have to wait and see how I feel on the day.'

In the 1490s a righteous Hawick priest by the name of Robert Irland warned the local lads against another absorbing game. 'Lang bullets' or road-bowls was very popular and a lot less muscular than the ba. Irland was anxious that his flock were ignoring mandatory archery practice and spending far too much time throwing balls along the High Street and the road leading out of Hawick.

Sixteenth-century Borderers loved horse-racing and just as the Jethart handba is largely unchanged, so too are the informal meets held at the summer common ridings. Called 'flappers' (perhaps on account of the all-action riding style) these races are run on grass tracks with only the most rudimentary layout. Betting was and is integral and a good deal of horse-trading also went on. Winners were awarded bells rather than cups and the oldest Carlisle bells are kept in Tullie House Museum. At the Peebles common riding a bell is still the

most prestigious trophy. The races were also important places of
business for Border reivers and it is said that the plans for the daring
rescue of Kinmont Willie Armstrong from Carlisle Castle were laid
when Walter Scott of Buccleuch met interested parties at Langholm
Races. On an April Saturday in 1596 he was seen talking to the
Grahams, probably negotiating safe-conduct through their territory,
and also giving instructions to his go-between, Willie Kang Irvine.

THE BA FRONTIER

The border between England and Scotland is often said to run from
the Redden Burn near Kelso down the midstream of the Tweed to
below Paxton House where it turns north and inland to form the
Berwick Bounds. This is not quite true. Between the villages of Wark
and Cornhill there is a blip. On the Ordnance Survey the border line
is shown to dip across the Tweed and take in two or three acres of
the south bank. Why? There is no building, settlement or unusual
feature. All that the curious can see over the hawthorn hedge is a flat
riverside meadow. On closer inspection, a rectangular area, once
enclosed by an ancient line of fencing (there is a tell-tale ridge
suggesting a ditch lost in modern ploughing) lies close to the
riverbank. Adjacent is a post which appears to have no purpose
or significance except that it lines up with one on the Scottish bank
opposite. What was this? An unlikely tradition might answer. This
parcel of land is known locally as the 'Ba Green' and it is said that
each year the men of Coldstream played a version of the ba or
handba against the men of Wark. Whoever won kept the piece of
ground for a year. And in this way it often alternated its nationality.
Eventually Coldstream grew much larger than the beautiful little
village of Wark and the Scots began to win every match. Where-
upon no contest was declared and the Ba Green stayed in Scotland –
a decision apparently recognised by the Ordnance Survey. It might
just be a true story.

In all these sporting events and excitements women are rarely mentioned. Like Mary Queen of Scots they probably watched the handba,
the bowls and the races, but they certainly never took part and the
record is largely silent about the general role of women in sixteenth-
century Border society.

The earlier ballads are more aristocratic in tone, like 'The Battle of Otterburn' with its protagonists, James, the Earl of Douglas and Sir Henry Percy, and when women are mentioned, they are cast as stereotypes and very definitely in supporting roles. As in 'The Dowie Dens o' Yarrow', they are often beautiful, romantic and ultimately tragic. Later ballads are more earthy, sometimes dealing with the lower orders in the sixteenth-century Border country, the working (or reiving) classes rather than earls or kings. But still women only appear as adjuncts to men, as objects rather than subjects.

Given the profound influence of the teachings of the church and the legacy of evil, tempted Eve and St Paul's unequivocal Letter to the Ephesians, 'Let wives be subject to their husbands because a husband is head of a wife, just as Christ is head of the Church', the lowly status of women is hardly surprising. In a normal household of the time even a widow was subject to her eldest son.

Evidence from European sources suggest that prostitution was part of rural life as well as urban, and that it was common. Many farm-workers, shepherds and lairds will have made their eager way to Carlisle and Berwick to buy the services of a whore. Both towns supported garrisons and the soldiers will have ensured a lively trade. In the early sixteenth century the Scottish king famously paid for sex. James IV's clerks recorded several cash sums to the account of Janet Barearse.

Contraception of some sort was undoubtedly practised, but was probably a matter left to women. There is evidence that breast-feeding was prolonged – for two years and sometimes three so that women could remain infertile.

BROGUES

Borderers with long memories can recall a time when shoes were a luxury, or at least only seasonal. Boots were worn in the snow and ice of the winter, but at Easter time bare feet became the norm. In the sixteenth century boots were much prized and often stolen on raids, passed on in wills or looted from the dead on a battlefield or after a skirmish. At Flodden, fought in the September rain, Scottish soldiers kicked off their footwear and hoped for better purchase on the boggy ground in bare feet. Most people wore brogues, boots being more expensive. These were not the clumpy, decorated (derby-fronted or bow-fronted are usually the options) brown or

black men's shoes of the twenty-first century, but a much simpler
ancestor. A piece of leather was cut and shaped to the foot and then
tied over the top with thongs. Sometimes these came up to the ankle
like espadrilles. This habit persists in the way that brogues worn
with kilts are still laced up to the calf. Sixteenth-century brogues
were pierced with holes so that water could easily run out of them.
Not meant to be waterproof, their main purpose was to protect the
feet from sharp stones. The holes are also still imitated in modern
fashion with a standard pattern of tooling on brogues.

Children were expected to work almost as soon as they could walk
and talk. On farm places many chores could be managed or made
easier by a child with a stick who could roar at beasts and daily jobs
like the collection of eggs or berry-picking in season could become
adventures. Ploughing with the 'auld Scotch ploo' (made from wood
tipped with iron and nothing like as efficient as the swing plough
which was invented in the eighteenth century) required a family to
work together. On late winter mornings someone had to lead the ox-
team or horses while father guided the plough, and behind him women
and children pulled out the worst of the weeds and bashed down the
big clods. Children certainly grew up much faster and boys were
expected to behave like adults when they attained their teenage years
and girls sometimes married when they were 12 or 13. Life expectancy
was also much shorter, and with a few exceptions society will have
looked much younger.

On 9 September 1513 King James IV led the Scottish army to Flodden
field and his nation to disaster. The outcome of that terrible day would
turn the history of the Borders in another direction and set a fertile
ground for the century of disorder which followed. As much as any
single political act, the battle at Flodden made the Border reivers
possible.

The battlefield lies only a mile or so over the English border, near
the village of Branxton. It is an unremarkable place, part of a series of
folded ridges rising up to the eastern end of the Cheviot range. When
the sky is overcast it can be difficult to pick out the memorial to all
those who died on that autumn day in 1513. But the fields themselves
have an atmosphere, a stillness, perhaps a memory of fear, of ancient
slaughter, of an immense, oppressive sadness. In a translation of a

Gaelic phrase, it is possible at Flodden to hear the music of the thing as it happened.

The alliance with France against Henry VIII had persuaded James IV to invade. Perhaps aspiring to be a player in international politics, he fulfilled an obligation he could easily have ignored and assembled a huge host, the largest army a Scots king had ever put in the field. But the English reacted quickly and the old warrior, the 70-year-old Earl of Surrey, raised a force of 20,000 and pulling out the banner of St Cuthbert from the nave of Durham Cathedral, he hurried north to meet the Scots. They faced each other across Flodden field.

Formed up in four battles, or battalions, on each side, 52,000 men – a huge number – stared across this undulating landscape, knowing that they were about to fight toe-to-toe for their lives. Close enough to see into the eyes of their enemies, close enough to smell the sweat and blood, close enough to feel the fear and panic. Medieval armies fought in ranks, packed dense, and usually their lords and captains led from the front, their standards snapping and fluttering in the breeze.

Gripping their pikes tight, endlessly checking their gear, fidgeting, glaring at their enemies across the shallow valley, men stood side by side, told each other to stand fast, encouraged their comrades around them. In the days before the army mustered, the older men will have listened again and again to mothers and sisters implore them to look out for their boys, to bring them home safe.

It is said that Flodden was a battle waited upon in silence, the usual barrage of insults and taunts were not exchanged between the Scots and the English. Only the roar of artillery and the blast of trumpets broke the tense quiet. But in the moment before the battalion of Borderers and Highlanders moved forward to begin the fighting, many men will have been literally sick with fear, retching and gagging, unable to stop it. Some will have undoubtedly soiled themselves.

Lords Home and Huntly and their captains in the front rank will have seen it all before and shouted over their shoulders to their men to stand fast and keep their courage. Before the first drum sounded the advance of the battalion of Borderers and Highlanders, it is likely that the Gaelic-speaking clansmen did a unique thing, something which will have baffled their enemies opposite. They began to recite their genealogy. Men could go back 20 generations: 'Is mise mac Iain, mac Rhuraidh, mac Dhomnaill. I am the son of John, the son of Rory, the son of Donald.' They did it to remember who they were and why their chiefs had brought them to Flodden to fight. And they roared their war-cries, the names of their places – 'Dunmaglass! Loch Moy! Glassaraidh!' – before they tore into the ranks of terrified English soldiers. Opening fatal gaps in the line, they were followed by Home's Border pikemen and the English battalion was knocked down. Most turned and ran for their lives. At first Flodden shaped to be a Scottish victory.

But when the battalion led by the Earls of Errol, Crawford and Montrose and that of King James IV advanced, matters began to go against the Scots. They were badly disordered by the boggy ground and the stream at the bottom of the hill. Crucial momentum was lost, their 17-foot pikes became unwieldy and the English began to work their shorter bills and poleaxes to deadly effect. Even though King James' battallion pushed the English back 200 yards, he was quickly surrounded and the slaughter began. In medieval warfare men were rarely killed outright, or even quickly. When a heavy blow or a cutting stroke was taken, it was vital to stay upright and often men wounded in this way would charge the man opposite and like a wrestler or tired boxer, use him as a support. When lines of battle engaged at close quarter, they often began to wheel round, like a rugby scrum. Because men are mostly right-handed and held their shields in their left hands and forearms, their inclination was to shove to the left – and this made the whole line tend to wheel to the left. Many battles were a matter of who pushed, shoved and hacked the hardest.

When a man was knocked down, the opposing ranks trampled over the top of him, cutting and kicking at him as they went. Often it was the second or third rank who bludgeoned a man to death or unconsciousness. Most died much later of wounds and the consequent blood loss. When fighting had stopped and the enemy put to flight, the exhausted victors found themselves masters of a battlefield strewn with the dead and many who were dying slowly, their lives bleeding away in a horrifically extended agony. Screaming and moaning men lay all around Flodden field in the awful aftermath. Plunderers and scavengers always carried daggers so that they could despatch the wounded and pillage their war gear and anything else of value.

JACKS

Border reivers rode in a fairly standard kit. Those who could afford them wore high, thigh-length riding boots and spurs. Wound around the legs of their breeches were lengths of wire or light chains, enough to turn a blow. On their heads most men wore a 'steel bonnet'. These caps could be elaborate with cheek-pieces, wide brims and high combs. But perhaps the most interesting item was a reiver's jack. This was not expensive to have made and men wore them over their torsos. A jack was made from layers of quilted cloth, sometimes leather, which had metal scales or even bits of hard bone sewn onto it. The wearer had far more freedom of movement than someone wearing armour and it reduced the burden on a pony. Jacks have a surprising history. In the medieval period the Lords of the Isles kept disorder to a minimum by despatching mercenary forces to fight for the warring local kings in Ireland instead of each other. It was a policy adopted a little too late in the Borders. These men were called Gallowglasses (from 'Gall-Oglaigh' for 'foreign warriors') and they developed as heavily armoured infantry able to repel and defeat cavalry. Their strategy was simple; the ranks of their regiments bristled with long spears and had the iron discipline to stand fast when cavalry charged. What helped that resolve was their jack. Sufficiently cheap for each man to afford one, they were the ancestors of what the reivers wore. Gallowglasses' jacks were long, stretching down to their knees. Below them they wore heavy boots which became known as 'jackboots'. And when the jack was adopted by horsemen it needed to be cut shorter and this coined the term 'jacket'.

When it became clear that Flodden was lost, many Scots turned and ran for their lives. These were mostly the men in the rear. King James' battalion was so large that it had 20 ranks but those at the back were usually poorly armed and had no captains to lead them. When they saw the Scottish pikes and standards going down in front of them and the beginning of a terrible slaughter, they scattered. Very few prisoners were taken at Flodden – only 400 – and very many died, perhaps more than 10,000 in total. Chroniclers thought it a cruel battle, worse than any fought at the time.

The day after the slaughter Lord Home led his Borderers back to Branxton, and it may be that they circled the English encampment, offering to continue the fight. Whatever their motives, they were driven off by artillery fire. Because of the terrible carnage and the fact that so many English soldiers had fallen or were badly wounded, Home might have thought Flodden could still be won.

Bands of other Border horsemen were waiting. Gathered on the ridges above the battlefield, keeping their distance, the so-called 'banditti' of Teviotdale and Tynedale were watching for an opportunity, biding their time. They later attacked the exhausted English camp and managed to carry off some plunder and a few head of horses. And as the defeated Scots were retreating northwards, the bandits shadowed them up the weary road to Soutra but eventually withdrew without launching an attack. These incidents were a prelude to what was to come in the sixteenth-century Border country. The dark days of the Border reivers were dawning.

Part II

5

Before Flodden

The night of 19 March 1286 was a night for feasting. A rainstorm had blown in from the North Sea, and the waves whipped up white tops out on the Firth of Forth. In the great hall of Edinburgh Castle King Alexander III of Scotland was drinking with his cronies. At the end of the evening, no doubt flushed with wine, he announced that he wanted to see his new, young wife. A few months before, Alexander had married the beautiful Yolande de Dreux. But the only difficulty was that she was in Fife, at the royal manor of Kinghorn. It was a foul, wild late winter's night, but the king would not be dissuaded. Clattering across the cobbles of Edinburgh Castle, he galloped through the sleeting rain to the Queensferry. Spindrift was spraying off the Forth and at first the ferryman refused to take the king across. It was dark, and far too dangerous a night to be out on the firth. At his insistence, and perhaps after some royal gold, the king got his way and the crossing was made. On the Fife shore the burgesses of North Queensferry implored the king to accept their hospitality and break his journey with them until morning. But he would not, and spurring his horse through the puddles of the coastal path, Alexander made his way to Kinghorn and the warm bed of his beautiful young wife. In the mirk and deafening wind, the king lost sight of his escort but did not stop and wait for them to catch up. Instead he kicked his mount on along the clifftop path on the headland at Pettycur. Perhaps he could see the lights of his manor house twinkling in the darkness. A sudden gust of wind buffeted them – the horse spooked and lost its footing and Alexander was thrown out of the saddle. He plunged two hundred feet though the darkness onto the rocks below.

When search parties found the king at first light, they picked up the lifeless body of the last of the macMalcolm dynasty. Alexander's only heir was a little girl who lived in Norway. His impetuosity had left

Scotland a kingless kingdom and it placed the Borders in the front line of almost three centuries of terrible and destructive war with England.

On the opposite shore of the Firth of Forth, entirely oblivious of the political catastrophe overtaking Scotland, the Earl of Dunbar and March sat by a roaring fire. His castle rose dramatically out of the sea, clinging to a rock by the ancient harbour of Lamerhaven, at Dunbar. Outside the wind whistled and big seas rumbled and crashed against the walls. It was a night for the fireside and Earl Patrick had gathered some of his captains and tenants for supper. Also summoned was a man of much lower status, a man who would also become more famous and revered than any of the noblemen who had dined in the castle hall. Thomas of Earlston, better known to history as Thomas the Rhymer, was probably a bard, a singer and poet whose role was not only to entertain but also to record important events in what he sang. Thomas and the other bards attached to noble households in Scotland could recite genealogies, historical ballads and tales which set his better born listeners in a glowing light. But on the night of 19 March 1286, Thomas would simply amaze them.

After supper Earl Patrick turned to his bard to enquire if the morning would bring anything interesting, a notable or important event. The chronicler, Walter Bower, reported a characteristic note of sarcasm in the earl's question but Thomas soon wiped the smirk off his face:

> 'Alas for tomorrow,' he exclaimed, ' a day of calamity and misery! Before the twelfth hour shall be heard a blast so vehement as shall exceed those of every former period – a blast that shall strike the nations with amazement – shall humble what is proud, and what is fierce shall level with the ground! The sorest wind and tempest that was ever heard of in Scotland!'

The terrible news arrived at Dunbar Castle at noon the following day. The king's death and the immediate proving of his prophesy made Thomas Rhymer famous. His sayings and writings were endlessly repeated and eventually printed over the coming centuries. Before Walter Scott and James Hogg made their marks, Thomas was the most widely known Borderer in history. Prophesy was part of the fabric of politics, taken very seriously and what he foretold was applied, reinterpreted and reapplied to explain, predict and even justify events. For example, the Rhymer's role was transformed from prophet to redeemer amongst the Celtic peoples of Britain, and the Highlanders in particular heard many resonances in what True Thomas uttered. Renamed Tomas Reumhair by the Gaelic bards who whipped up support for the 1715 Jacobite Rebellion, they claimed he had predicted victory, and in 1745 the army of Bonnie Prince Charlie was known as 'the Rhymer's Children'. Famous now only for the sweetened up and watered down ballad of Thomas the Rhymer, he was a powerful influence on Scottish politics for the best part of five hundred years.

The prophet may have been wrong about Culloden, or at least his Gaelic interpreters were, but he correctly predicted the outcome of the battle of Flodden and a score of other bloody defeats across the war-torn Borders landscape. The death of Alexander III was a disaster for the people of the Tweed Basin, Annandale and England north of Hadrian's Wall. With only short respites Borderers would watch a dismal procession of armies tramping across their fields, stealing their corn and cattle, molesting their women and killing their menfolk. For nearly three centuries they lived in a war zone and learned the arts of survival. The international politics of the late thirteenth and early fourteenth centuries laid a fertile ground for the rise of the reivers and a society based on fear, crime and feud. And after the Union of the Crowns in 1603, politics would destroy it.

Frontiers were different in the middle ages. Far more porous and less formal, they also depended on local relationships as much as national, either with individual lords or corporations like the great abbeys. And the Anglo-Scottish border made less sense than most. It divided people who were essentially similar, spoke the same language, farmed in the same way and for centuries had formed part of the old kingdom of Northumbria. It was the magnetic ambitions of the Gaelic-speaking kings in the north and the dynasties to the south which had pulled this polity apart and eventually drew a frontier line along the Tweed and the Cheviot tops.

The battle of Carham in 1018 is seen as a convenient watershed for the history of the border. In a bloody fight by the Tweed near Kelso, the spearmen of Northumbria were cut to pieces by Malcolm II of Scotland's axemen. The Scottish annexation of the Tweed Basin was never seriously in doubt after that date and even though all sorts of anomalies (to say nothing of long-term English occupation in the future) remained, kings in the north gradually asserted themselves over the Borders.

In the later eleventh century William the Conqueror and his sons had difficulty in gaining control of the north of their new kingdom. It lay far from their power-base around London and still attracted the ambitious attention of the Scandinavian dynasty which had ruled England in the first half of the eleventh century. But the Norman kings moved to meet the expansiveness of the macMalcolm dynasty and William Rufus reclaimed Carlisle, making it a plantation town. Communities of Flemings, Normans and Irish settlers were given land in the old Roman city, the castle was rebuilt and the walls repaired. At the eastern end of the Hexham Gap, on the site of the fort on Hadrian's Wall known as Pons Aelius, William Rufus' brother, Robert Curthose, built a new castle. Rising on the high ground to the north of the Tyne Gorge, the Newcastle protected the lowest crossing point over the river. In this way Northumberland and north Cumberland were also understood as potential areas of dispute and conflict. This status was confirmed throughout the twelfth century by the macMalcolm kings' claims on both areas. Often they were successful (due in large part to English distraction and weakness) and David I controlled much of the north of England. In 1153 he died in Carlisle Castle. But by 1157 the northern counties were back in English hands.

Control on either side of the border depended on a series of interlocking relationships of obligation. The church played a clear and progressively determinant role in drawing the Borders into Scotland and the northern counties into England. The bishops of St Andrews and Glasgow claimed independence from the Archbishops of York by maintaining pressure on the papacy in Rome, and they insisted on making all the important ecclesiastical appointments in the Borders. The jurisdiction of the Prince-Bishops of Durham extended right up to the Tweed (and in places beyond it) and they built a powerful castle at Norham to protect what they owned. As much as any other agency the church helped make the border a political reality.

In 1235 Alexander II married Joan, sister of Henry III of England. Two years later he agreed to the terms of the Treaty of York. In return for lands in Cumbria and the right to hang on to the old Liberty of Tynedale (as vassals of the English king), Alexander surrendered all of his claims to the earldom of Northumbria. The line of the Anglo-Scottish frontier was at last settled on the Tweed in the north-east and the Cheviot watershed, the Liddel Water and the little River Sark in the south-west.

This consolidation persuaded kings and their counsellors to organise. To cope with wrongdoing by Englishmen in Scotland and vice versa, the neighbouring jurisdictions needed a special legal mechanism. In 1248 six Scottish knights met with six English knights to discuss the formulation of what became known as the 'laws of the marches', and the following year these were codified and promulgated. In essence they insisted on the return of fugitives from justice, the recovery of debt and the regular production of accused parties at the ancient trysting places on the border line. Some of these, like the Reddenburn near Kelso, were well established and well known. Between 1249 and 1596 the laws of the marches were reviewed and recodified eight times.

Broadly the central transaction was simple. If an Englishman committed a crime in Scotland, for example a robbery, the Scot who had been robbed complained to the Scottish authorities. They in turn passed on the case to their English equivalent, who then investigated. If the charge was found to have substance, the English authorities were bound to produce the accused at a trysting place to answer for it. When it was followed through, this principle could work well and fairly. But it was not always followed through.

This comparatively civilised spirit of international cooperation did not last long. After the death of Alexander III's only close heir, the little Maid of Norway, and the harassed and miserable reign of King John, war clouds began to gather over the Borders. In 1296 Edward I arrived on the banks of the Tweed at the head of a huge army, probably the largest to invade Scotland since Agricola's legions marched north. While English armoured knights took Berwick in a matter of hours, riding right over the top of flimsy defences, no more than 'a ditch and a barricade of boards', a Scottish army mustered at Caddonlea near Galashiels. Less than half the size of Edward's force, the Scots had no intention of moving east to confront him. Instead they adopted a strategy which would become standard. In their council of war at the camp at Caddonlea, the seven earls who led the Scots decided to attack England's western frontier, advancing as far as Carlisle, and – redoubling the misery of ordinary Borderers – to burn, steal and kill in the countryside around. There was no escape, it seemed.

Between 1296 and 1328, what became known as the Wars of Independence trailed destruction in their wake, and on both sides of the border as armies crossed and recrossed. After the dreadful summers of 1315 and 1316 and the failure of the harvests, and the frequent passing of rapacious regiments of soldiers, ordinary Borderers must have despaired. These 34 years of destruction, the span of almost two generations, were another turning point, a time when the fundamental nature of society changed – and for the worse.

What did farmers and their families do in the face of an approaching army or raiding party? The sources are scant, almost silent. Chroniclers recorded the burning of dozens (sometimes hundreds) of farms, villages and towns, the beseiging of castles and the outcome of battles, but they have little or nothing to say about the people caught in this incessant crossfire. They must have fled. When Edward I returned to Berwick in 1298, it was said that the town was deserted, and when the Scots were mustering to raid into north Cumberland after Bannockburn, the English king's officers assisted in moving farmers and their stock south and out of the way. This was almost certainly a general pattern. Quickly gathering up what was valuable and portable and driving their beasts before them, farmers and their families must have retreated to remote places and hid and sheltered as best they could. Perhaps they made for the summer sheilings up on the high pasture. Foraging parties will have found some but at least there was a chance of survival.

HAY FEVER

Seasonal allergic rhinitis is the posh name for hay fever, a condition which has nothing to do with hay. Airborne pollen from grasses, weeds and flowering trees causes about 20 per cent of the population of Britain (more than 12 million and rising) to sneeze in May and June each year. Hay fever is new, the first cases were only reported in 1819. Warmer winters and wetter springs have been causing plants to flower earlier and produce more pollen to be blown around in early summer breezes. One of the few advantages of living in the period of the little ice age was that you were very unlikely to suffer from sneezing and eye irritation. It was too cold and wet for hay fever to present much of a problem.

In 1308 Edward II was at York, ordering his sheriffs of Northumberland, Cumberland and Westmorland to raise 'posses' to repel and pursue raiders, but not lead their men into Scotland unless absolutely necessary. This was most likely a measure to discourage the desperate, bands of riders looking to lift cattle after their own had gone.

Government papers carried reports that English borderers were forming criminal alliances with Scots raiders, becoming 'their companions
and guides', and sharing in plundered goods and stock. Simmering
under the surface was a question of loyalty. Were Borderers more
likely to be loyal to their surnames and their neighbours than to their
nationality? It seems so.

In November 1315, after the first sunless summer and its unripened
harvest, Edward II wrote to the Bishop of Durham asking that he
forbid his tenants on the border from making local truces with their
Scots neighbours. So that some sort of subsistence agriculture could go
on, it appears that landowners had been reaching accommodations
with each other, people they knew well. 'The calamitous and helpless
state' of the people had driven them to ignore the state of war between
England and Scotland and ignore their king's wishes. And no wonder.

Famine had one thing to recommend it. It had at least prevented
Edward II from reinvading Scotland in pursuit of revenge in the year
following Bannockburn, but it probably encouraged more raiding
across the border. Edmund de Caillou, the Captain of Berwick and a
Gascon serving in the English army, led an expedition up the Tweed as
far as the mouth of Teviotdale and Jedburgh. Returning with many
head of cattle and much plunder, he was intercepted by Sir James
Douglas. As a deliberate tactic the Scots commander sought out the
Gascon and fought him in what amounted to a single combat.
Douglas' force was much smaller and he needed to decapitate the
English raiders if he could. And he did.

HEATH PEA

The first pioneer bands of hunter-gatherers who colonised northern
Britain at the end of the last ice age lived off the land, the sea and the
seashore. Their skills and lore were never lost, and in times of
famine were especially valuable. Those who knew where to find
mushrooms, raspberries, hazelnuts and crab apples might stave off
starvation a little. There was a wide range of what we might now
call weeds which could also supply much needed sustenance. Silver-
weed has a carroty, crunchy root which can be boiled or dried and
ground into a sort of flour. It was so commonly used in the
Highlands that the Gaels called it 'an seachdamh aran', or 'the
seventh bread'. In 2006 it seems that these nutritious plants are back
on the menu. Dietitians are investigating the properties of Heath

Pea. Its roots have an aniseed flavour and were said to give those who chewed them the ability to perform superhuman feats of strength and endurance. Highland armies apparently munched Heath Pea on the way to victories at Prestonpans and Falkirk in 1745 and 1746. However, all that may be, but 21st-century society is of course investigating the humble pea not as a source of nutrition but as a means of facilitating weight loss.

A familiar pattern of raid and reprisal began to establish itself. Sometimes it baffled outsiders – and locals. In July 1317 two Italian cardinals were sent by the new Pope, John XXII, to England and Scotland to attempt to broker a peace and gather support for a crusade. Travelling through Northumberland, John de Ossa and Luca de Fieschi were ambushed by 'banditti'. When confronted by two urbane Italian princes of the church in their scarlet skullcaps, the 'banditti' were somewhat nonplussed. Of course they robbed them of everything worth having, but failed to see the potential for a large ransom. Instead they abducted two local lords and left the cardinals, no doubt dazed but relieved, standing in the road.

No medieval community could survive a perpetual state of war and after another abortive English invasion in 1319, the terms of a truce were hammered out at Newcastle. Local contact between English and Scottish borderers was forbidden but the general heads of agreement look very much like a restatement and reinstatement of the laws of the marches. For the first time the appointment of officers to administer them is recorded. Known as 'Conservators of the Truce', two were drawn from Cumberland and Westmorland and four from Northumberland. They were bound to hear complaints about truce break-ers, investigate them and seize and detain whoever was believed to have serious charges to face. So far so familiar. But 1319 saw an early organisational structure created to complement the old laws of the marches. These Conservators sound very like versions of the later March Wardens, the royal officers who would become central figures in sixteenth-century reiver society. No record of matching Scottish appointments survive, but for the reciprocal arrangements to work at all, these were likely to have been in place.

The arrangements did not work in 1322 when the truce was shattered by Edward II and his invading army. His men wasted the countryside as far north as Leith, but a year later negotiations resumed. Contact between Scots and English was again expressly forbidden – although one concession was made to practicality. The Conservators might meet their opposite numbers and hold 'truce days' to transact business. These could be held at the ancient trysting places along the border – at Kershope, Carter Bar and Reddenburn and elsewhere. By 1327 a famous name appeared on the scene. Henry de Percy was appointed as 'the Principal Keeper of the Truce' and paid 1,000 merks to maintain 100 men-at-arms and their 'hobelars' or ponies. The institutions of reiver society were slowly taking shape.

Another famous Border name emerged in the early fourteenth century. The Douglas family had been steadfast supporters of Robert de Bruce and tradition holds that the red heart in the centre of their coat of arms represents the great king's. After his death from leprosy in 1328, Bruce's heart was cut out of the hideous, decaying corpse and taken on crusade against the Moors in Spain by the Douglases. For many years the king had been under sentence of excommunication for his murder of John Comyn at the altar of Greyfriars Church in Dumfries, and even in death it seems that Bruce's remains were employed in penitent works.

After Bannockburn, the Douglases received more material rewards, taking over ownership of the forests of Selkirk, Traquair and Ettrick in 1321-22. By the end of the fourteenth century, they had built up a wide patrimony which included estates in Teviotdale, Eskdale, Lauderdale and around Kelso. Over in the west a closely related branch of the family became powerful in Wigtownshire, the wonderfully named Archibald the Grim taking the old title of Lord of Galloway. This was all a deliberate but dangerous royal policy. To buttress the border, Scottish kings needed bulwarks, concentrations of substantial military capability, and so on the Scottish side, the Douglases grew mighty – and as war rumbled wearily on they became mightier still.

Robert de Bruce and his immediate successors were forced to contend with a serious dynastic complication. Edward Balliol had a legitimate claim to the throne of Scotland, and as the son of King John, it was in some ways a better claim than Bruce's. After the hideous murder of his father, Edward III of England and his counsellors took over the simmering war with Scotland, and they found Edward Balliol a very handy political pawn. And because of geography and Balliol's own claims to family property, much of this fascinating political sub-plot was played out across the Borders landcape.

THE MEN WHO WOULD BE KING

At least three different sorts of royal claimants were important in fourteenth- and fifteenth-century politics. A rival claimant such as Edward Balliol, or Edward I of Scotland, presented a serious threat to the Bruces who felt their own royal status in constant need of bolstering. Across the Scottish nobility there were several families who had grounds for believing themselves as royal as the king's. But none had a father who had actually been crowned King of Scots. The second sort was the straightforward imposter. Far from being one of the princes in the Tower (escaped), Perkin Warbeck was not a legitimate claimant to the throne of England but evidently a Frenchman, born in Tournai. His position was perhaps the weakest. The most mysterious claimant was the man known as 'The Mammet'. This was the strange name (it may simply mean 'imposter') given to a man claiming to be Richard II. After having been deposed in 1399 by Henry IV Bolingbroke, Richard was said to have escaped from prison in London and sailed to sanctuary in the Western Isles. He was immediately taken under the protection of the Regent, the Duke of Albany, who paid him a handsome pension. Richard's presence in Scotland was a useful political counter, especially when the king of England was so clearly a usurper himself. The Mammet died in 1419 and was accorded a royal funeral in Stirling. Modern historians now believe that he was no imposter. In an age long before photography or the mass production of printed images, what mattered was not so much likeness as manner and knowledge. If the Mammet behaved like a king and had plausible personal recollection of his part in the major events of his reign, such as the Peasants' Revolt, then many will have bowed to him as Richard II of England.

With the death of the old warrior-king, Robert I, Scotland faced shifting phases of political uncertainty. The new king was a four-year-old boy, David II, and his Regent, Donald Earl of Mar, had only a shaky grip on power. Encouraged and funded by the English, Edward Balliol sailed out of the Humber Estuary in the summer of 1332 at the head of an expeditionary force. Known as 'the Disinherited', the invaders sought to reclaim the estates they believed were rightfully theirs. Many had been driven out of Scotland by Robert I, their lands seized and given to the king's supporters in the Wars of

Independence. Others were English magnates who had lost their Scottish holdings.

At Dupplin Moor, on the River Earn near Perth, the Disinherited unexpectedly defeated the Earl of Mar's larger army. Balliol had not the resources to grasp outright control and set about subduing the rest of Scotland, but he did understand the great power of symbols. A month after his victory at Dupplin Moor, Balliol's supporters had organised a traditional coronation ceremony at Scone. In the footsteps of ancient kings from Kenneth I onwards, he climbed the 'hill of faith' and had himself anointed by a bishop and crowned Edward I of Scotland by the time-honoured kingmaker, the Earl of Fife.

The coronation created a political mess which promised nothing but problems for those living on either side of the Anglo-Scottish border. Balliol granted the sheriffdoms of Roxburgh and Berwick to his sponsor, Edward III of England, 'for all time coming', and the two major towns and castles passed into English occupation. Roxburgh was lost to the Scots between 1334 and 1460 (with one short break) while Berwick was never recovered. Stranded far to the north of other population centres in Northumberland and cut off from its natural hinterland in the Tweed Valley, the town remains a historical anomaly. Lying to the north of most of the Border country, like an island unto itself, it is neither Scots nor convincingly English.

Two kings in Scotland and a powerful and expansionist king of England ensured that the economy of the Borders could not recover its former vigour. Based on the growing of wool, its sale at Roxburgh's markets and export through the port at Berwick, trade had been busy, international and lucrative. The great Border abbeys survive as monuments to God but also to all those business transactions with Flemish and Italian merchants on the quays at Berwick and in the shadow of Roxburgh Castle. But with the frequent tramp of soldiers keeping cartloads of woolpacks and hides off the roads into Scotland, and the long-term presence of English garrisons, the medieval sheep ranches in the Cheviots, Lammermuirs and the uplands never regained their scale and output. And with the customs revenues at Berwick and Roxburgh going to the royal treasury in London, Scots kings had little motivation for the reconstruction of the local economy and the wool trade. In this way fourteenth- and fifteenth-century politics sowed more seeds for the growth of the criminal society of the sixteenth century.

Edward Balliol's triumph lasted only a few months. Having arrived to celebrate Christmas at the town of Annan, part of the family's extensive estates in Dumfriesshire, the royal retinue was attacked by a thousand-strong force of David II's supporters. After his brother, Henry, had been killed, Balliol only just managed to escape. Scrambling onto the back of a horse, wearing nothing but a shirt, and hanging desperately onto its mane, he splashed bareback across the Solway sands to the English shore and was given refuge by Lord Dacre in Carlisle Castle.

By July of the following year Balliol was back in Scotland, this time with Edward III and a huge English army. And this time wearing his crown and riding under his royal banner. By-passing (temporarily) Scots-held Berwick, the invaders plundered their way far to the north, reaching Perth and all the while supplied and supported by a large fleet off the North Sea coast shadowing their advance and putting in at convenient harbours. When Edward III and Balliol returned to Berwick, they found the siege still in progress, and despite the cruel tactic of hanging two Scottish hostages (including the sons of the governor, Sir Alexander Seton) each day in full view of the walls and their defenders, the town held its nerve and held out.

When a relieving army finally arrived under the command of Sir Archibald Douglas, the English took up a powerful position on Halidon Hill, a mile north of Berwick and offered battle. The slaughter was unrelenting. As the Scots fought their way up the hill, they fell under a murderous hail of arrows. Echelons of English archers stood in the new 'harrow' formation which allowed them to fire to their flanks as well as directly in front. Able to loose at least ten arrows a minute from their tremendously powerful longbows (more than 6 foot long and with a draw weight of between 80 and 120 pounds) and send them prodigious distances, his archers won the battle at Halidon Hill for Edward III. Their technique of firing high into the air to harness gravity to the terrifying impact of the arrows brought down rank after rank of Scots foot soldiers and cavalry. Casualty estimates for medieval battles are usually unreliable, but thousands were shot dead or fatally wounded and many noblemen died on the bloody slopes of Halidon Hill, at least five Scottish earls and their commander, Sir Archibald Douglas.

Berwick fell the following day, and in its castle Edward I of Scotland established his puppet court. In reality his master seemed determined to leave him little to rule over. Edward III allowed his soldiers to plunder and burn over wide areas of Scotland south of the Forth. Unlike his grandfather, who sought to subdue by installing a pro-

English party in government, Edward opted for scorched-earth brutality instead of politics. His garrisons in the castles of the Borders terrorised the countryside around, creating a wasteland instead of cultivating a profitable colony – and thereby failing to gather support for Balliol.

ARMOUR PIERCING

From the early experiments at Halidon Hill through to the unexpected triumph at Agincourt, English archery dominated the battlefields of Britain and France. Scots kings tried hard to create similar skills in the north and several Border towns have streets which remember the practice areas for bowmen: the Butts, the Bow Butts. But it never happened. The immense hitting power and accuracy of English (and Welsh) archers, their ability to fire rapid volleys and also to send very long and heavy arrows into the air was unparalleled. Often an arrow might pierce plate armour but use up so much of its energy in so doing that it could not quite get through a mail shirt and pierce the abdomen of a charging knight. Recent tests at Kelso showed a different effect – which was almost as disabling. When an arrow pierced outer armour and mail and its sharp tip was wedged in place and touching the skin, the movement of riding a horse made it impossible to keep the armour on. As a knight moved, the arrow scratched and lacerated his skin until the agony forced him to dismount, if he could in the midst of battle, and tear off his breastplate. At Agincourt so many French knights dismounted and disarmoured that the lines behind them piled up into mounds of screaming men and horses.

In the years that followed the defeat at Halidon Hill, the regency of David II and ultimately the young king himself developed the policy of building up powerful local lordships along the English border. Douglases, Scotts, Humes and Kers grew accustomed to acting on their own initiative when trouble came north, and instead of a remote, often absent and weakened central royal authority, their more immediate ability to protect the countryside and its people fostered strong local loyalties around them. Some began to manipulate international relations to their own ends. Sir William Douglas of Liddesdale had cleared Teviotdale of English occupation by 1343 and began to call himself

Warden of the Scottish Middle Marches, a very early use of the office and title. His neighbour, Sir Alexander Ramsey, Warden of the Scottish East Marches, was made Keeper of Roxburgh Castle and Sheriff of Teviotdale by David II's government. Douglas was outraged. His men attacked Ramsey as he presided over a sheriff court at Hawick and bundled him off to Hermitage Castle. Confined in a filthy cellar, he was starved to death.

David II was allegedly furious. Sir Archibald Douglas calmly withdrew into 'the inaccessible wilds of the Border' and opened a correspondence with the court of Edward III of England. Within months he was restored to favour and granted the keeping of Roxburgh Castle. A familar political pattern was developing.

More military disasters waited for the hapless David II. While Edward III was embroiled in France in the early exchanges of the Hundred Years War, the Scots had recaptured much territory and were attempting to establish royal authority. But in 1346 the young king over-reached himself. At Neville's Cross near Durham, English archery again proved decisive and David II was badly wounded in the face by an arrow. Worse, he was taken prisoner.

The way at last seemed open for Edward Balliol and he immediately moved 'to recover his realm'. At first he tasted dramatic success, overrunning southern Scotland and reaching as far west as Glasgow. But always seen as an agent of the English king, his support remained slight and despite five years of guerrilla warfare, Balliol was never able to take a firm hold of his realm.

In 1349 his subjects had other, much more pressing concerns than rival claims to the throne. At Caddonlea near Galashiels, the traditional muster-place for the Scottish host, soldiers pitched their tents by the stream and waited for their captains to make plans for an invasion of England. Their purpose was to take advantage of the devastation in the south caused by the arrival of what they called 'the foul English pestilence'. Hundreds of thousands had died, communities were reeling at the impact of what historians came to call the 'Black Death'. Bizarrely, the Scots believed that it was a disease which respected nationality and frontiers, only affecting the English. The Tweed had been used as a cordon sanitaire, the fords and bridges closely guarded and the ferry boats pulled up on the northern bank.

When the disease suddenly erupted around the campfires at Caddonlea, the soldiers panicked and the army scattered. And thereby spread the plague much more quickly throughout Scotland. The contemporary chronicler, John of Fordun, believed that a third of all Scots died in 1349. Later historians estimated a quarter. By either reckoning it was a cataclysmic event, reducing the population from around a million to 750,000 or even less in a matter of weeks. Far more devastating than any military campaign or famine, the Black Death changed medieval Scotland radically, and for the worse. Around 30 per cent of the agricultural labour force disappeared, literally overnight, and the remainder lived in terror of following their agonising fate – at any moment. The economy must simply have ruptured and the rural cycle left badly damaged.

GROSS, GRIM, BLACK AND A LOSER

The Douglas family attracted nicknames like no other. Perhaps as a result of using the same Christian names in succeeding generations, the genealogies sprout soubriquets like Archibald the Tyneman (the Loser), Archibald Greysteel (fought well at the Battle of Ancrum Moor in 1545) and the splendid Archibald the Grim (fought well most of the time). There was also James the Gross (fat but long-lived) and – surely the worst of many Douglas nicknames – that attached to Hugh, Lord Douglas, who lived from 1294 to 1342. He has gone down in history as Hugh the Dull. In the early 1600s, the Border historian, David Hume of Godscroft, set the seal on Hugh's dismal reputation: 'Of this man, whether it was by reason of the dullness of his mind, we have no mention at all in history of his actions.' Oh dear. But perhaps the most extravagant transition was that of Charles the Wellbeloved, King of France until 1422. Because he began to lose his mind, attacking his courtiers without warning, he first became a tentative 'Charles the Silly' and then, after he had killed four of them – only desisting when his sword broke, definitely 'Charles the Mad'. Perhaps his wife drove him to it. Queen Isabella's great bulk and even greater sexual appetite conferred the title 'The Great Sow'.

In the Borders, as elsewhere, those who caught the disease were left to die a lonely and excruciating death. Priests were not allowed to administer last rites and families forbidden to sit by the beds of the dying. Those who recovered – and around 40 per cent did – must have been in danger of dying of thirst and starvation as they were left to their miserable fate. In a very short time thousands were thrown into mass graves, houses gutted and the possessions of the dead burned on huge pyres. It was a holocaust.

Here is John of Fordun's account of what happened:

> For, to such a pitch did that plague wreak its cruel spite, that nearly a third of mankind were thereby made to pay the debt of nature. Moreover, by God's will this evil led to a strange and unwonted kind of death, insomuch that the flesh of the sick was somehow puffed out and swollen, and they dragged out their earthly life for barely two days . . . Men shrank from it so much that, through fear of contagion, sons, fleeing as from the face of leprosy or from an adder, durst not go and see their parents in the throes of death.

In the weeks following the arrival of this lethal illness few people travelled unless they had to and market days must have been sparse and trade doubtless declined sharply. A labour shortage soon took hold and while it benefited those who were left, the economic downturn was bad for everyone. Food prices rocketed, land values fell and cultivation shrank back. After the dismal effects of climate change from 1315 onwards, this new calamity only added more momentum to the decline of the Borders in the fourteenth century. The plague returned regularly and outbreaks were reported as late as the eighteenth century.

Edward Balliol was a tough old bird and his ambitions survived, but support in England was waning. The captured David II was much more valuable to Edward III if he was recognised as the legitimate sovereign of Scotland. As the Hundred Years War absorbed more and more resources, a king's ransom became very attractive to the English. They needed the money and Balliol became expendable.

In January 1356 Edward III held court in his castle at Roxburgh and summoned Edward I of Scotland into his presence. For the times Balliol by then was a very old man indeed at 76. But 'like a roaring lion', wrote the chroniclers, he tore the crown of Scotland from his head and with the symbols of earth and water, he gave them up to Edward III. And having resigned his kingdom and all his Scottish possessions, he was awarded a pension so that he could retire to his family estate at Bailleul in northern France, as his father had done. A remarkable man – who might have been king – he died almost ten years later at the immense age of 85.

By the terms of the Treaty of Berwick, concluded in 1357, the

English finally got their money. David II was ransomed for 100,000 marks, a vast sum whose payments further crippled the economy. Officially the treaty also stipulated that there be a 20-year truce between the kings of England Scotland. But not necessarily between Borderers. The Scots in particular ignored it and before the ink was dry and the wax had set on the new treaty, the reconquest of Berwickshire and Roxburghshire began.

Nibbling at the margins of English occupation, local lords re-imposed themselves and forced English garrisons to stick close to their castles. By 1364 the Chamberlain at Berwick was reporting that no rents could be collected at Hawick because of the actions of Scots lords, and in 1369 the Earl of Dunbar and March repossessed his old estates around Earlston. Two years later the Chamberlain was accounting only for rents paid within a 5-mile radius of Berwick – the minimum effective range of regular patrols.

In Roxburghshire the English held onto the powerful castles at Jedburgh and Roxburgh itself, and controlled the countryside in a ten-mile corridor between them. Attacks on these strongholds were likely to sting the English into large-scale military action and the new king, Robert II, was in any case bound by the terms of the treaty which released his predecessor. But privately the first Stewart king condoned what the Border lords were doing and he rewarded them.

The fourteenth century saw the consolidation of the 'Auld Alliance' between Scotland and France against England. Edward III, his son 'the Black Prince', and successor, Richard II, pursued territorial wars against the French for more than 60 years. It was in Scotland's direct interest to give aid to her enemy's enemy and vice-versa. But this only rarely worked in any practical way, although it did force the English into a mindset of fighting a war on two fronts. And when a truce had been declared or the war had gone well in France, the English kings could turn their attention northwards.

In the early 1380s the Earls of Douglas had been active on the border, retaking Wark Castle and even extending control over parts of north Northumberland. Richard II of England retaliated with vigour. At the head of a huge army of 14,000 men, the largest to march north since Halidon Hill, he led a full-scale invasion of Scotland. Once again the Borders suffered. At Hoselaw near Kelso the English pitched camp, their banners snapping in the breeze, their 'thousand fires' twinkling in the night sky and sending a chill of terror around the countryside. Many Border lords and prelates hurried to make their peace.

As Richard II pursued Douglas and his supporters, the Scots scorched the earth in front of his huge army. Quartermasters sent out foraging parties but there was little to be gleaned. Perhaps out of frustration, the English king ordered the destruction of Melrose and Dryburgh abbeys. He also tightened his hold over Roxburghshire and Berwickshire.

A repeating, highly destructive and depressing pattern of raid and retaliation had become entrenched and for fully four generations fire, rack and ruin had blighted the Border country.

Born in 1316, two years after the sensational victory at Bannockburn and while his grandfather was in his martial pomp, Robert II was an old man when he succeeded to the throne of Scotland. Fifty-five was a venerable age in the fourteenth century. By the 1380s Robert had attracted an unflattering nickname. Known as 'Auld Bleary', he clung to kingship long enough to frustrate the ambition of his eldest son, John, the Earl of Carrick. In 1384, exasperated, he orchestrated a palace coup which removed the old king from the effective exercise of power and forcibly retired him to Dundonald Castle on the family estates in Ayrshire.

TAILZIE

Disputed successions to kingdoms, estates, titles or privileges were a continuing source of conflict in medieval Scotland and England. One solution was the mechanism known as 'entail' in England, and it essentially nominated an alternative line of succession should the principal line fail to produce heirs. In Scotland it was called 'tailzie' (the original meaning was 'a slice of meat') and it worked in much the same way. So, when David II failed to produce an heir, an agreed tailzie meant that the children of Robert the Bruce's daughter, Marjorie, could pick up the succession to the throne. This sort of sideways move could be problematic but it caused less dissent than the old Celtic principle of tanistry which operated in Scotland until the mid-twelfth century. Tanistry broadened the succession very much more by including all those whose great-grandfather had been a king as possible heirs. It certainly guaranteed the line of succession but also sparked endless, vicious, blood-spattered incidents. Unknowingly, William Shakespeare dealt with the consequences of tanistry in 'Macbeth'.

Auld Bleary lived long enough to see his son punished for his presumption. Badly injured by a kick from a horse, the Earl of Carrick was left so crippled that he could take no active part in warfare. It was as much a blow to prestige as a practical matter for a medieval magnate. This allowed his younger brother, Robert, Earl of Fife, to take up the reins of authority and become Guardian of Scotland. One of his earliest acts was to organise a huge raid over the border into England which culminated in the famous battle at Otterburn.

This was not an invasion in pursuit of political advantage or the annexation of territory: the campaign of 1388 bore all the marks of a raid, plain and simple, and it owed much more to the growing habit of reiving than to the policies of Robert I or Edward III. And its climactic battle was fought in moonlight.

The events of that summer were exceptionally well recorded. Jean Froissart, the French chronicler, had spoken to two Gascon esquires who had fought for Sir Henry Percy at the battle at Otterburn, Jean de Castelnau and Jean de Cantiron. Their conversation took place only a year later and memories must have been sharp. And like a good historian, Froissart sought a balanced view. Also in 1389 he interviewed a Scottish knight and two esquires who had fought for the Earl of Douglas. In addition, seven other medieval accounts survive and these are further supplemented by one of the best and very earliest of the Border ballads, 'The Battle of Otterburn'. It is a strange and significant story, and the seeds of much of what was to come lay at its core.

When the Earl of Fife mustered the Scottish host in the high valley of the Jed Water, retaliation was much on his mind. Richard II of England's invasion of 1385 had achieved few strategic purposes but it had been tremendously destructive. Borderers in particular responded to the new Guardian's call to arms and many joined him in the Jedforest in the summer of 1388. They had suffered at the brunt of the English advance and had scores to settle. Under the command of James, Earl of Douglas, many surnames came. Led by their heidsmen, both Johnstones and Maxwells rode in from the west, and there were Kers and Humes from the eastern marches. The opening stanza of the ballad and its hunting metaphor bears repetition for it makes it very clear what was being planned around the campfires in the old forest – a raid:

> It fell about the Lammastide
> When muir men win their hay,
> The doughty Douglas bound him to ride
> Into England to drive a prey.

Fife and Douglas decided to divide their forces. From Southdean Kirk, the larger division made for the Larriston Fells and the head of Liddesdale. The Guardian and Sir Archibald Douglas would lead them down towards Carlisle and the fertile farms of the English west march. They had no siege equipment and would make no attempt to take the town and its squat, well-made castle. James Douglas sought his prey by moving his troopers up over the Carter Bar and down into Redesdale and then on to Tyneside. The strategic intention may have been to tie up English defenders on both sides of the north Pennines and thereby disable any flanking incursion into Scotland.

Both divisions moved with lightning speed. On the morning of 28 July Douglas crossed into England and late the same day his small army camped only a few miles north of the Tyne. By midday on the 29th they were across the river and raiding almost as far south as Durham. The Earl of Fife and Sir Archibald had made 40 miles on their first day and driven many to take refuge behind the stout walls of Carlisle.

What made this medieval blitzkrieg possible was something simple. These armies travelled on horseback. Carrying little or no baggage, their troopers lived off the land and their ponies ate the summer grass. Jean Froissart reported that these huge raiding parties could strike over a range of 60 or 70 miles in a day and a night and since they were pulling no baggage carts, they could move quickly over the hill trails, avoiding towns, their garrisons and delaying trouble until they reached their objective.

The western division bypassed Carlisle on 3 August and rode up the Eden Valley, plundering and raiding as they went. They burned the town of Appleby and advance parties reached as far as Brough before wheeling their ponies northwards again.

Douglas had been busy in the east and by 1 August his men were driving hundreds, possibly thousands of head of stolen cattle across the Tyne fords at Prudhoe. The bridge at Ovingham may still have been standing. From that moment on, the campaign took on all the lineaments of a classic raid. Douglas further divided his forces and sent on a party with all of the plunder to make as much haste as possible up the line of Dere Street and on towards the border. The old Roman road turned down into Redesdale at Otterburn and Douglas and his chosen men would rejoin them there.

Once their plunder had begun to move north, the remaining Scots rode east along the north bank of the Tyne. Much of Hadrian's Wall was still upstanding in 1388 and the military road which paralleled it enabled Douglas to reach the great West Gate of Newcastle's walls in little more than an hour, probably on the afternoon of 3 August. There was no intention to make any attempt to break into the city. The Scots had come to stall, to play for time. While their comrades made slow progress with all those cows up the Roman road, Douglas would bottle up the English behind Newcastle's walls, buying a precious day or even two to allow his men to get as far north as possible.

Sir Henry Percy, made famous by Shakespeare as 'Harry Hotspur', no doubt knew exactly what was going on. Froissart and others relate a tale of single combat between the two commanders outside the West Gate. Perhaps it is true. Douglases had done it before. Hotspur's soldiers certainly sallied out of the city to harass the Scots and it may be that he himself challenged the Earl of Douglas. Single combat took place before Bannockburn and Halidon Hill, and notions of chivalry were very fashionable at the end of the fourteenth century. Here is Froissart's account:

> The Scots returned to Newcastle and rested and tarried two days, and every day they skirmished. The Earl of Northumberland's two sons were young lusty knights and were ever foremost at the barriers to skirmish. There were many proper feats of arms done and achieved: there was fighting hand to hand: among others there fought hand to hand the Earl of Douglas and Sir Henry Percy, and by force of arms the Earl of Douglas won the pennon of Sir Henry Percy, wherewith he was sore displeased and so were all the Englishmen.

Whatever the truth, it all wasted time, and by the morning of 4 August it was enough. Defenders looked out from the West Gate and saw nothing. The Scots had gone before dawn. Two days was judged to be sufficient for the plunder to have reached the rendezvous at Otterburn.

Douglas led his riders and their surefooted ponies through the grey hour before first light, and when they reached Ponteland, they overran the sleeping village and its castle. Both were torched and the local lord, Sir Raymond Delaval, captured and carried off for ransom. Without any more delay the Scots remounted and hurried up the north road to Otterburn.

Percy had sent scouts to shadow Douglas and when they reported a much smaller force than he had assumed, it was resolved immediately to give chase. Hotspur would earn his nickname. Otterburn and Redesdale lie more than 30 miles north of Newcastle and Percy knew that only a mounted force had any chance of catching the Scots before they could slip over the Carter Bar and down into the Jed Valley and safety. A muster-call rang around the city and some time around midmorning Sir Henry Percy's banner dipped under the Pilgrim Gate and his men spurred their ponies into a canter. Douglas may already be climbing the winding road up to the Carter. No time to be lost.

While they waited for their comrades to arrive from Newcastle, the Scots attacked Otterburn Castle. But having travelled light with no siege equipment in tow, they made little impression and the defenders held the castle described by contemporaries as 'tolerably strong and situated among marshes'.

Elsewhere the Scots had used the boggy ground to their advantage. A large corral had been built for their plundered cattle, probably on the higher haughland still visible in a loop of the River Rede. Workgangs of servants had improvised a stockade of sorts with cut branches and brushwood, and watered by the river, bitten by the midges, the cows were protected by the surrounding treacherous marshes. Froissart wrote of the stockade being 'at the entrance to the marsh on the road to Newcastle'. This was significant for what was to take place later. Just as Otterburn Castle was well defended by its surrounding marshes, the Scots' cattle corral made use of the undrained land, keeping the animals in and attackers out.

Meanwhile, Percy's troopers kicked their ponies on up the north road, passing the charred and smoking houses at Ponteland, on up to Belsay and beyond. As the terrain rose after the Scots Gap, the English commanders no doubt sent ahead a screen of scouts. Ambush was a favourite tactic and there were several likely places. By the afternoon Sir Henry Percy's mounted army, perhaps 4,000 strong, was climbing up past Kirkwhelpington onto the moorland above Redesdale. Dere Street and its wide, hard roadway lay well to the west and his troopers will have had to trot along much narrower paths. Sometimes no wider than sheepwalks, the hill trails of the middle ages may have forced

Percy's horsemen to travel in single file in places. This slowed progress tremendously and would later have sore consequences. But it was the Scots who would make the first mistake.

Probably convinced that it was far too late in the day for Percy or any other pursuer to be approaching, Douglas' scouts may have made their way down off the hills to the camp at Otterburn by the early evening. Perhaps the English outriders took care to conceal themselves well. As afternoon shaded into evening, the Scots unbuckled their kit, lit cooking fires and gathered round them to sit, talk over the excitements of the last days and take their ease.

Peace was shattered when a rider tore into the camp at full gallop, whooping and hollering that a huge English force was closing fast. Seven standards fluttered in the breeze, according to the ballad, as Percy spurred on towards Douglas and his thieving band. A day's hard riding – and he had caught them!

Chaos crackled through the Scottish camp as men fell over themselves to buckle on their armour, fiddle with fastenings, pull a mailshirt over their heads and find their weapons. Many managed to lay hands on only part of their war-gear as their captains screamed at them to stand to. The Earl of Moray fought without his helmet, the Earl of Douglas without much of his body armour, others were without gauntlets, greaves, some had spears but no dagger, others went barefoot across the heather. But the Scots did not lose their composure or forget their common sense.

Henry Percy did. The sun was setting fast, and as soon as Sir Matthew Redman's vanguard arrived at Otterburn, they attacked the Scots' cattle corral. When Percy's horsemen galloped up out of the village, they dismounted and massed for an immediate attack. Without waiting for all of his long column to gather and quickly pushing his men into a line, Percy became Hotspur and led his men over the moorland. His fatal problem was organisation. Not enough time had been allowed for his captains to form up their men into battalions. Most of the heavily armoured men-at-arms bunched together at one end of the line while at the other lightly armed archers found themselves unsupported and very vulnerable. According to the Westminster Chronicle they 'straggled into action in irregular order'.

As the light faded, the Scots scrambled into a much better drilled battle formation. Seeing that Percy's front was badly unbalanced, they quickly wheeled and attacked him on his flank, driving their spears into the company of archers and knocking them down before they could begin firing. As Percy's late-comers arrived and dismounted, they rushed into the battle piecemeal, making no dramatic difference. By contrast the Earls of Moray and March calmly rallied their contingents as a strategic reserve and waited for their moment.

The battle soon became a bloody scrummage as the two lines locked together in the hacking, shoving and kicking of close-quarter fighting. In the midst of all that intimate fury James, Earl of Douglas, was felled and, incompletely armoured, done to death by wounds to his body. Few noticed in the melee. Few could see further than what was at their front and immediately beside them. As darkness descended and the big harvest moon rose over the moor, Percy's men began to tire. They had ridden all day to fight at Otterburn while many of their enemies had rested. After the failure of the disordered first charge, their chances of victory hung in the balance.

Then Sir John Swinton broke the line. A tough, battle-hard soldier from Berwickshire who had fought in English armies for pay and plunder in the Hundred Years War, he hacked his way through Percy's men-at-arms and turned them. The chroniclers reported that the death-blow followed quickly when the Earls of March and Moray and their reserves drove into the dying battle and all in a moment Otterburn became a rout.

English soldiers threw down their weapons, turned and ran for their lives. Many noblemen, exhausted in their heavy body armour, held up their hands, yielded and were captured for lucrative ransoms. One of these was Harry Hotspur, Sir Henry Percy. And it was then that Sir Walter Scott's strange, (and, of course, retrospective) prophesy for James, Earl of Douglas, came true:

> But I hae dreamed a dreary dream,
> Beyond the Isle of Skye;
> I saw a dead man win a fight,
> And I think that man was I.

Late in the afternoon of 5 August, the likely date of the battle, the Prince-Bishop of Durham left Newcastle with several thousand soldiers (almost certainly not the 10,000 claimed by Froissart) to reinforce the impetuous Percy. But they had not gone far before they met streams of fugitives from the disaster at Otterburn. So many of the Prince-Bishop's men turned and fled with them to the safety of Newcastle's walls that his force was reduced to fewer than 500. So rather than face the pursuing Scots, the wise prelate realised he had no choice and he retreated through the Pilgrim Gate.

Having recovered their self-possession by the following day, Durham's soldiers mustered and rode hard for Otterburn. This time the Scottish scouts were alert. They warned their commanders of a second approach and this time they set to strengthening their temporary fortifications. When the Prince-Bishop and his captains rode into view, the Scots taunted them from behind their barricades, blew trumpets and issued dire threats. It was enough. Durham retreated and Douglas's men eventually made their way over the Carter Bar. What was perhaps the greatest raid in the long story of reiving ended profitably – but with the death of their captain, the Scots had paid a heavy price for all that plunder.

Archibald the Grim gained most. After a perilous crossing of the treacherous Solway fords with the Earl of Fife, he returned from the western raid to Cumbria to discover that he would inherit vast tracts of land from the dead Earl James. To add to his Galloway estates between the Cree and the Nith, the new Earl of Douglas became master of Douglasdale, Eskadale, Lauderdale, the old royal Forest of Selkirk and many farms and villages in the Tweed Valley. It was an immense and valuable domain – but almost all of it lay in a war zone.

Archibald the Grim got his nickname for an apt quality. Said to be grim, or in its older meaning 'merciless', in battle, the English also called him Archibald the Black. The latter tag came to apply to his descendants and that branch of the family were known as 'the Black Douglases'. This distinguished them from the Earls of Angus who were called 'the Red Douglases', very much junior cousins.

DUKES PUT UP

Towards the end of the fourteenth century English and Scottish kings began creating dukes and dukedoms, probably in imitation of the French. In 1398 the Duke of Albany was first north of the border, but the title lapsed on the execution of his son, Murdoch, in 1425. It passed through various royal hands until it finally became extinct in 1917. Leopold, the Duke of Saxe-Coburg and of Albany was a German and like Duke Murdoch he was forced to forfeit the title. Dukedoms were created as a pinnacle for the aristocracy and only kings could make them. The word derives from the Latin 'dux' meaning a leader. Richard II created his uncles Duke of Buckingham and Duke of Cambridge at Hoselaw near Kelso in the course of his invasion of Scotland in 1385. Little good it did him. Dukes have precedence over all other aristocratic titles. They are followed by Marquises, then Earls, Viscounts, Barons, Knights, then Esquires and finally Gentlemen. Titles like these go before names and letters after. And the letters which have precedence over all others are VC.

The year after Otterburn, Earl Archibald and George Dunbar, the Earl of March, mustered their soldiers to raid into England and exploit the weakness of Richard II's administration, but their plans were thwarted when a French envoy arrived in Edinburgh. A three-year truce between the kings of England and France had been concluded, and as partners in the Auld Alliance, the Scots were bound by its terms. Robert II's sons forced the Douglas/March army to disband. Furious, the two earls began to enter into private arrangements with the English, and these were designed to deliver advantage to their families and their possessions in the Borders. International relations and the wider cause of Scotland as a whole came a very distant second.

Auld Bleary finally died in 1390 at his retreat at Dundonald Castle. He was 74 and 'broken by age'. His eldest son, John Earl of Carrick, who had been broken by accident, took the regnal name of Robert III. He and his counsellors wished to avoid the issue of the legitimacy of King John Balliol's short reign. The names 'John I' or 'John II' both had baggage attached. The former would have denied Balliol's existence and the latter recognised it and also the claims of Edward Balliol and his descendants. Dupplin Moor lay only two generations in the past.

Robert III was anxious to prolong the truce of 1389. He and his family needed time and the opportunity to exert their authority inside Scotland and not allow themselves to be distracted or destabilised by war across the border. And just as important, the powerful southern earls of Douglas and March must not be given the chance to become more powerful.

On 11 March 1398 Scots and English commissioners met at Hadden Stank near Kelso. Like the nearby Redden Burn it was a customary trysting place on the line of the border. David, Earl of Carrick and heir presumptive, arrived with a bishop, another earl, a baron, two clerks, two knights bachelor, and a squire. This carefully compiled list was balanced by a deputation of exactly equal rank on the English side. It was led by the Duke of Lancaster and Guyenne, John of Gaunt, the king's uncle. Known by contemporaries as 'Days of Trewe' or Truce Days, these were the ancestors of the sixteenth-century meetings held by March Wardens or their deputies.

With royal dukes and earls in charge and great magnates in tow, the deliberations at Hadden Stank would have been formal, showy affairs. Heraldic standards, pavilions, perhaps fanfares, announcements, processions, oaths and the fixing of waxen seals. If the March weather was unusually benign, it must have been an impressive spectacle.

The grander business of state was speedily concluded (having been agreed beforehand) but the grit of cross-border relations took more time. Complaints from Scots about alleged English wrongdoing and vice-versa had already been lodged. In a stark geographical quirk, English bills of complaint were handed to the Sacristan of Kelso Abbey and Scots bills to the Governor of Roxburgh Castle – which lay just across the Tweed, less than a mile distant. Such were the awkward realities of everyday life in the eastern Borders. At Hadden Stank these bills were heard and adjudicated upon. The old term of 'Conservators of the Truce' was used and deputies appointed to see that the peace was kept.

It was not. The Truce Day of 11 March 1389 failed, despite its high-born cast list and its high-flown language and intentions. Truce-breaking of all sorts went on and another meeting was scheduled for the autumn in an attempt to bring criminals to justice. Certain customs were reaffirmed and the second Truce Day of 1389 heard mention of what became known as 'hot trod', the right to pursue 'with horn and hound' thieves and stolen goods from one realm into another without impediment.

The following year all was thrown into even greater confusion when Richard II of England was deposed and the usurper, Henry Bolingbroke, assumed the crown and called himself Henry IV. Henry Percy, Earl of Northumberland, and Ralph Neville, Earl of Westmorland, both supported the new king and were confirmed by him as Wardens of the East and West Marches respectively. Immediately they found their hands full as Scottish reiver lords took the opportunity to raid into England. In Coquetdale a band of reivers were happily rounding up cattle when they were attacked and taken prisoner by Sir Robert Umfraville. One of the Scots was John Turnbull, known as 'Out With The Sword', a very early example of a classic reiver nickname.

DUEL OR NO DUEL

Deals were sometimes done over long-term sieges. They were expensive and an early resolution was welcomed by both parties. Defenders would calculate how much food, water and resolve they had left and occasionally negotiate surrender by a certain date if no relieving force had arrived before then. This happened at Berwick and Roxburgh. The quid pro quo was usually an agreement that lives would be spared and property respected. In the aftermath of a battle at Humbleton Hill near Wooler, Harry Hotspur laid siege to the tower of Cocklaws in the Scottish Border. When it held out, he agreed that it should surrender by 1 August 1403 if neither the Duke of Albany or Robert III came with an army to relieve it. Albany raised an army, and Percy did the same. A victory on the scale of Bannockburn was promised. The Scots army marched south to relieve Cocklaw – but the English did not turn up. Percy had been raising his army to fight Henry IV at Shrewsbury and the whole thing was a ruse. In 1394 Sir William Inglis briefly took Jedburgh Castle for the Scots but lost it soon afterwards to Sir Thomas Strother. Over some now lost point of honour the two men agreed to fight a duel with the winner taking the castle. At Rulehaugh, a flat piece of ground nearby, an audience including the Earls of Northumberland and Douglas gathered. After a furious fight lasting no more than a few minutes, Inglis killed Strother. But for some reason Jedburgh stayed in English hands and Robert III compensated Sir William with the old barony of Manor, not far from Peebles.

One of the heroes of Otterburn, the Earl of March, was anxious to make contact with Henry IV and involve him in a serious domestic dispute. In exchange for a large sum in gold, Robert III had agreed to give his eldest son, the Duke of Rothesay, in marriage to March's daughter, Elizabeth Dunbar. Archibald the Grim immediately outbid him and the old king changed his mind, and promptly added injury to insult by refusing to repay March his handsome dowry.

The earl did not waste time or mince his words. In a letter to Henry IV, he invited the new English king to take sides in a family feud in Scotland. In exchange for his support, March would immediately defect and throw his weight behind English ambitions in Scotland. By midsummer the Duke of Rothesay had married Archibald the Grim's daughter and March had been joined by the Percies in raiding in the Borders and East Lothian. Thus the winner and loser of Otterburn disregarded national politics and combined in pursuit of family interest. Like true Borderers.

Henry IV then invaded Scotland, laid siege to Edinburgh Castle, issued a few irritated letters, marched up and down and then hurried south to Newcastle. Nothing was resolved and a year later a peace conference assembled hopefully at the village of Kirk Yetholm, near the border. Prior diplomacy had not prepared the way and when the English commissioners trotted out the tired old formula which stretched back into the mists of myth-history and which – self-evidently – proved that Scottish kings had in fact been subject to English kings since the time of Athelstan of Wessex and likely long before, the reaction was less than polite. When arbitration on the matter was suggested, the Bishop of Glasgow replied with a question. Would Henry Bolingbroke's claim to the English throne also be subject to the same scrutiny? In such an atmosphere, there was nothing to be achieved.

In any case Henry IV had more pressing problems elsewhere. In 1400 he had been forced to abandon his siege of Edinburgh Castle and lead his army south to Wales to deal with a serious rebellion. Owain Glyn Dwr and his men had attacked the hated English towns in the north and burned Oswestry and Welshpool. His cousins, Gwilym and Rhys ap Tudur took Anglesey and were strong enough to confront Henry IV and drive him behind the walls of Beaumaris Castle. The gold dragon-standard of Uther Pendragon was unfurled in all its ancient glory and it led Owain Glyn Dwr to many victories over the Sais, the despised English, between 1402 and 1404.

English distraction, whether in France or in Wales, usually encouraged the belligerent Border lords into bouts of military opportunism, and amid the labyrinthine complexities of Scottish domestic politics, the seemingly ever-present need to raid into England was at least a constant. It was becoming a habit of mind, and for those who had to suffer its dismal consequences, a fact of life, year in year out.

THE WOLF OF BADENOCH

Alexander Stewart, the Earl of Buchan and brother of King Robert III, became notorious in the 1380s as 'the Wolf of Badenoch'. Having abandoned his wife and taken 'a concubine' known as

Mairead, Stewart began to turn himself into what he saw as a Highland chieftain. When the Bishop of Moray reproved him for his adultery, the Wolf destroyed the town of Forres and burned the episcopal cathedral at Elgin. Alexander Stewart, most certainly not a Gael, did much to develop the reputation of the Highlands as a lawless, savage society. It was a description soon to be applied to the Borders. What compounded the actions of the Wolf was a grisly affair known as 'the Battle of the Clans'. To settle a territorial dispute, two groups, probably Camerons and Mackintoshes, met near Perth to fight to the death. Thirty men stood on each side. They were not allowed to wear armour – this was to be a decisive encounter – and carrying Lochaber axes, dirks and crossbows, they were watched by grandstands crammed with a specially invited audience. There was to be no quarter and no mercy. At the end of this appalling spectacle only two Camerons and ten Mackintoshes were left standing. All the others had been hacked to pieces. Every Scottish chronicler reported this, as did many English.

Archibald the Grim died in 1400, but his son, also Archibald but not yet grim, continued a close alliance with his father's old reiving partner, the Earl of Fife. He had lately been elevated with the grand title of Duke of Albany.

As King Robert III's grip on power slackened, Albany's grew tighter. Douglas supported him and in return was allowed to plunder into Northumberland despite the fact that a truce was theoretically still in place. In June of 1402 a party of Scots raiders were driving their spoils up the old Roman road of Dere Street. As they crossed the River Teviot, north of Jedburgh and near the hamlet of Nisbet, they were ambushed by the renegade Earl of March. Several notables were killed and others captured for ransom. In itself this incident was part of the small change of Border politics but it did sting Douglas into action and was the first move in a fascinating sequence of events.

In August 1402 he entered England at the head of a large force and raided down as far as the Tyne. Somewhere, somehow, more booty was found and the Scots made their way north by the low road, the trail which skirted the eastern end of the Cheviot ranges. To their astonishment, Douglas and his captains ran into a substantial English army arrayed directly across their route north, barring the way up the valley of the River Till. There was no way round, and Harry Hotspur and the Earl of March were sitting on their ponies in the front rank, itching for revenge.

Encumbered by loot and fearful that they were badly positioned the Scots panicked themselves into a bad mistake. Seeking higher ground, they rushed to occupy the site of a prehistoric hillfort, Humbleton Hill, its grassy old ramparts still visible. Hotspur and March moved quickly to entrap the Scots and – as at Otterburn – the former showed that he had learned nothing and advocated an immediate charge. March calmed Hotspur and instead brought forward the lethal companies of English archers. As the Scots cowered powerless on the hillfort, they fell in their hundreds under the incessant, murderous whoosh loosed on them from below.

That hard-bitten old campaigner, Sir John Swinton, was sheltering under his shield amongst the carnage and he knew that if the Scots made no move, they would be cut down where they stood. Protecting themselves as best they could, his 'chosen lances' climbed into the saddle. Kicking their terrified horses into a gallop, yelling their war-cries, he led them in a desperate downhill charge towards the ranks of archers and English men-at-arms. The archers lowered their aim and firing heavy bolts more like small javelins at the Scots' horses, they brought down most of them before they could engage. It was said that some bolts could pierce plate-armour at close range. Old Sir John disappeared into the ruck of the fighting, going to ground with his horse to be trampled and hacked to death.

Along with four other earls and a hundred or so knights, Archibald Douglas was captured at Humbleton Hill. Soon after the battle he acquired a nickname very different from his father's. Douglas became known as 'the Tyneman', a Scots word meaning 'the Loser'.

SOLDIERS OF FORTUNE

The Hundred Years War greatly encouraged the use of professional soldiers, or mercenaries. Campaigns fought in France were not attractive to an amateur English medieval host mustered to do its mandatory military service. The logistics did not work for part-timers. Back home crops needed to be sown, harvests led in and winter ploughing done. Bands of battle-hardened fighting men evolved, usually under the command of English knights. Sir John Hawkswood had pursued a successful career with his 'White Company' fighting in Italy for one city against another. The

Florentines gratefully remember him as 'Giovanni Acuto' and he sits on a prancing warhorse in a fresco on the wall of their great cathedral, the Duomo. But he could see more lucrative work across the Alps in France and he led his company northwards. Sir John Swinton has no similarly splendid memorial but he was engaged in the same business, fighting for the English kings in the Hundred Years War. Mercenaries were supremely realistic and when they saw which way a battle was going, the last thing they wanted to do was fight to the last man. In the midst of the din and chaos of battle opposing commanders would have no hesitation in holding up their right hand (the accepted signal of surrender) and making sure it was seen – and sometimes they were quickly hired by the winning side. Daft amateurs must have worried mercenaries most.

The nationalism so robustly evident at Bannockburn and in the masterful person of King Robert the Bruce appeared to have fragmented into family factionalism by the end of the fourteenth century. The Earl of March's defection to the Percy power complex gave rise to a blood feud with the Douglases. In the opening decade of the fourteenth century this sort of rivalry blurred the idea of the border. The extent of a noble family's reach seemed as important as the limit of more formal jurisdictions.

In 1403 a remarkable meeting in North Wales took place, an occasion later given vivid form by William Shakespeare in his play *Henry IV Part One*. Owain Glyn Dwr, Henry Percy and Edward Mortimer, the grandson of Edward III, each signed an agreement known as 'the Tripartite Indenture' at Bangor. They resolved to topple the fragile and illegal regime of the usurper King Henry, replace him with Mortimer (whose claim was legitimate) and divide England and Wales between them. Percy was promised all of the north beyond the Trent for his family fiefdom and, to bolster his position, he abandoned George Dunbar, Earl of March and drew Archibald the Tyneman into the conspiracy.

His ill-luck was contagious. Percy and Douglas met Henry IV at Shrewsbury, Glyn Dwr failed to turn up and the battle went badly wrong. The Tyneman lost yet again, was captured and spent five years under arrest before returning to Scotland in 1408. Percy was killed in the fighting and Glyn Dwr retreated into the mists of the Welsh mountains to bide his time.

These events seem to be outlandish, to run against the grain of history. But in the political reality of the time, they certainly did not. The great magnates of the borders – Percy and Douglas – had huge ambition and would not have hesitated to remove a crowned king if their family's interests were threatened. Henry IV was weak, broke and his regime very unstable. If Percy had not perished at Shrewsbury and Glyn Dwr's Welsh archers had come to the fight, it might all have fallen out very differently. And the Tyneman might have lost his reputation and his family might have waxed even more powerful even more quickly in Scotland.

The intensity of cross-border raiding begs a difficult question. Where did all that loot come from? In the late fourteenth and fifteenth centuries the same territory was continually plundered, year after year, but there are no indications of the law of diminishing returns. Surely the same beasts did not trek wearily over the Cheviots only to trek back where they came from the following year. Perhaps they did.

More likely was the operation of a vicious downward spiral. As Border society gradually descended into organised criminality, it became progressively poorer. And its governing dynamic turned from production to larceny – which bound it to become poorer still.

Economic indicators, such as they are, support a darkening picture of the Border countryside in decline. The appalling devastation that followed in the wake of the Black Death of 1349 was compounded by repeated visitations. Between the first outbreak and 1420, there were eight 'plague years' in Scotland. Eight times the virus cut its way through communities and mortality rates could sometimes be as high as 10 per cent.

For the fifteenth century, records of rural life in Northumberland are better than those for Cumbria, Galloway, Dumfriesshire and the Tweed basin and they show a general retreat from cultivation. Some of this was a consequence of the Black Death and labour shortages but contemporaries cite raiding as the prime cause. Farmers who worked the land in a frontier zone could occasionally expect to see foraging parties of soldiers stealing their crops, but it happened year after year; some felt forced to give up their tenancies. This trend was certainly recorded in Northumberland but it was probably widespread over the whole Border region, perhaps so common it passed without comment.

In the Tweed basin the shifting political map had a direct impact on the local economy. The levels of customs revenues measured import and export activity and before the Wars of Independence Berwick-upon-Tweed's volume of trade had been very substantial. Ships from north-western Europe landed a colourful array of cargoes on the quaysides at the mouth of the Tweed. Thousands of gallons of wine, spices, exotic foods, high-value metal goods and much else arrived in the holds of merchant ships. These were refilled with bulging wool-sacks for the continental textile factories and hides for the leather trade. In 1286 the customs revenue for Berwick was £2,190 compared with £8,800 for the whole of England.

What made all of this trade possible was a hinterland. Reaching 70 miles westwards up the Tweed Valley, an immensely productive and well-organised rural hinterland grew all that wool and leather for export through Berwick. But when the town became a political prize, batted back and forth between English and Scots occupation, the trade gradually evaporated. When in English hands, as it was for most of the late middle ages, Scottish kings did not want to see Tweed and Teviotdale wool exported through Berwick and supplying their enemy with customs revenue. Instead they promoted Edinburgh, and despite the difficult upland routes over Middleton Moor and Soutra Hill, such Border wool as could be harvested did go north.

To the English kings, Berwick was not only a northern Calais, it was also an opportunity to make money – if they could gain control of its productive hinterland. If the garrisons at Roxburgh (the main inland wool market) and Jedburgh could only extend their power over the whole area then trade would boom once more. It was eminently possible in more politically stable circumstances. English kings and magnates had made fortunes from the wool trade in the stable south. If only they could incorporate the Tweed basin into England, much needed revenue would flow.

As it was, neither side gained anything – and between the two the Border economy suffered badly. From the 1370s to the 1450s the total Scottish customs revenue declined sharply – by around 70 per cent, from £9,000 per annum to only £2,500. This decline undoubtedly created the conditions and led to the causes of crime.

One of the prime engines of economic growth in the twelfth and thirteenth centuries had been the great Border abbeys. Only magnificent ruins survive now, but in their time they were majestic churches. A description of Kelso from 1517 talks of a huge cathedral-like structure with a double crossing and 12 side-chapels each with its own altar. It was an opulence made possible by the wool trade.

The Border abbots had been princes of the church, influential in national politics. But in the fourteenth and fifteenth centuries little is heard from these men. Their surnames suggest that some were certainly local, probably minor aristocrats. Few made any impression beyond their abbey precincts and religion and the influence of its wealthy prelates appeared not to mitigate the developing criminal atmosphere of the times.

ROXBURGH

Perhaps the most dramatic – and poignant – casualty of the bloody centuries of cross-border warfare and raiding is now completely invisible. Across the Tweed from Kelso lies a green and empty park studded with mature trees and grazed by sheep and cattle. Twice a year race-horses thunder around a point-to-point track. It is now known as Friar's Haugh and the Fairgreen, but in the middle ages it was the site of a large medieval town. It has entirely disappeared, right down to the foundation stones of its many houses and churches. Nothing at all remains of Roxburgh – despite the fact that for at least 200 years it was one of the most vibrant and prosperous places in medieval Scotland. It served as the inland market for the profitable wool and leather trades, the prime destination for the shepherds and stockmen who drove their flocks and herds down from the high valleys and the western ranges. Roxburgh's hinterland was huge and as an animal processing centre on an industrial scale, it brought together primary producers and merchants, and many of the latter were European. With its port of export at Berwick, Roxburgh was the axis of a busy and booming economy. Dominated by its tremendous castle, the town had at least three major streets: King Street, the Headgate and Market Street. There were four churches: Holy Trinity in the centre of the town, St James to the north, near the Tweed, the Friary of St Peter to the south, and inside the castle walls, the Chapel of St John. One of Scotland's very earliest schools was set up and a royal mint turned out currency. Yet it has all gone. After 350 years of ruin and war, the town is entirely effaced. By 1649 St James Church had only six communicants and in the nineteenth century its ruins were removed to make way for a racecourse. Roxburgh gave its name to a county and a ducal title but the ghost-town has seen no sensible archaeology and the site remains essentially mysterious, an inland Atlantis lost under the grass.

The Synod of St Andrews in 1400 published a list of prohibitions which shed a glancing light on the church and its community at the outset of the fifteenth century. Most of all the synod was anxious that priests should understand their role clearly, be able to say mass correctly and minister to their communicants in a proper manner. This was extremely important in a society which believed absolutely in Heaven and Hell. And with the growing importance of the idea of Purgatory (where sins were, literally, purged) in the middle ages, the church reached into the afterlife and became an active agent in the transit of souls.

The horrors of the Black Death had sharpened perceptions immeasurably and the starkness of Heaven and Hell had softened. Purgatory was not eternal, it offered the chance to cleanse earthly sins and the living took part directly in influencing this process. The chapels in Kelso Abbey saw many masses said and sung for the souls of the dead in Purgatory. The more the better, and the shorter the time spent in the cleansing fire. In return, the dead spent their time in prayer and this lightened the burden of sin on the living. It was a straightforward spiritual transaction with clear outcomes, and the Synod of St Andrews attempted to deal with any abuses by forbidding priests from accepting cash payments from those with recently dead relatives to celebrate several masses a day.

MYSTERIOUS MASS

The chantries in the Border abbeys and churches where mass was sung for the souls of the (wealthier) departed were busy. The word for them comes from the Latin 'cantana' meaning 'a place for singing'. It was no doubt very beautiful and very atmospheric. Some early Irish churches sang what was called the 'Laus Perpetuus', or 'the eternal praise' when monks worked in relays around the clock so that the music never stopped and the building was never silent. Mass was intended to be mysterious and until the modern era, it was celebrated behind a screen (often called a rood screen because it was topped by a rood or cross) and the laity could not see the service. The word 'mass' is from the dismissal, also mysterious, which runs 'Ite, missa est', or 'Go! It is sent.'

The more sinful of the early Border reivers could also hope for another method of redemption, especially if they were wealthy and willing to endow the church. An ancient belief persuaded people that the place of burial was very important. The more sacred the ground, the more effective the soil itself would be in purging the body of sin. This is why many aristocratic tombs are to be found inside churches, often as close to the altar as possible or even under it. When James Douglas' body was brought back from Otterburn, it was interred close to the high altar in Melrose Abbey. This was thought to be one of the most deeply sacred places in the Borders because of the association with St Cuthbert and others. Some noblemen went to the trouble of becoming novice monks towards the end of their lives (almost always they endowed the abbey with gifts at the same time). This guaranteed burial inside the precincts, in the cleansing soil.

The St Andrews synod also demanded that priests should behave with more dignity. They should not visit brothels and also put away their common-law wives. They should not go about armed, at least not with long (and obvious) daggers attached to their belts.

Other prohibitions occasionally strayed into what seems to be excessive solemnity. The church was at the centre of community life in the middle ages and a regular focus for social events. At festivals, such as Whitsun, special cakes and ale were taken in the churchyard and games often played. Perhaps handba was, they certainly had hurling in Cornwall and Wales. But the Synod of St Andrews set a ban on dances in the churchyards and also on wrestling and other sports, which must have made the world a duller place.

In other ways life for ordinary Borderers in the later middle ages was unchanging. As an overwhelmingly rural society, the turns of the year dominated. In the hungry months of late winter and spring, most subsisted on grey rye bread, porridge and dairy products such as butter, curds and cheese. Replenished by root vegetables and onions, potage always bubbled by the hearth-side and meat was rare. Summer saw fruit, mostly apples and pears, and beer was drunk by all ages, not so much for its alcoholic nature (although that was no doubt welcome) but for the calories. Made from barley or oats, it was very nutritious. Historians have reckoned that the daily intake was three pints.

By 1406 Robert III had died, and it seems his passing went unlamented. Even at a distance of six centuries there is a palpable atmosphere of personal misery and political failure around the early Stewart kings. An oft-repeated quote sets the tone. When Annabella, his Queen, asked Robert III what arrangements he had in mind for his tomb and a suitable epitaph, this mournful reply came back. It was reported by Walter Bower, a contemporary chronicler:

> I have no desire to erect a proud tomb. Therefore let these men who strive in the world for the pleasures of honour have shining monuments. I on the other hand should prefer to be buried at the bottom of a midden, so that my soul may be saved on the Day of the Lord. Bury me therefore, I beg you, in a midden, and write for my epitaph: 'Here lies the worst of kings and the most wretched of men in the whole kingdom.'

It reads like a passage of invented dialogue, but rings true as a general judgement which appeared to be current at the time. But they are extraordinary sentiments from a King of Scotland.

With the same sort of miserable luck which dogged his father, James I had been made a prisoner by the English. Sent away to France allegedly for the furtherance of his education but more likely for his safety, the young prince's ship had been boarded by 'pirates' off Flamborough Head. They handed James over to Henry IV and commodious and secure lodging was found in the Tower of London. When news of his heir's capture was brought to Robert III, 'his spirit forthwith left him, the strength waned from his body, his countenance grew pale, and for grief thereafter he took no food'. Three weeks later the king was dead.

His brother, the Duke of Albany and former Earl of Fife, was made Governor of the Realm. In the continued absence of James I and the consequent lack of a coronation, Albany ruled over 'a kingless kingdom'. And he did so in quasi-regal style, occasionally attaching the phrase 'by the grace of God' to his title.

As Governor, Albany encouraged the annual meetings at Hadden Stank and even entertained discussions of a more lasting peace. All of this diplomatic talk was interspersed with sporadic incidents of Anglo-Scottish violence. Ships were seized and anchorages raided, and on 7 May 1409 Jedburgh Castle was at last prised from the grip of its English garrison. The successful assault was led by 'mediocres Thevidaliae', literally, 'the middling people of Teviotdale'. Some historians have mistranslated this into the peasants of Teviotdale being swept along on a rising tide of Scottish nationalism and storming Jedburgh castle to evict the hated English. In reality the 'mediocres' were lesser lairds, younger sons and the like, and were led by Sir

The lonely farm of Ovenshank in Liddesdale, the quintessential reiver valley
(*All photographs taken by Liz Hanson*)

A hardy Galloway bullock in the foothills of the central ranges of the Cheviots

The ruins of a tower house at Edgerston, at the head of the
Jed Valley, below the Carter Bar

Falside, in the central ranges of the Cheviots

A hailstorm over Cheviot

Carewoodrig Valley

Late winter on Hownam Law in the Cheviots

Sourhope at the head of the Bowmont Valley in the Cheviots

The Cheviots just before a winter storm at the head of the Jed Valley

The modern road from Langholm to Newcastleton through the Tarras Moss

The Tarras Burn

Late spring on the high pasture of the Lammermuirs,
in the Allan Valley

Spring in Upper Teviotdale

Late autumn, after the harvest in fertile Berwickshire with
snow on the Cheviots to the south

Wild country at the head of Annandale, the lair of the Johnstones

The Devil's Beeftub at the head of Annandale

Goldilands Tower in Upper Teviotdale, a Scott stronghold

The ruins of Dryburgh Abbey, near St Boswells

River mist over Berwick-upon-Tweed

Flodden's fertile fields as they are now

Smailholm Tower and its commanding views over the Tweed Valley

Even in a watery sunshine Hermitage Castle still looms

The remains of the Hume's castle inside the walls of the folly now known as Hume Castle. Its exaggerated crenellation still dominates the Border skyline

The Victorian Mercat Cross at Jedburgh, the site of the royal herald's humiliation

Mary, Queen of Scots' House at Jedburgh

Norham Castle standing guard over the Tweed

Berwick-upon-Tweed and its walls

Greenknowe Tower near Kelso

Modern hill farming in Upper Teviotdale

Limiecleuch Farm in Teviotdale shows how even in summer the land looks inhospitable

Evening at Priesthaugh Farm in the Cheviots

Sunset over the Border hills

William Douglas of Drumlanrig, who would have been affronted to be thought a peasant.

The middling sort and their impetuosity were perhaps preferred to anything more formal or deliberate because they were deniable in the event that Henry IV of England planned a hefty response. These things just happened in the less lawful frontier zone. In any case, Albany stepped in quickly to order that Jedburgh Castle be entirely effaced. At only 8 miles from the border up on Carter Bar, it was too exposed to leave standing, and its removal erased any argument over reoccupation. An early nineteenth-century county jail now stands on the impressive site.

Berwick and Roxburgh still remained in English hands and the latter began to come under increasing threat. In 1410 the Douglases and the Dunbar families (now on speaking, or at least raiding terms) broke into the town of Roxburgh and set it on fire, and retreating across the bridge over the Tweed to Wester Kelso, they pulled it down.

BRING BACK BERWICK

In 2003 a group of Border Scots hatched a plan to offer to buy back Berwick. No one was sure about where a cash offer should be made and it was suggested that a donation might go to the League of St George. A press release was issued and amongst the world's media, the story caught fire. As far away as New Zealand, it was reported that the Scots were about to march over Berwick Old Bridge and retake the town. Perhaps they would occupy the Guild Hall, or somewhere. TV crews arrived, the Vicar of the Parish Church offered to mediate, and eventually – nothing happened. It was all a jolly PR stunt designed to highlight the attractions of the Borders and persuade tourists to come back after the devastating epidemic of foot and mouth disease. But such is the strange position of Berwick, out on a limb, that the story was just credible enough to be widely believed. Some in Berwick supported the initiative. No wonder. Sociologists from Edinburgh University have carried out a scientific and systematic survey of attitudes to nationality in the town. Lying so close to the Borders Berwickers were expected to embrace an English identity more enthusiastically – for precisely that reason. More than 100 household interviews showed that Berwickers were ambivalent, preferring to take on a local identity rather than an English, or even Scottish, one.

When Henry V ascended the English throne, he seemed determined to revive the Hundred Years War, and as the heir of Edward III, he claimed the crown of France. His expedition of 1417 across the Channel sparked events in the Borders. Archibald the Tyneman attacked Roxburgh Castle, but true to his nickname, failed to make any impression. This despite a survey of the fabric in 1416 which discovered that much of the old stronghold was crumbling. Sections of walls and towers were thought to be on the point of collapse and the timber shoring down the shaft of the castle's well had completely rotted. Roxburgh even lacked iron gates. Yet the immense strength of its position between Tweed and Teviot was enough, and the English held on. Twenty miles to the east the Duke of Albany attacked Berwick and was also repulsed. Considering the absence of the English king and his army in France, it was a feckless episode.

When James I returned from captivity in 1424, he quickly neutralised the power of the Albany Stewarts and began to show himself as a determined, courageous, perhaps even tyrannical king. After the pitiable miseries of Robert III, it was a shock to the Scottish political system.

James was ruthless. In order to divide the great magnates he offered preference and support to the Douglases and had Albany's son (the Duke had died in 1420), his two sons and his 80-year-old father-in-law, the Earl of Lennox, arrested and tried at Stirling Castle. They were all dragged out onto the esplanade and publicly executed. Nothing like this had been ordered by a Scottish king for more than a century and it signalled the arrival of a Stewart resolved to rule without opposition from a powerful nobility.

In 1436 James mustered the royal host and marched on Roxburgh Castle, where and it all promptly went wrong. Queen Joan arrived in the camp with news of a conspiracy against the king. Surrounded by his nobility and all their soldiers, James suddenly felt uncomfortable, squabbled with his captains, and to the amazement of the garrison watching from Roxburgh's battlements, abandoned the siege and made his way back north. A year later it all came true. In the Dominican Priory in Perth, hiding in the sewers, James was found by assassins and stabbed to death. Members of his own household were involved and had left doors unbarred and without servicable locks.

James I left a surprising legacy. Despite his ruthlessness and blood-spattered end, he was one of the best educated of Scottish kings, having passed much of his 18-year imprisonment in England in reading, music-making and writing. *The Kingis Quair* (from 'quire', a gathering of leaves of paper) is a long poem composed by James in English and much influenced by the work of Geoffrey Chaucer. It also contains several identifiable Scotticisms and along with the work of other poets and writers, it signals the increasing use of Scots and the retreat of French as the language of the court. This process was clearly underway when the Earl of March wrote to Henry IV in 1400. He apologised for not writing in French, and he did so because 'the English tongue is more clear to my understanding'.

At that time Scotland was a patchwork of speech communities. While the court and most people living in central Scotland spoke a form of Scots, the Church wrote and celebrated mass in Latin, and most official documents were also set down in Latin. In the north and west Gaelic was widespread and a dialect of Irish Gaelic was the speech of Galloway and Carrick. It is said that King Robert the Bruce was fluent in it. In the Northern Isles Norse predominated, and in the Borders it is likely that the same dialect of northern English was spoken on both banks of the Tweed. This apparently caused confusion at the battle of Otterburn in 1388, but it must also have bound English and Scottish borderers together.The ancient tongue of Old Welsh had long fled from the lowlands but pockets of use may have survived in isolated upland communities.

MERLIN AND THE ASH TREES OF MEIGION

Owain Glyn Dwr, Edward Mortimer and Harry Hotspur Percy drew up an agreement in 1403 known as the Tripartite Indenture. It set down the three-way partition of England and Wales for each man who attached his seal to it. So that there could be no possibility of forgery, the document was divided up by a zigzag or indented line to produce jagged edges. This meant that only the genuine pieces would fit together. So called because of this procedure, indentures were made like this up until well into the nineteenth century. Owain Glyn Dwr wanted a substantial share and his 'Greater Wales' reached far into England. Like most of his countrymen, he knew that Old Welsh had been spoken all over Britain, especially in southern Scotland – the place known as 'Yr Hen Ogledd' or 'the Old North', and that Welsh kings had once ruled in London. Owain believed in prophesy and especially in the words of Merlin. Under

the command of the mighty King Cadwallon the Welsh had won a
great victory at the Ash Trees of Meigion, and Merlin said that they
would win there once more. Owain insisted that the boundaries of
Greater Wales should reach Meigion. To their amazement, Percy
and Mortimer agreed. The Ash Trees of Meigion lay in the Peak
District, deep in the heart of England. But this old attachment was
not as odd as it sounds. The Peak District is one of the most Celtic
areas of England. Ancient and pagan customs like well-dressing,
where flowers are arranged around the many natural springs of the
district, survive and on the Ordnance Survey many Old Welsh
places-names are plotted.

James II was seven years old when his father was assassinated in Perth.
A fractious elite of the most powerful noble families, including the
Douglases contrived somehow to run Scotland, but immediately there
was disaster to contend with. The plague returned. And Archibald,
Earl of Douglas, was one of its victims. Concerted periods of bad
weather in the spring and summer of 1437 meant the harvest failed. In
1438 it failed again and the countryside was gripped by famine. It
must have been a miserable time for ordinary people.

Power politics scarcely missed a beat and James II and his counsellors entered upon an aggressive campaign against the Black Douglases. In 1440 what became known as 'the Black Dinner' was held in
Edinburgh Castle. The king invited the young Earl William of Douglas
and his brother to join him in a banquet. In a memorable moment of
melodrama, the king's chancellor, Sir William Crichton, placed a
bull's head on the table. The Douglas boys were arrested, tried on
trumped up charges and decapitated on the executioner's block on the
Castle Hill.

The effect of this outrage was surprisingly muted. James the Gross
became earl and did much to restore his family's position. By 1448 the
Douglases were back raiding in north Northumberland. In the tit-for-
tat warfare of that time Percy and Neville incursions into the west
march was balanced by attacks in the east. A system of warning
beacons was set up in Dumfriesshire.

In 1452 James II summoned the Earl of Douglas to Stirling Castle
Reassurances were sought and given by means of a safe-conduct. A
discussion of the Douglases' alliance with the Earl of Crawford and
Ross quickly grew heated. The king lost his temper with the earl and

'did stert sodanly till him with ane knyf and strake him in the collar and down in the bodie'. The wounded Douglas was immediately stabbed to death by Patrick Gray, James II's bodyguard, and others.

It was a sensational and utterly outrageous act, a second earl murdered after some royal deception. The Douglases found them-selves themselves under the command of a new earl, James, and he led 600 men into Stirling. After denouncing the king, he had the worthless safe-conduct issued to Earl William tied to a horse's tail and dragged through the muddy streets. It was a declaration of civil war. But instead of seeking to create an alternative to James II's tyranny, the Douglases burned the town of Stirling. It was not good politics.

James II was more adroit and carried hostilities to appropriate targets. He mustered the royal host and marched into Douglas territory, attacking Peebles, Selkirk and Dumfries. By means which remain unclear some sort of reconciliation was effected whereby Earl James forgave the murderers of Earl William and promised to dissolve the contentious alliances with other magnates, and for his part the king gave assurances of fair treatment. The Douglases guaranteed that they would defend the Borders and honour the truce with England. None of it lasted.

In 1455, presumably when he felt strong enough, the king went on campaign against the Douglases, bombarding their castles, raiding their territory, especially the Forest of Selkirk. In what seems to have been a failure of nerve, the earl capitulated very quickly. James fled to England while his three brothers were caught near Langholm by a band of Johnstones, led by their heidsman. Two were killed and the third escaped to join Earl James in exile in England. The Johnstones sent the severed head of Archibald Douglas to the king. No doubt he was pleased to see it.

Within only three months the immensely powerful and resilient dynasty of the Black Douglases had been utterly defeated and James II ruled unchallenged in his kingdom.

A parliament convened in August 1455 and waved through acts of formal disinheritance of the Douglases. Much of their territory and most of their castles (Threave in Galloway was the most famous and it had been a model in its time. Archibald the Grim's massive fortress was much admired and widely copied) passed into the hands of the king. James II's annual income increased substantially and the royal domain now reached far down into southern Scotland.

In local government a longer-term effect of the fall of the Black

Douglases slowly became apparent. Such was the grip of the earls on the Borders and Galloway and so great were their resources that they were able to keep order amongst the lesser nobility. But when their leadership was removed – virtually overnight – a patchwork of names, small lordships, old resentements and budding ambitions replaced it. Kers, Pringles, Humes, Scotts, Johnstones, Maxwells and others emerged – and began to compete, squabble, and eventually feud with each other in the power vacuum left by the departure of the Douglases.

James II was determined to use the profits of suppression to cement his own kingship. Instead of the great magnates, he would provide effective central government. Parliament passed ordinances on the defence of the Borders. Fords were to be watched and a system of warning beacons maintained. Three companies of troops (spearmen and archers, both mounted) would be paid for by the royal exchequeur and deployed to the three Scottish marches.

In 1456 the king mustered the host and marched into the small enclave controlled by the English garrison of Roxburgh Castle. With no attempt to lay a siege and in what seems to have been no more than a show of force, he then moved on to encamp on the Kale Water, near Morebattle and not far from the northern terminal of Clennel Street. English envoys arrived and for reasons which are unclear, James was induced to retreat from what was shaping to be an invasion of northern England. Two months later the army was marched south again, and this time they crossed into Northumberland on a raiding expedition. A year later Berwick was unsuccessfully assaulted. Business as usual for the long-suffering farmers of the Borders.

It may be that the royal council decided at that point to take a more considered approach. In the toppling of the Black Douglases, James II had used artillery to deadly effect and he was evidently fascinated by cannon and how they worked. Materials for cannon-founding were bought from European specialists and arrangements for the manufacture of gun carriages put in train.

DOE OR DIE

The rise of the Douglas family has left a small legacy in a Border town. The motto of Kelso High School is 'Doe or Die' and it encircles a representation of a heart. Both are taken from the Douglas coat of arms and the local association is with the beautiful Springwood Estate near the town. It belonged to the Douglas family

and looked across the Teviot to Roxburgh Castle, which is historically very appropriate since in 1314 Sir James Douglas captured the
stronghold from the English in a daring assault. He fulfilled Robert
the Bruce's dying wish that his embalmed heart should be taken on
crusade against the Moors. The promise of such pious actions, even
after death, were important to the king as his life slipped away.
After his murder of John Comyn at the high altar of the Greyfriars
Kirk at Dumfries, Bruce had been excommunicated by the Pope and
he must have feared the fires of Purgatory. When fighting against
the Moors at Teba de Andales, it is said that Sir James Douglas
threw the casket containing the king's heart deep into the ranks of
the Unbelievers and challenged his men to cut their way through to
rescue it. They were forced to 'doe or die', and they did, both.
Recently Bruce's heart was found buried at Melrose Abbey, the site
of the fourteenth-century Douglas tombs.

When Henry VI was captured in 1460 by the Yorkist faction in one of
the many twists of the Wars of the Roses, James II believed that an
opportunity had presented itself. Once again he summoned the royal
host and this time substantial artillery pieces were trundled down Dere
Street to Melrose. The target was Roxburgh Castle, and the aim to
remove the English garrison. It had become nominal but remained
irksome, and was sustained by the defensive excellence of the site of
the ancient fortress. Much strengthened and expensively maintained,
the fabric of the mighty ramparts was in good repair and an immense
effort would be needed to breach them. James and his bombardiers
dug in their guns on the north bank of the Tweed, below where Floors
Castle now stands. The trajectories were plotted, the elevations
calculated and the king spent much time fussing over his elaborate
artillery battery.

On Sunday 3 August, Queen Mary of Gueldres arrived to support
her husband in what promised to be his hour of triumph, a success in
the place where his father had so humiliatingly failed in 1436. To
welcome his queen, James ordered a salvo on the castle walls. He
stood by one of the largest guns, known as 'the Lion', and:

King James hauing sik plesure in dischargeng gret gunis past til a
place far fra the armie to recreat him selfe in schuiting gret pieces,
quhairof he was verie expert, bot the piece appeiringlie, with ouer

sair a chairge, flies in flinderis, with a part of quhilk, strukne in the hench or he was war, quhairof (allace) he dies.

It seems likely that the king bled to death. But such was the unity he had welded together, Mary of Gueldres was able to rush her nine-year-old son across the Tweed to the great church of Kelso Abbey and in the assembled presence of all of Scotland's great magnates, have him crowned as James III. Thereafter, the royal host remained sufficiently resolved and purposeful to complete the siege of Roxburgh successfully. After more than 160 years of enemy occupation the great fortress was once again in Scottish hands.

It all came too late for the once-thriving town. With the loss of much of the lucrative wool trade and the continuing occupation of its port at Berwick, Roxburgh had shrivelled into little more than a village. It was a spectacular casualty of international politics since 1296 and the Wars of Independence. Now, nothing at all remains to be seen, not a single stone stands above ground.

Immediately after the siege Roxburgh Castle was 'doung to the ground'. Like Jedburgh Castle it lay close to the frontier and would have presented a tempting target for English re-occupation. By 1488 it had become a place of such small importance that 'the castle and the place called the castlested' could be granted to Walter Kerr of Cessford, heidsman of a reiving surname.

Queen Mary of Gueldres was the dominant influence at court after 1460 and as she and Bishop Kennedy of St Andrews dabbled for advantage in the Wars of the Roses, armies tramped regularly back and forth. Berwick was retaken and then quickly lost. Eventually James III grew into his period of personal rule and he began to alienate sections of his magnates. In the process of all this, the Humes of Berwickshire became embroiled in dynastic politics. Because they objected to the appropriation of the ancient church at Coldingham by the crown, Lord Hume gathered an army of Borderers about him. The dispute was allowed to spiral rapidly into a civil war. The disaffected heir apparent, James Duke of Rothesay, joined Hume's forces while his father mustered an army. They met at Sauchieburn, near Bannockburn, in 1488.

The royal standard flew on both sides. James III had rallied support from the north of Scotland, including detachments of Highlanders, while at his back Prince James had men from Galloway, the Borders and the Lothians. In the confusion and din of battle the king became detached from his bodyguard, fell off his horse and was probably injured. Isolated, and in mysterious circumstances, it seems that he was stabbed to death by a priest. Young Rothesay found that he was James IV well before his time and in penance for his part in his father's death he went often on pilgrimage to saintly shrines and wore an iron belt during Lent.

Those Borderers who had helped the new king overthrow his father were rewarded, and the rise of a new aristocracy in the aftermath of the fall of the Black Douglases was consolidated.

Although James IV was only 15 years old at Sauchieburn, he was determined there would be no faction-ridden regency and that his personal rule would begin on the morning after the battle. Like most young men he could be headstrong and in 1495 James welcomed the pretender to the English throne, another young man called Perkin Warbeck. It was an ill-advised, potentially dangerous friendship. Warbeck claimed to be the son of Edward IV, one of the murdered princes in the Tower. Despite the fact that he was an imposter, the claimant had gathered support. Enemies of the Tudors, such as the Irish earls and the Holy Roman Emperor, Maximilian, had even supplied him with troops. For his part, James IV gave help, a base for operations into his usurped kingdom of England and also a Scots wife. The board seemed set for yet more cross-border conflict.

Henry VII of England was a canny politician, and when Warbeck's pretensions fizzled out after an abortive invasion of the West Country, the king imprisoned him in the Tower of London. It was only when he attempted to escape in 1499 that Warbeck found himself on the scaffold at Tyburn with a rope around his neck.

Meanwhile Henry and James had agreed a peace treaty 'of perpetual amity', sometime also known as the 'Treaty of Perpetual Peace'. When this was consummated in 1503 by a marriage between Margaret Tudor, Henry's daughter, and James, Borderers must have breathed a collective sigh of relief. Perhaps the long, weary years of near-constant warfare were at last drawing to a close. The royal houses of Scotland and England were uniting and both kings seeking cooperation rather than conflict.

But it was a false dawn. A hundred bitter years would have to pass before the marriage of Stewart and Tudor could change the course of history for the better. And it would be a century of unprecedented slaughter, violence and waste along the whole length of the border. It would be the century of the Reivers.

6

The Wild Frontier

Hob the King and his brother, Dand the Man, had cheek. Nicknamed like the Chicago gangsters they so closely resemble, the Elliot brothers had forayed far out of Liddesdale in the winter of 1502. The charge-sheet recorded that they had led a raiding party 'beyond Tweeddale and Lauderdale', probably up into the Lammermuir Hills above Edinburgh and there they had lifted nine score sheep. And it seems that they did it with impunity. Halbert Elliot and Andrew Elliot – to give them their Sunday names – appear never to have answered for their crimes, or at least not that one. All that contemporaries could do was record who had done what and approximately where. They could not catch them or bring them to any sort of justice.

The raid was audacious, even reckless. Stealing livestock within sight of Edinburgh's Castle Rock, the traditional seat of royal govern-ment, and removing them southwards down Lauderdale, Tweeddale, Teviotdale and home to Liddesdale without let or hindrance – it must have galled James IV as he attempted to assert himself over all of his kingdom. Even more galling was the fact that Hob and Dand's raid was only remarkable because it brought the chronic problems of lawlessness in the Borders so close to Edinburgh. Raiding was growing rife and one family became particularly hard-riding – 'ever-riding' according to one contemporary historian. When the king was in Jedburgh on the 5 and 11 November that year, he had heard grievous complaints against the Armstrongs of Liddesdale, Elliot allies and neighbours. Edmund Armstrong and his brothers were commanded to appear before James and defend the charge that they had burned Borthwickshiels near Hawick, the property of the Scotts of Buccleuch. They were also accused of stealing 300 sheep, 60 oxen and cows, 20 horses and mares, and goods to the value of 100 merks. More Elliot allies and neighbours, the Crosers or Crosiers, were also named as horse-riding thieves at the Jedburgh Assizes. Whether or not any of them turned up to hear the charges is less clear. It is unlikely.

It was a weary, dreary roster of disorder, what had become a way of life for many Borderers, both perpetrators and victims (who could easily exchange roles). The use of such clearly criminal names as 'Hob the King' and 'Dand the Man' in official records speaks of unwelcome familiarity. As James IV prepared for his marriage to Princess Margaret Tudor, these unchecked raids were an embarrassment. Such an obvious inability to control the Border country through which his bride was to travel did not say much for the king's ability as an effective ruler. A solitary consolation was that lawlessness seemed at least as substantial a problem on the English side.

MARGINAL DISORDER

Scottish kings had difficulties asserting themselves in the north and west of their kingdom as well as in the south. Their nominal subjects had no hesitation in making alliances with the English. In 1462 Edward IV signed the Treaty of Westminster-Ardtornish. If James III of Scotland could be deposed, then the co-signatory, John Macdonald, Lord of the Isles and King of Man, would take over half of the kingdom, that part lying to the north of the Forth–Clyde line. From his castle at Ardtornish, on the mainland opposite southern Mull, John ruled an Atlantic principality. He could command 10,000 soldiers, but more important, a navy of 250 galleys. The Stewart kings had some success in 'the daunting' of the isles but the threat from the west remained constant in the first half of the sixteenth century. By 1545 Donald Dubh, the Clan Donald heir of John, rallied the Highlanders and Islesmen to his banner, and at a Council of the Isles on Islay, he and his allies negotiated with the agents of Henry VIII. The gathering rebellion only fizzled out when Donald unexpectedly died of a fever in Ireland. The Border surnames never presented an equivalent political threat even though they could muster highly mobile cavalry armies at lightning speed. They were too busy squabbling amongst themselves ever to consider unifying against the crown.

Relative distance also allowed James IV a course of action usually denied to the Tudor kings based in London. He could personally lead punitive expeditions to the Borders and use all his royal authority to press hard on the worst of the reiving families. More than eighty such expeditions tramped south from Edinburgh in the sixteenth century and they generally met with only temporary success. But James IV's marriage contract, the 'Treaty of Perpetual Peace' was at least optimistic, containing clauses about curbing lawlessness in the Borders.

The Armstrongs shrugged their shoulders at all this breezy diplomacy, and by the early 1500s they had forged themselves into the most feared of the riding families. With the Elliots, Nixons and Crosiers, they had made Liddesdale their redoubt and last resort. When royal expeditions commanded the heidsmen of the Armstrongs to appear and answer for their crimes, the summons was routinely ignored. Seventy of the name were listed as outlaw. This meant a good deal more than it does now, basically a synonym for criminal. In the sixteenth century to be branded an outlaw, that is to say, placed beyond the protection of the law, could be very dangerous and exposed. Any man, an officer of the law or not, could attack and kill an outlaw with impunity, perhaps even receive a reward. In addition, his dependants and property were similarly fair game. But in the Border country the effects of outlawry were much mitigated by membership of a large and aggressive family like the Armstrongs and also the general – and widespread – reluctance to do anything which might spark a deadly feud.

In 1509 the political weather changed. Canny Henry VII died and was succeeded by the very different character of his son, Henry VIII. Headstrong, bellicose and initially highly able, he plunged into the maelstrom of European war, alliance and intrigue. The loss of England's possessions in France still smarted and Henry was anxious to set about reclaiming them. An immediate diplomatic difficulty was his brother-in-law. James of Scotland was close to the French, and while the terms of the Treaty of Perpetual Peace carefully allowed both England and Scotland to give aid to their respective allies, it looked in reality as though they were set on a collision course.

Momentum began to gather on both land and sea. Scotland's new naval capability was challenged by Henry VIII's captains and Scots ships were boarded and seized. James' naval commander, Andrew Barton, was accused of piracy and died in English captivity. On the border, a long-running dispute flared into significance. At a truce day, probably in 1509, Sir Robert Kerr was presiding as Warden of the Scottish Middle March. For reasons now lost he became involved in a fatal scuffle with three Englishmen. They were Lilburn, from near Wooler, a man called Starhead and the splendidly described John Heron, the Bastard of Ford. After Kerr had been killed, the Scottish contingent rallied and managed to lay hands on Lilburn, but the Bastard Heron and Starhead escaped. It was all very embarrassing – and the incident is said to have enraged James IV. Kerr had been a close courtier, principal cup-bearer to the king and master of the royal artillery.

The Bastard Heron's half-brother, the legitimate Lord of Ford, was Warden of the English East March and he was either persuaded or felt compelled to act honourably. He therefore gave himself up to be a hostage for the Bastard and with Lilburn was detained in Fast Castle on the Berwickshire coast north of Eyemouth. Lilburn then died, but far from giving himself up and thereby freeing his half-brother, the Bastard Heron was reportedly seen desporting himself in public, and even worse, was sending raiding parties over the Tweed into Scotland.

Meanwhile two associates of Andrew Kerr, the son of the murdered Sir Robert, had been busy. The brothers Tait had been on the trail of the third wanted man, Starhead, and they found that he had fled to York. Following him – and showing the long reach of deadly feud – they murdered the man in his house and then hacked off his head, put it in a sack and rode back to Ferniehurst with grisly proof that the hit had been made. Such was the intricacy of serial violence in the sixteenth-century Border country.

THE GREAT MICHAEL

Between 1505 and 1511 James IV spent huge sums to create a Scottish navy. Its most impressive ship was The Great Michael, and it was huge, far outstripping Henry VIII's Mary Rose or any other contemporary craft then afloat. At Newhaven, near Edinburgh, an immense keel was laid down: it measured between 150 and 180 feet and on it the skeleton of The Great Michael was slowly built up. At 1,000 tons, it could carry 27 cannon and needed a crew of 300 to sail it. The cost was staggering at £30,000 Scots. The huge ship took five years to build, but it never fired its guns in anger. Only three years after the launch, the battle of Flodden changed everything and The Great Michael was sold to the French for only £18,000. Eventually it was left to rot to pieces in Dieppe harbour.

The feud between the Herons and the Kerrs would grind on for another sixty years, but more immediately its beginnings gave James IV ample excuse, as he and his counsellors saw it, to ignore the Treaty of Perpetual Peace if and when it suited them. However, more straightforward causes for war were soon on hand.

Perhaps prompted by the Bastard Heron, an English raid struck deep into the Scottish east marches, carrying off many beasts and successfuly driving across the Tweed. The fords were no doubt running low in the summer of 1513. Under the command of Alexander Home, the Lord Warden of all the Scottish Marches, the response was rapid and designed to be stunning. Hume put at least 3,000 men in the saddle and hurried over the Border. With such a large force, there was no need – or indeed possibility – of stealth. Seven villages were torched in north Northumberland and much plunder taken. Given that most herds and flocks would have been out summering on the hills, the most attractive and readily available prize for Hume's raiders was horses, and very many were herded together and driven north.

Sir William Bulmer mustered a small force of Northumbrians and in a classic reiver tactic, rode around and ahead of the slow-moving Scot, their plunder weighing down and delaying them. When the English riders reached the Milfield Plain, Bulmer chose a place by the track where broom bushes had grown thick and gave good cover. It was probably somewhere near where the modern A697 skirts the foot of the Cheviot Hills, not far from Flodden Hill. Bulmer had archers with him, and when the Scots rode into the ambush, they let fly. The volleys were deadly. Perhaps 500 Scots fell and 400 were captured. Home lost his banner and only just escaped.

Known as 'the Ill Raid', it took place only a few days before James IV finally decided to call on the royal host of Scotland to muster, before he took the first step down the road to disaster at Flodden.

At first all went well. Sieges were laid at Wark, Etal and Ford castles, and at the strongest of the Border keeps, at Norham, James's army scored a brilliant success, breaking through the solid defences in only five days. Harrying the north Northumberland countryside, carrying off plunder, and the king even finding time to dally with Lady Heron at Ford, the Scots expedition behaved at first like a raiding party, albeit one of gigantic proportions. But that cannot have been James' main purpose. United behind him, the Scottish magnates sought battle, the chance of a signal victory over the English and a degree of freedom of action in the north not seen since the days of the Bruces. James seemed ambitious to make himself a player in European politics, and he advanced into England as an ally of France. No one reckoned with the old warrior, Surrey, and his tactical brilliance on the day of battle.

Historians often aver that the English army could not exploit their stunning victory by invading Scotland because they themselves had taken heavy punishment at Flodden. The walls frantically thrown up to protect Edinburgh were never needed, and, short of provisions, the Earl of Surrey was forced to turn his army south and disband it. Historians of the Borders see the aftermath of Flodden quite differently.

In command of a small but battle-hard troop of mounted soldiers, Thomas Lord Dacre, Warden of the English West March, was instructed to bring fire, sword and plunder to the Borders. And he did it with a vengeance. In the winter of 1513/14 plumes of black smoke billowed on the chill winds as Dacre's men burned hundreds, perhaps thousands, of Borderers out of their homes, and as families hid in the damp woods or sought refuge in the sheilings of the grey upland valleys, they waited for the fires to die. When they straggled back to their farmsteads, many saw that the English troopers had rounded up their livestock and driven it away. And not just English riders. In Dacre's small army were four hundred Scots, 'outlaws . . . which should be under the obeisance of Scotland'. No doubt many were Armstrongs, and no doubt their intelligence reports and advice settled many an old score with the help of English spears. It must have been a desolate, freezing and hungry winter in fire-blackened farms and villages of Tweeddale, Teviotdale and Annandale.

TOE-ROPE

A military historian once wrote that the invention of the stirrup was 'the most significant development of warfare between the taming of the horse and the invention of gunpowder.' Alexander the Great and Julius Caesar and all their cavalry rode without stirrups. Until around AD700 military riding techniques in western Europe were completely different: troopers held on with their legs and one hand on the reins to guide their ponies. That of course meant that they could only fight with one hand, and that in turn restricted the range of weapons they could use. Stirrups changed all that. They were invented in India around 200 BC, initially as a method of mounting the horse. They were called 'toe-stirrups' at first and the word derives from the Old English 'stigan', meaning to climb up, and 'rup' is a near-synonym for 'rope'. When Attila and his Huns tore through Europe in the fifth century AD, their devastating success came from the ability to control their nimble ponies with their legs and feet – secure in stirrups. This left both hands free to fire arrows while moving very fast around the battlefield. Border Reivers were also adept as using weapons with both hands, and like those of the Huns, their little ponies responded readily to leg-aids, able to stop, move and change directions without a pull on the reins.

Sometimes Dacre's men met resistance. While raiding around Hawick, a troop of riders was intercepted at Hornshole, two miles east of the town. Tradition holds that they came from Hexham and that the Hawick callants not only won the skirmish but also carried off their banner. Much of the Hawick Common Riding is founded on this incident and the 'banner blue' held up high by the Hawick Cornet is said to be a replica of what fluttered in front of the Hexham men at Hornshole.

The most ancient of the Border common ridings have strong traditional connections with the battle at Flodden. And however real or imagined these may be, it is significant that the common ridings at Selkirk and Peebles first come on record in the early sixteenth century (and when those at Hawick and Lauder are first noted in the early eighteenth century, they seem to be already very old). The central purpose was to walk or ride around the boundaries of the common land belonging to the town. Surrounding lairds sometimes encroached on the common or pastured their beasts on it without permission. The procession of townspeople was led by a principal, in the shadowy beginnings probably the provost, and then later a young man when ceremony gradually replaced necessity. They carried a flag and the principals of the ancient common ridings, with one exception, are all called 'Cornets', a term for a cavalry officer first used in the seventeenth century. Flags were centrally important and the Hawick Cornet may indeed have plundered his in 1514 from a detachment of Lord Dacre's men.

Flodden threw Scottish politics into a dizzying, faction-ridden spin in which Border heidsmen were intimately involved. James V was an infant and frantic power-broking crackled incessantly around his cot. At first the Queen Dowager, Margaret, the sister of Henry VIII of England, claimed the right of regency and attempted to direct matters of state. In 'a triumph of passion over policy' she married the much younger Earl of Angus. This combination presented a clear threat to the Earl of Home and he began to encourage the entry of John, Duke of Albany, into the bitter intrigues whispering around the Edinburgh court. Educated in France, unable to speak English, he was nevertheless a legitimate candidate for the regency. As James V's cousin, he stood very near the throne in the male line of succession.

KING SAM

In the sixteenth century kings listened to various forms of address – 'Your Royal Highness', 'Your Majesty' or sometimes 'Your Grace'. Capital letters also seemed to be optional. Looked at with a lexical eye, these terms seem daft to us now, 'Your Majesty' literally meaning 'Your Bigness'. But in the late middle ages and beyond, the aristocracy insisted on their rank being recognised. Modern forms of address can be found in the excellent *Debrett's Review*. 'Madam' seems to cover most women (even the Queen – 'Ma'am' is only an abbreviation) and 'Sir' most men. One of the most complex entries in this fascinating and definitive list is for titled ladies who are divorced. Amongst the general tables of precedence and relative ranks in the armed forces is the order of succession to the throne. Sixteenth in line is a young man called Samuel Chatto. 'King Sam' has a certain ring to it but seventeenth in line, his little brother's name has even more of a resonance. His name is Arthur.

But it all went quickly wrong for Home. Courtiers – almost certainly those fluent in French – began to sway Albany away from supporting the interests of the Border heidsmen, and when Home persuaded the Queen Dowager and the Earl of Angus to abduct the infant king, the game grew very dangerous indeed. The plot failed and Home and the Anguses fled to the Borders. After more clumsy attempts to out-manoeuvre Albany, Home mustered a raiding party of seasoned riders. In November 1515, as the first blasts of the winter blew in off the North Sea, 'banditti of the borders' rode north over the Lammermuirs and plundered Albany's town of Dunbar. Shut up in the castle was a small garrison of French soldiers and also Home's captured mother. As a flourish of reiver power, the Dunbar raid appeared to have its effect and Home was forgiven his treasonable transgressions.

The outbreak of peace did not last. Trusting Albany's assurances of safe-conduct, Home and his brother, William, arrived at court in Edinburgh. They were accompanied by their fellow Border heidsman and ally, Dand Kerr of Ferniehurst. All were immediately arrested, the brothers forced to go through a farrago of a trial – in which Home was charged with treacherous inactivity during the course of the battle of Flodden – and on 11 October 1516, sentence was carried out. Home mounted the scaffold and was decapitated. A day later his brother was forced to kneel and lay his neck on the headsman's block. Seeing how bloodily politics was playing out and fearful of the same fate, Dand Kerr bribed his guards and rode hard for Ferniehurst and safety.

A few weeks later the Duke of Albany followed Dand to Jedburgh where a general assize was held to deal with the worst of the reiving families and their excesses. Then the Regent made a bad mistake. The glamorous Sir Anthony Darcy, styled 'Le Sieur de Beaute', was a Frenchman much favoured at court. With Home's execution, the east marches of Scotland lacked a warden and the man Borderers called 'Bawtie' was appointed. He did not prosper.

When the castle at Langton, near Duns, was unlawfully seized by William Cockburn, Bawtie gathered a small posse and rode out of Dunbar Castle to set matters to rights. Arriving below Langton's walls he instructed that the castle be returned to its rightful owner, Cockburn's young nephew. But what seemed to the Frenchman a simple, black and white business began to turn nasty when Sir David Home of Wedderburn turned up with a troop of horsemen. Not only was Wedderburn kinsman to the recently executed Home, whose job Bawtie had taken over, but he was also a close ally of William Cockburn. After a few harsh words, the Home horsemen made short work of the Dunbar posse. Bawtie turned tail and galloped northwards for his life, but not knowing the countryside, he found himself riding full pelt into a trackless bog, somewhere east of Duns. Frantically pushing his horse on through the maze of pools and tussocks, he was slowly surrounded by Wedderburn's troopers. One of them charged, with his sword flailing, and decapitated Bawtie where he stood. It was said that Wedderburn took the Frenchman's head by its fashionable flowing locks, plaited them and tied the trophy to his saddle pommel. Many centuries before, the same gory habit had been seen amongst the Vikings of the north of Scotland, and long before that amongst the Celtic cavalry warriors of western Europe.

Border heidsmen were utterly ruthless in pursuit of their family's interests, and when opportunities presented themselves, they rarely hesitated. On the desperate night following the battle at Flodden, Dand Kerr and his men broke into the Abbey of Kelso and claimed it and all its far flung possessions for their own. The king of Scotland lay dead on the field and his heir was an infant of only seventeen months. Who was to stop Kerr from throwing out the servants of Andrew Stewart, Bishop of Caithness? James IV had gifted the revenues of Kelso to his bastard son, but he too had fallen at Flodden and Dand Kerr knew a chance when he saw one. Before the high altar he had the small congregation of monks witness the installation of his brother, Tam, as the thirtieth Abbot of Kelso. When the mitre was placed on his head, the great monastery passed into the pastoral care of a local bandit.

Founded by David I in 1128, dominated by the immense church with its cathedral-like double crossing, Kelso had been one of the richest and most venerated abbeys in Scotland. Its abbots held the hard-won right to wear the bishop's mitre and their community was seen as a special daughter-house of the Holy See in Rome. But as news of the slaughter at Flodden spread like wildfire throughout the Borders, the Kerrs took advantage. Their descendants, the Dukes of Roxburghe, now control a wide patrimony based on the gifts of land made to Kelso Abbey during the middle ages. The glory of God became the pride of the Kerrs.

The Humes were similarly quick to see what was possible after Flodden. John Home had been installed by his brother, Alexander, as Abbot of the Augustinian Canons at Jedburgh, but when Lord Home was executed, John was forced to flee north of the Tay.

HUME, HOME, KERR AND CARR

The twenty-first-century descendants of the reiving aristocracy are sometimes slightly disguised. Homes became Humes – the confusion in pronunciation began early, in the twelfth century – and they became earls. But they were no longer based at Home Castle and are instead Earls Home, pronounced Hume, of the Hirsel, a very beautiful house near Coldstream. The Kerrs became Dukes of

Roxburghe, with an 'e' for some reason, and they say their name as
Carr. Deborah Kerr, the demure Hollywood actress, also affected
Carr. Ferniehurst Kerrs became Marquises of Lothian at Monteviot
House, near Jedburgh while Elliots became Earls of Minto, near
Hawick. Most widely landed of all, the Scotts graduated to Dukes
of Buccleuch. Their house at Bowhill near Selkirk and their vast
estates might be seen by the cynical as first prize for reiving. The
largest and arguably most active reiver surname, the wild Armstrongs of Liddesdale, failed to keep up: dukedoms, earldoms and
marquisates eluding them. They are even a headless surname, with
no heidsman or chief. But at least they got to go to the moon.

While Thomas, Lord Dacre, had a clear commission from Henry VIII to
stoke the fires of disorder in 1513, he also held the office of Warden of the
English West March and was therefore responsible for keeping order. As
such he kept a close eye on the riding families of Redesdale and Tynedale.
Charltons, Robsons, Milburns, Storeys and others were every bit as
thrawn and independent-minded as the Scottish surnames. In fact their
reputation was bad enough to prompt the Merchant Adventurers
Company of Newcastle to brand them as unemployable in an ordinance
of 1554. They were expressly forbidden 'to serve. . . any who are born of
brought up in Tynedale, Redesdale or any other such like places'.

In 1518 Dacre sent an expedition into the wilds of north Northumberland and it captured ten of the leading reivers. Determined to
bring them quickly to trial, probably at Morpeth, Dacre's troop of
eighty horsemen picked their way carefully down Redesdale, straight
into an ambush. At a narrow place the warden's posse was trapped
and attacked by a force from the Redesdale surnames of Halls,
Headleys, Storeys and others. The captured reivers were immediately
freed, the Bailiff of Morpeth killed and five others forced to travel
north to Scotland, possibly to be held for ransom.

By 1520 the faction fighting at the Scottish court had paralysed
government to such an extent that ambassadors could not be sent to
England to negotiate a truce. Instead, Tam Kerr, Abbot of Kelso
(styled 'Thomas') was instructed to treat directly with Lord Dacre and
conclude a short-term agreement. This was no more than a recognition of the realities of power in the Borders. Bluntly, the Kerrs and the
Dacres were in a better position to monitor and enforce an international truce than any in Edinburgh and London.

By 1521 Tam appeared to be sharing the office of abbot. According to contemporary records his brother Dand held an extraordinary combination of offices which recognised his family's dominance of mid Tweeddale. When he met Dacre at a truce-day at the ancient trysting place at Redden, Dand was simultaneously Abbot of Kelso, Warden of the Scottish Middle March and Heidsman of the Kerrs. It was local, not central authority which counted.

When the Duke of Albany returned from France in 1521 to take up the office of Regent once more, the truces negotiated by Dand and Tam Kerr were set aside. With the promise of French backing (a substantial force did arrive, but too late in the year to campaign), the Regent rekindled the smouldering war with Henry VIII's England. But the Scots were reluctant to invade – not only because of the risk of another Flodden but also because sympathies were divided. There were those who were uneasy at being a pawn of French foreign policy and others who believed that England would make a better ally than an enemy.

Where Albany did succeed was in provoking Henry VIII. And the Borders paid dear for his pro-French diplomatic posturing. In 1522 Dacre and the Earl of Northumberland made plans to have the village of Wester Kelso (most of it now invisible under the walls, lodge houses and policies of Floors Castle) burned but were anxious not leave any fingerprints. Here is Northumberland's letter to the king:

> I . . . have devised that, within these three nights, God willing, Kelso shall be burned, with all the corn in the said town, and then they [the Scots] shall have no place to lie any garrison near to the border. And this burning of Kelso is devised to be done secretly, by Tynedale and Redesdale.

The raid was aborted but wind of it reached whichever Kerr was Abbot of Kelso. He wrote to the Queen Dowager, imploring her to persuade her brother to desist, and Margaret passed on the plea: 'Also my Lord, the Abbot of Kelso has prayed me to write to you to be his good lord, and for my sake you will not let any evil be done to that place, which I pray you to do.'

The plea was ignored. A year later the Earl of Surrey and Lord Dacre rode into the eastern Borders in great strength, blazing another trail of terror and destruction. This time, however, it was systematic and very devastating. Some of its effects can still be seen.

HORSESHOE LUCK

Old and worn-out horseshoes were often nailed over a country doorway. They are believed to bring protection from bad luck as well as good luck and the origins of that belief turn out to be very old. An upturned shoe, making a u-shape, is thought to represent horns, specifically the horns of the Celtic god, Cernnunos. Despite the Christian appropriation of his headgear for the Devil, people persisted in believing that he could protect a house and the family in it. Horseshoes set in the opposite position, with the gap at the bottom, were thought to bring luck – and also to be protective. From the earliest prehistoric days of blacksmithing, it is likely that touching iron warded off evil, a bit like touching wood. And many touched the shoe as they entered and exited the doorway. The upside down position was protective because it resembled the shape of the female genitals. Just as over the entrances to medieval churches where carvings of female figures with exaggerated pudenda are found (known as 'sheela na gig'), the horseshoe was placed to distract evil spirits from coming into the house. However unlikely that might sound there exists plenty of evidence from several cultures to support the interpretation.

By the spring of 1523 Dacre was at Kelso, his men torching the wooden and thatched houses. What made this more than a raid was the time and trouble taken to inflict lasting damage: 'In the morning of the day which was yesterday, we set forward and we went to Kelso where we not only burned and destroyed the whole town that would burn by any labour but also cast down the Gatehouse of the Abbey.'

Dacre's men became even busier. They fired the abbot's house and then demolished the blackened ruin. In the great church itself the beautifully worked wooden stalls from one of the many side-chapels, the Chapel of the Blessed Virgin, were ripped out and burned, while the lead covering the roof was stripped, probably for use as artillery shot. By itself, that last action probably caused most damage. And so that the monks might endure as much discomfort as the townspeople, their dormitory was wrecked and burned to the ground.

What might have converted a sacred place like Kelso Abbey into a legitimate target was the Kerr takeover after Flodden. The Earl of

Surrey noted that Dand Kerr was Dacre's 'mortal enemy' and the ancient abbey was no more than another of his possessions. But piety, or the lack of it, likely made little difference. It was no defence ten years later when Henry VIII's commissioners dissolved and destroyed England's monasteries and nunneries.

Jedburgh fared little better. When the Earl of Surrey's forces reached the town, they saw a place they reckoned was twice the size of Berwick. In addition to its venerable and beautifully sited abbey, Jedburgh boasted six defensive towers. Perhaps they were the possessions of different families (possibly rivals, as in many of the northern Italian cities and towns of the same period), or perhaps they formed part of a fortified perimeter. In any case, the town was 'cleanly destroyed, burned and thrown down', though but only after bitter street-fighting.

While Jedburgh burned, Dacre led his small army south to nearby Ferniehurst, the stronghold of Dand Kerr. As now, the approach to the tower is thickly wooded, and in the early sixteenth century it was very vulnerable to artillery. When the English force trundled their guns within range, the Kerrs attacked them in the woods, desperate to prevent their deployment. The trees also prevented the much superior English numbers from being automatically decisive. Dacre's men joined what was said to have been a vicious fight. Ferniehurst eventually fell and Dand Kerr was captured.

As darkness came down the English picketed their horses, around 1500 of them, in the woods around the tower, but they failed to set a proper watch. No sentry heard the approach of a small force of Borderers and at dead of night, they cut loose the tethered horses and whacked and hallooed them into a stampede. Hurtling through the dark woods, they bolted, some racing through the burning streets of Jedburgh, others galloping over the river-cliffs by the Jed Water. The English lost half their mounts, and Dacre ascribed the attack to an appearance of the Devil. Dand Kerr must have smiled.

NIGHTMARE

Nightmares have nothing to do with female horses. 'Mare' is an Old English word for an incubus, an evil spirit which sat on the chests of women while they slept. Later it came to mean a Demon Lover who ravished women during the night, a handy explanation for unwanted pregnancies. The confusion with horses grew up in the nineteenth century with a series of very popular engravings by the Swiss artist, Fuseli. They show an incubus sitting on a sleeping woman's chest while a strange, blind horse watches.

A year later the Duke of Albany returned to France. And with him went most of France's influence on Scottish foreign policy. Peace negotiations were soon underway. Here is a report sent from Berwick to Cardinal Wolsey, the royal chancellor:

> The confirmation of the peace on the part of the Scots was brought hither by the Abbot of Kelso, the Headsman of the Kerrs of Teviotdale, well accompanied by honest men to the number of 60 persons to whom I made such cheer as I could that day at dinner. And forthwith we examined our commissions and made collation of the other of our greater writings. And so, at night we departed and kept our lodgings. And because the companions with the said Abbot were Borderers, I bid them to be well accompanied and good cheer to be made unto them. The said Abbot being a sad and wise man, brother to Dand Kerr of Ferniehurst.

With the conclusion of a temporary peace and the departure of the Francophile Albany, power swung towards the pro-English party and its leader, the Earl of Angus, first amongst the Red Douglases. As de facto Regent, he led several punitive expeditions to the Borders, and in 1526 blundered into the convoluted tangle of local politics.

The young James V was effectively the prisoner of the Douglases, but his agents were able to negotiate the help of Walter Scott of Buccleuch. Plans were laid for the rescue of the king. When the Earl of Angus rode south at the head of another expedition and stopped at Melrose, the Scotts were waiting. With 600 riders they launched themselves at Angus' force, somewhere near the Tweed fords. The assault faltered, lost momentum and ranks closed around the king. With the help of the Kerrs of Cessford and Ferniehurst, the Red Douglas and his men beat off the Scotts. When the skirmish turned into a panicky rout, Kerr riders galloped in pursuit. One of the Scotts' confederates, an Elliot, wheeled his pony and turned to fight. Couching his lance, he charged at Dand Kerr of Ferniehurst and killed him. The incident ignited a feud which lasted at least two generations. Intermittent efforts were made to patch it up and a marriage was contracted in 1530 between Walter Scott of Buccleuch and Janet Kerr, daughter of Dand. But bitter resentments still burned and in the High Street of Edinburgh, 26 years after the fight at Melrose, a gang of Kerrs and their allies set upon Walter Scott and stabbed him to death.

The late 1520s saw Liddesdale increasingly become the central focus of lawlessness, the Armstrongs, the Elliots, Crosiers and Nixons able to ignore and even publicly belittle an ineffectual royal authority in Scotland. Even though the Earl of Angus led two well-organised and powerful expeditions, in 1525 and 1527, which hanged several notorious reivers out of hand and captured Sim the Laird of the Armstrongs of Mangerton in Liddesdale (probably the high heidsman of the whole surname) and his brother, Davy the Lady, his efforts had little lasting impact. In fact his plundering of 4,000 head of cattle only prompted more retaliatory raiding.

Such was their collective disdain for national authority that the Liddesdale surnames began to make common cause with the reivers of Tynedale. The Armstrongs and Elliots rode with the Charltons and Dodds, mustering large bands of riders, not troubling to act in secret or with stealth, and flying their own standards as they scoured the Borders for plunder. This sense of a cocky, semi-independent principality of thieves flickered briefly into real substance in 1527.

Tynedale and Liddesdale reivers are recorded as mounting a concerted attack on Tarset Hall in north Northumberland. Soon after they became even more bold. When Sir William de Lisle, heidsman of a prominent English surname and a sometime ally of Liddesdale, was imprisoned in Newcastle, the Armstrongs and Elliots rode into town and freed him. It was an act of amazing audacity – and self-confidence. For much of 1527 Lisle led large bands of riders on either side of the border, and it appeared that no government official or force could check their excesses. A descent into anarchy seemed finally to have taken place, the Borders had become the badlands, a no-go zone of utter lawlessness.

Sir William de Lisle's brief but spectacular reign as the reiver-king of several allied surnames was brought to an end in early 1528. Rousing itself into action, the English crown appointed Henry Percy, Earl of Northumberland, as Warden of all the Marches and he quickly weighed in with a heavy hand. Forays were intercepted and raiders summarily hanged. When Percy threatened to invade Liddesdale, the Armstrongs saw that the game was up and without hesitation they surrendered de Lisle and his leading men to the English warden. They appeared before Percy with symbolic ropes around their necks and he wasted no time in converting the symbolism into brutal reality when he hanged the lot of them.

Across the border, the Armstrongs remained unpunished. For some forgotten tactical reason, they left their fastness of Liddesdale and chose to occupy the Debatable Land. This was an area of about 40 square miles in the western marches, lying between Gretna Green and Canonbie. As the name suggests it was disputed territory, neither English nor Scottish. In 1528 the Armstrongs moved in, claimed it and determined to defend themselves.

CLANS AND SURNAMES

Ancient Border surnames wishing to form themselves into societies in order to maintain their historical links and shared past have unfortunately taken to calling themselves 'clans'. There is a Clan Elliot, a Clan Armstrong, and for goodness' sake, a Clan Moffat. They are in fact nothing of the kind. The misappropriated Highland nomenclature has brought all sorts of misleading connotations: clan chiefs, clan pipers, clan tartan, gatherings and the whole biscuit-tin lid kit and caboodle. The central problem is that the use of 'clan' appears to establish a connection, to suggest that the Gaelic-speaking Highland families were somehow linked to the great Border surnames. They were not. Perhaps the only tangible contact was made by Walter Scott, who publicised tartan Scotland in the nineteenth century, and the Border textile mills who made most of it. The central difference was in relation to land. Highlanders of the same surname had an umbilical attachment with a particular place. This old notion of 'duthchas' is difficult to translate but it wraps up the way in which a clan had collective customary title to the glen or shoreline where they had lived since a time out of mind. Border heidsmen had tenants in the sixteenth century and sometimes even moved to take over different areas. What bound them together was the name itself and the loyalty it commanded. When Highlanders raised their broadswords to charge, they roared the names of their places: Loch Moy! Dunmaglass! When Borderers fought in battle, they shouted out who they were and rallied all of that surname to them. They were most certainly not clansmen and would not have been seen dead wearing tartan.

When William, Lord Dacre, the Warden of the English West March, heard of this flagrant annexation, he planned an attack. Mustering more than 2,000 riders, he advanced up the little River Sark, and into an ambush. The English surname of Storey had wind of what was afoot, warned their Armstrong allies who beat back Dacre with ease. A single surname had defeated a small English army.

In the 1520s the Border Reivers were becoming increasingly notorious across the north of Britain. News of their crimes and lawlessness had spread all over Scotland and much of England. They had become a national disgrace and were the target of a remarkable reaction from the national churches. Gavin Dunbar, the Archbishop of Glasgow, had been tutor to the young James V. When the king began his personal rule, free of the Red Douglases, Dunbar was appointed as Lord Chancellor of Scotland. Where military solutions had failed to make much impact on the perennial problem of the Borders, perhaps the spiritual power of the church might do better. It was certainly cheaper, and worth a try.

Some time in the late 1520s the Archbishop promulgated 'a monition of cursing' against the reivers. He did not hold back:

> I curse their head and all the hairs of their head: I curse their face, their eyes, their mouth, their nose, their tongue, their teeth, their neck, their shoulders, their breast, their heart, their stomach, their back, their belly, their arms, their legs, their hands, their feet, and every part of their body from the top of their head to the soles of their feet, before and behind, within and without.

And that's not all:

> I dissever and part them from the Church of God, and deliver them alive to the Devil of Hell, as the Apostle Paul delivered Corinthian. I interdict the places they come to for divine service, the ministrations of the sacraments of Holy Church, except the sacrament of baptism only, and forbid all churchmen to shrive or absolve them of their sins, until they be first absolved of this cursing.

Because they are nothing but

> common traitors, reivers, thieves, dwelling in the south part of this realm, in Teviotdale, Eskdale, Liddesdale, Ewesdale, Nithsdale and

Annandale. They have been in several ways pursued and punished by the temporal sword and our Sovereign Lord's authority, and do not fear it.

The vehemence of the language is palpable – even at a distance of five centuries – but it should not be allowed to distract from the importance of Dunbar's actions. Not only were the reivers placed outside the temporal legal system, they were now also cast out of the church.

Excommunication was an extremely serious matter. Marriages could not be blessed or contracted, funerals would lack a priest, last rites could not be administered or a final confession heard and the sins absolved. The sole consolation was that the monition of cursing was very general, no individuals were named and many no doubt claimed that it did not apply to them.

English reivers did not escape. Perhaps as a deliberately timed complement, the Bishop of Durham delivered himself of a similar curse on the surnames of Tynedale and Redesdale, but again it was not practical to name specific names. Apparently Hector Charlton, a Tynedale reiver, held a communion where he himself took the service and served all those who attended with wine. In a time when – even on the eve of the Reformation – religion and the church played a central role in the lives of everyone, it was a surprising and shocking example of blasphemy.

When Gavin Dunbar determined 'to strike with the terrible sword of Holy Church', he probably struck harder than we can imagine in this Godless age. The curse was never lifted and the fell sentence of excommunication remained in force throughout the sixteenth century. When in 1596 Robert Carey listened to Geordie Burn's recital of all his crimes, it sounded like a confession which might have been made to a priest.

CARLISLE CURSES

When the Archbishop of Glasgow cursed the Border Reivers in 1525, he made it comprehensive, an invective which could easily have found its way into a Monty Python film. Carlisle City Council recently created an underpass and had it decorated by a pavement inscribed with many of the Border surnames. At the end of the underpass there is a polished, pink granite boulder with the Archbishop's curse beautifully carved around it. In 2001 a Christian group in the city petitioned to have it removed. They claimed that the curse was still working, nearly 500 years later. The outbreak of foot and mouth disease in 2001, the Carlisle floods of Christmas 2004 and the recent poor form of Carlisle United FC were all cited as evidence. Perhaps they have a point.

By the end of 1528 the three-year truce concluded after the devastating raids on Kelso, Jedburgh and elsewhere was about to expire. Official commissioners met at Berwick and agreed terms. At Alnwick an unofficial meeting took place between Sim the Laird, the Armstrong heidsman, and the Earl of Northumberland. If they could not agree, then the truce made at Berwick would not be worth the wax melted to seal it.

Northumberland was an appointed government official, Warden General of the English Marches and directly responsible to Henry VIII and the royal administration in London. Sim the Laird had no such status, and held no equivalent office of any kind in Scotland. The December meeting in Alnwick was the stuff of realpolitik, and it was fascinating. The heidsman of the Armstrongs, a surname riding high in its pomp, in some ways the successor of Sir William de Lisle as a reiver-king, the ruler of Liddesdale and many of the valleys round about, Sim was probably the most powerful man on the Scottish side of the frontier. It made every sort of sense for the Earl to talk directly to him. If they could do a deal, it would stick.

Very unusually some sense of what actually passed between the two was recorded. Northumberland's account may suffer a little from an English bias, and Armstrong's words may have been intended for effect as much as substance. But what he said was remarkable.

The fundamental problem of disorder in the Borders was caused not by the crimes of the riding surnames. No, that was only a symptom, an effect. According to Armstrong, the root cause was the ineffective rule of the Scottish kings. Neither James V nor his predecessors had been able to deliver justice properly, either in its administration or its enforcement. And those counsellors and regents who had ruled while the Stewarts were minors were no better. Sim could produce first-hand, convincing evidence for this governmental failure. He and his riders could raid unchecked over great distances, destroy churches and generally act with impunity. It was a scandal – and also a political version of Groucho Marx' view of clubs and his membership of them.

The best solution for the Borders was a radical one. The whole area should become part of England. If only Henry VIII were to replace James V as sovereign over the Scottish marches, then the rule of law would prevail. Presumably the Armstrongs would then lay down their spears, swords and pistols, yoke their ponies to the plough, become peaceable farmers and convert Liddesdale into an agrarian paradise. Possibly.

Sim the Laird's analysis must have been disingenuous, and Northumberland might have laughed, though he probably didn't believe it either. The Armstrongs' interests would have been ill served by the agents of a powerful monarchy, English or Scottish. His game may have been to play off one against the other. Sim knew fine that his words would be reported to London, and by indicating that the Armstrongs might be willing to become allies of the Tudor kings, he may have hoped to bolster his position against the Stewarts. Liddesdale was undoubtedly in Scotland, at least for the moment, but if its inhabitants aspired to be English, or threatened to, then that could only foster their ability to act independently. Three thousand riders galloped behind Sim the Laird. That fact alone persuaded London and Edinburgh to listen to what he said in Alnwick.

TAIN BO

One of the oldest stories in Europe survived in Irish Gaelic and takes cattle reiving for its theme. Some things never change. The 'Tain Bo Cuailgne', or 'The Great Cattle Raid of Cooley' is set in the north of Ireland and it describes prehistoric reiving and a society which existed in the first millennium BC. The boy-hero is Cuchulainn and he defends the cattle of Ulster single-handedly against the raiders of Connaught. Queen Maeve is after more wealth, and like the Borderers of the sixteenth century, she saw it as having four legs. When in bed with her lover, the queen talks of the measurement of wealth and they agree on its ultimate expression in a particularly fine bull. This habit of counting wealth in cows is culturally widespread and historically persistent. Sheep and goats are intrinsically more useful, versatile and easier to manage, but a man (or an Irish queen, or a Border Reiver) who owned cows was a man of real substance.

Nationality mattered in sixteenth-century Scotland, and England. After the Wars of Independence, and all the blood shed since, and especially after Flodden only 15 years before, Borderers had a keen sense of Scottishness. But when set against family loyalties, this appeared to slacken. The same was true in the north of Scotland, amongst the Highland clans. Family or clan came first, and if it was in the best interests of family to change national allegiance, then so be it. But it was no trivial matter.

English and Scottish Borderers were also often related. Major surnames such as the Nixons, Grahams, Bells and Halls had large branches on both sides of the frontier, and a weary Warden of the English West March noted that the Armstrongs were in the habit of intermarrying with their allies, the Tynedale families.

Even if distorted and exaggerated, Sim the Laird's remarks gave voice to actions and previously unspoken policies. In all they did, the Armstrongs and the other great surnames put their own interests before any other. And despite all the violence, the thieving and the feuds, such undying fidelity to family is not entirely unattractive.

Sim's opinions were probably also intended for the ears of James V and his allegedy feckless counsellors. They may well have been passed on directly by the Earl of Northumberland himself. He met the Earl of Moray, James V's bastard brother, at one of the trysting places on the eastern border only three months after the conversation in Alnwick. On the agenda at the Reddenburn near Kelso were the terms of the truce agreed at Berwick, but the meeting broke up in acrimony. Northumberland refused Moray's insistence that such meetings ought to take place in Scotland. If heated words were exchanged, some of Sim's assertions might have spiced the atmosphere.

In any event James V resolved to take firm action. The Borders would be tamed and the heidsmen brought to heel. Before a parliament convened in Edinburgh in May 1528, Scott of Buccleuch, the Kerrs of Cessford and Ferniehurst, Maxwell, Home, Johnstone, and other leading heidsmen were all summoned and then immediately imprisoned. William Cockburn of Henderland, in the Yarrow Valley, and Adam Scott of Tushielaw up Ettrick were both executed and their severed heads spiked on the Edinburgh Tolbooth. Scott must have been a notorious reiver for the records attach the label 'King of Thieves' to notice of his death. He was particularly accused of 'taking Blackmail', and his royal title may have stemmed from his central control of a widespread protection racket.

The heidsmen seem to have been detained to guarantee the submission and good behaviour of their surnames. Soon after their arrest James V embarked on yet another expedition to the Borders and it was important that all went forward well. Eight thousand strong, his men advanced quickly into Upper Teviotdale, above Hawick, to a place known as Carlenrig.

Black Jock had agreed to meet the king there. Better known as Johnnie Armstrong of Gilnockie, he was one of the most famous – and notorious – reivers ever to ride the marches. Plays were written about him – one of them is still much performed. *Armstrong's Last Goodnight* (1964) by John Arden has Johnnie as the central character. Songs and poems have also been composed about Black Jock and they paint him in romantic, even heroic, colours. He only raided in England, and, Robin Hood-style, robbed the rich to pay the poor. Just, in his own rough and ready way, and brave, Johnnie was the very epitome of reiver romance.

Most of what has been written about Black Jock (using the name conferred by contemporaries is salutary and places him properly alongside the likes of Hob the King and Dand the Man) is simply ahistorical. But there must have been something more, something which sparked the romance that swirls around him and no other reiver. Perhaps it was a dark glamour, a memory of style, manner and dash.

No Armstrongs had submitted to James V's parliamentary court in Edinburgh. It may be that Black Jock and his retinue of leading riders came to submit to the king at Carlenrig. Certainly some sort of assurance or guarantee must have been sought and received. Black Jock was a seasoned criminal and he cannot have willingly ridden to meet the king if he thought his life was in danger. But it most certainly was.

Carlenrig lies just off the modern A7, about 10 miles south-west of Hawick. A well-set kirk stands on one side of a narrow country road. Near the wrought iron gates into the kirkyard, the road widens considerably to allow space for ample parking – and not only for use on a Sunday. On the opposite side of the road there is a much-visited shrine. In a small, walled graveyard, which seems much older than the kirk, stands a monument to a notorious thief. Such is the power of Johnnie Armstrong's posthumous (and largely confected) reputation that someone guilty of many very serious crimes finds himself warmly remembered in a Christian cemetery.

Alongside the sober tombstones of generations of God-fearing farmers stands a defiant and even assertive memorial to one of the most rapacious and ruthless of all the Border Reivers. The raised and armed arm of the Armstrong emblem, designed to look as though it is about to strike, is much in evidence. No one appears to see any irony.

Why? The bare facts of what happened at Carlenrig offer little convincing explanation. That most discursive and informative of Border historians, the Rev. George Ridpath, wrote that the king caused '48 banditti to be hanged on growing trees' and that John Armstrong was one of them. That is all.

But stories began to elaborate the incident very soon after 1530. They told of trickery, bad faith and bitter exchanges between the king and Johnnie Armstrong before he and his men were strung up. The essence of the embroidered tale was that by some device, an invitation to join a hunting party or a promise of safe conduct, Armstrong and thirty or forty of his leading men were lured into the royal presence. Dressed in their flashy finery (the sixteenth-century equivalent of the sharp and shiny suits of Mafia mobsters), their cockiness seems to have offended the king. Here are the details from the ballad which described the event:

> John wore a girdle about his middle,
> Imbroidered ower wi' burning gold,
> Bespangled wi' the same metal:
> Maist beautiful was to behold.

> There hang nine tassles at Johnnie's hat,
> An ilk ane worth three hundred pound.
> 'What wants yon knave that a king should have,
> But the sword of honour and the crown?'

> 'O, where got thou these tassles, Johnnie,
> That blink sae brawlie abune thy brow?'
> 'I gat them in the field fechting,
> Where, cruel king, thou durst not be!'

The incendiary dialogue is obviously invented, but it does sound a small, faint note of authenticity. Perhaps insulting words were exchanged and a hot-tempered king ordered a summary execution.

The royal soldiers closed in around Johnnie and his retinue. Once he realised how perilous the situation had suddenly become, the reiver started talking, for his life. Border Reivers were renowned for their gifts of oratory – or at least persuasion, and the ballad gave Johnnie some eloquent lines:

'Grant me my life, my liege, my king!
And a brave gift I'll gie to thee –
All between here and Newcastle town
Shall pay their yeirly rent to thee.'

But it was no use:

'To seek het water beneath cauld ice,
Surely it is a great folie –
I have asked grace at a graceless face,
But there is nane for my men and me.'

The king turned his back and left Armstrong and his men to wriggle and choke on the end of a rope. It is a puzzling episode. An unmistakable odour of dishonour and betrayal drifts around the old trees at Carlenrig. Even though he was scarcely an honourable figure himself, there persists a powerful sense that Johnnie Armstrong was hard done by. And it might be true.

Amongst all those who report the incident, even the laconic Rev. Ridpath, one phrase is repeated. Historians record many executions in the long story of the reivers, but what was remarkable about that of Armstrong and his men is that they were 'hanged from growing trees' or 'growand trees'. Ropes were slung not over a gallows beam but over what was handy at that moment, the stout limbs of the mature trees around Carlenrig churchyard. This speaks of an impulsive act, of something unplanned and unexpected. Perhaps Johnnie Armstrong and James Stewart really did exchange insults. Like most of his royal ancestors, James V was apparently hot-tempered. And in 1530 he was only 17 years old. In the sixteenth century boys grew into men much earlier than they do now but even so there is more than a hint of youthful impetuousity in stringing up the Armstrongs from growand trees.

In any event, it would have made more sense to deal with a famous reiver in a considered way – the same way in which William Cockburn and Adam Scott had met their fate. Better to make a public spectacle of the dispatch of Johnnie Armstrong on a scaffold at the mercat cross of Edinburgh and spike his severed head on the Tolbooth walls for all to see. Or hold him in detention as a guarantee for the good behaviour of his surname. Killing him at Carlenrig looks like an indulgence and bad politics.

The role of Lord Maxwell in this business is also suggestive. Immediately after his death, within three days, Armstrong's goods and lands were made over to the Dumfriesshire family. The Maxwells and the Armstrongs had long been associated, and even after Carlenrig, remained close. But there is a hint that Lord Maxwell (even though he was probably still in prison in Edinburgh at that time) had had a hand in arranging the meeting of Johnnie and King James. Perhaps he guaranteed the reiver's safety. This only adds to the sense of a spontaneous altercation in the churchyard. Surely if Maxwell had played false a blood feud with the Armstrongs would have followed. Others had been pursued for much less.

THE REIVER TRAIL

The broadcaster and writer, Fiona Armstrong, owns a resonant reiver name and she is fascinated by all that history attached to it, good and bad. Fiona has helped create 'The Reiver Trail'. It begins at the bleak mass of Hermitage Castle and climbs west, up through a high valley where stock-rearing farms like Carewoodrig (still in the hands of Elliots) still run the tough little cows known as Galloways (not the big beef cattle called Belted Galloways – these are all black or sometimes brown with dense coats). These beasts did not look much different in the sixteenth century. The trail then joins the A7, takes in Carlenrig where Johnnie Armstrong was strung up and swings down to Langholm and the Armstrong Museum. It passes the beautiful tower at Hollows before turning east into Liddesdale, the quintessential reiver valley. The landscape looks different now, much less wild, cars whizz by and that hard-bitten life is long fled. But there are places on the trail, like the lovely, lonely road up to Carewoodrig, where the past rushes in with the swirling mists, where the whaups cry on the wind, and where at an early winter twilight no one would be surprised to hear the thump of hoofbeats on the grass.

The lynchings had little lasting effect. There is a tradition that King Henry VIII had asked James V to deal with Johnnie Armstrong. Evidently his surname had been overdoing their forays into England and causing mayhem. Perhaps there was concern at the alliances with Tynedale and Redesdale. This sort of intervention is unlikely on a number of levels. Especially against a background of hostility in the 1530s, one sovereign king would scarcely be anxious to take instruction from another in how to keep order in his own kingdom, unless there was a deal, and there is no evidence that there was. In any case Henry was usually happy to see the Stewarts in difficulty in the Borders. In fact, in 1532, the English were doing their best to foment disorder. The Warden of the English West March, Lord Dacre, was advised to encourage the men of Liddesdale to raid into Scotland 'as may annoy the King of Scots'.

The tradition of Henry VIII's involvement in the lynching at Carlenrig was later employed as shaky evidence to back the assertion that Johnnie Armstrong's demise was all the more unjust because he was some sort of rough and ready patriot who raided only in England and never so much as harmed a hair on any Scotsman's head. Simply not true.

Significantly, Sim the Laird, Johnnie's elder brother, was still at large and still active. If James V had hoped to inhibit the Armstrongs, he failed. More worrying for the Scots king was the escalation in the nature of cross-border raiding in the 1530s. The Douglas Earl of Angus, leader of the pro-English party in Scotland, had fled when James began his personal rule. In 1532 he was in Berwick mustering a large raiding party. In the October of that year, they rode into the eastern Borders with fire and sword. This was evidently in retaliation for a previous Scottish raid which had penetrated as far as Wooler. In the familiar sequence of hit and counter hit, the Earl of Northumberland also led 1500 riders into Teviotdale. The Scott stronghold of Branxholm, near Hawick, was burned and much plunder taken. Like the tower and dozens of farm steadings, deep resentment smouldered in the Borders. When it came, the retaliation was stunning, and on a new and extraordinary scale.

Buccleuch sought and received support from both the Cessford and Ferniehurst Kerrs. Together they mustered what amounted to a small invasion force of 3,000 riders. With no need for or possibility of stealth and concealment, Buccleuch led his huge raiding party over the Cheviots and down into Northumberland. Establishing themselves at a central location, the identity of which unfortunate village is uncertain, the reivers proceeded on a plan for systematic looting. Forces of two or three hundred detached themselves to attack and pillage the surrounding towns and returned to their base to pile up their gains. Despite local resistance, the Buccleuch raid was so imposing that when the area had been exhausted, his riders could return northwards without fear of serious attack. There were simply too many of them.

This pattern, the Big Raid, repeated in the following decade. It became a way of prosecuting an undeclared war between Henry VIII and James V, and the reivers were content to exploit the situation for their own reasons. Fuelled simultaneously by the inherited hurts of long-standing family rivalries and the turns of international politics, the Big Raids did immense and lasting damage. The older habit of running small forays with dozens or scores of riders was frightening enough, particularly during periods of special intensity, but when thousands of soldiers descended on a valley or a wider area, they stripped it like locusts and often destroyed its ancient fabric.

Royal prompting was unmistakable – and unwise for anyone to ignore. When King Henry wrote to his warden, Sir William Eure, requiring him 'to let slip as many under his rule as should do the Scots three hurts for one', he let them slip across the border in force and regularly.

BOOKS AND BORDER BOOKMEN

The occupation of southern Scotland by English troops had an unexpected and initially non-violent effect. Protestant literature spread around the countryside, and although it was forced underground by the alliance with catholic France, its circulation helped to turn people towards the reformed religion. A new printing industry had taken root in Edinburgh. Walter Chepman and Andrew Millar, both originally Borderers from Selkirk, had set up the first printing press in the Cowgate in Edinburgh. Dating to around 1508, Scotland's oldest surviving books were made by them. They are very small, only 15 centimetres tall, varying in length from 8 to 48 pages. Mostly poetry, and some prose, they appear to have been popular. Millar was a bookseller and Chepman a merchant, both well suited to making a business out of publishing, and they laid a fertile ground for the mushrooming of religious literature as the sixteenth-century Reformation gathered momentum.

By 1534 a truce temporarily halted the alternating cycle of big raids. The English king needed relief on his northern frontier. Henry VIII's continuing inability to sire a male heir to sustain the Tudor dynasty began to drive all his policy. While James V was busy hanging Johnnie Armstrong at Carlenrig, Henry had called what became known as the Reformation Parliament. Because the Pope would not grant a divorce from Catherine of Aragon (inconveniently, she was the aunt of the Emperor Charles V, the most powerful catholic prince in Europe) and allow the fertile Anne Boleyn into his bed, the king was preparing to change the church in England into the Church of England. And to kill anyone who stood in his way. The likelihood that Henry himself was the problem, probably becoming infertile as a consequence of bouts of syphilis, never crossed the mind of this most ruthless of monarchs.

In a series of parliamentary acts the church was disconnected completely from Rome and the Pope. As Henry himself was confirmed as the head of the new Church of England, all its revenues, appointments and properties came into direct royal ownership. Doctrinally there were few changes and worship carried on much as it had always done.

To retain the vital support of his aristocracy throughout all these upheavals, Henry and his brilliant Chancellor, Thomas Cromwell, devised a simple strategy. All of England's monasteries were to be dissolved – allegedly because they were nothing but nests of corruption – their monks and nuns expelled and their vast landed wealth become the property of the crown or sold at knock-down prices to the nobility. The strategy worked well and as England's ancient network of social and educational welfare was swept away, thousands of minor landowners became major ones – and also loyal supporters of good King Harry.

Except in the north. Rebellion stirred – but not very violently. In a strangely pious and passive atmosphere, the rising known as the Pilgrimage of Grace gathered momentum. Many were appalled that a vital part of Holy Mother Church was being summarily and sometimes brutally dismantled – and at dizzying speed. Drawing recruits from Carlisle, Cumberland and Northumberland, as well as Yorkshire and Lancashire, and marching under the banner of the Five Wounds of Christ, more than 40,000 pilgrims were led south by Sir Robert Aske. Henry VIII and Cromwell were terrified. The Duke of Norfolk was packed off to Doncaster to parley with Aske and told to concede whatever he wanted, except for the restoration of monastic lands. He did. The pilgrims immediately tore off their badges of the Five Wounds, rejoiced that the king had seen the light and rejected evil counsel, dispersed and rode home to the warmth of their winter hearths.

A year later Henry VIII repudiated all that Norfolk had agreed to, executed Sir Robert Aske and the ringleaders of the pilgrimage and set up the Council of the North. This was an extended arm of the ever-centralising government based in Tudor London and designed to deal with the unruly, disloyal and half-savage north. The pilgrimage had persuaded the royal administration to appoint March Wardens from anywhere except the Borders. Locals were not to be trusted or raised up too high and made powerful. Ignorance on the part of incomers was to be compensated for by more even-handedness and for the rest of the sixteenth century many of the English wardens were often highly competent, professional royal officers from the south.

The north almost certainly retained another suspect loyalty – to the doctrines of the catholic church, whatever the structural changes forced through by Cromwell and his king. Protestantism tended to thrive in the towns and in London, while the more conservative rural areas clung longer to the old faith. In the remote valleys of the southern ranges of the Cheviots such piety as there was (or was possible) remained predominantly Roman Catholic for generations. On the northern side of the frontier famous Scottish reiver surnames also stayed loyal. In Dumfriesshire the Maxwells kept their catholicism into the early seventeenth century, refusing to expel the Abbot of Sweetheart Abbey until 1607, long after Scotland's reformation had triumphed. The Kerrs of Ferniehurst also took some time to convert, but when the monastic houses of Scotland were also dissolved, they grabbed their share when the family came into possession of the abbey at Newbattle, near Dalkeith. Since the progressive emancipation of catholicism began in the early nineteenth century, other Border families have reconverted.

James V had matrimonial difficulties of his own, and when he married Mary of Lorraine, a French princess, Henry VIII was un-comfortable with the match. He himself had made overtures but after the execution of Anne Boleyn for the crime of giving birth to a little girl, few eligible aristocratic European women could have failed to notice the English king's high turnover of wives. Alliance between Scotland and France was also troubling, and diplomatic approaches were made. Would James of Scotland meet his uncle Henry at York?

Could the Scots be persuaded to embrace a similar reformation to England's? James finally agreed to talk. A date was set in 1541.

As was his habit, Henry VIII made an elaborate royal progress to York. Lavish preparations were made for the arrival of his Scottish nephew. And the king waited, and waited. Probably as a result of European diplomatic pressure and certainly influenced by his bishops who were determined to keep intact the hard-won independence of the Scottish church, James was persuaded not to keep the appointment. Humiliated, enraged and determined to use force where words had not even been given the chance to fail, Henry made his plans.

Despite at least two Scottish embassies, both laden with explanations and soothing excuses, there was scarcely a delay. Plenty of pretexts for action offered themselves to the English wardens. Liddesdale riders had attacked Bewcastle and killed seven Fenwicks during the course of the raid, and Scots families had illegally colonised the Debatable Land. The Tynedale and Redesdale riders were encouraged to set about their old allies in Liddesdale – but in a remarkable exchange they refused. Such a foray would only spark a debilitating feud. Instead the Charltons, Milburns and others proposed and carried out a raid on Teviotdale and the Scotts and Kerrs. In turn they retaliated and the familiar cycle began to spin.

DIPLOMATS

Ambassadors had been used by kings and prelates for many centuries, but they had generally returned home after their missions had been completed – or not. As the Tudor and other European states centralised in the sixteenth century, a need for permanent embassies grew. They could send back political, military and commercial intelligence. The growing Tudor civil service was able to process all this material and to act on it. As royal courts settled more or less in a principal or capital city, a diplomatic corps developed. It could sometimes be dangerous work and all sorts of reciprocal immunities and exemptions were devised and agreed. The Pope tried to claim that his nuncios were the most senior ambassadors and that all others should be ranked according to the date of their country's conversion to christianity. This was plainly daft, did not reflect contemporary power politics and squabbles broke out. In the Hague the retinues of the French and Spanish ambassadors confronted each other in the street, each refusing to let the other pass – since that would imply precedence. For a whole day they stood glaring at each other until the city authorities demolished a set of railings to make the street wider and therefore avert 'a diplomatic incident'.

In response to these routine raids, Sir Robert Bowes, the Warden of the English East March and Captain of Norham Castle, began to muster a large force. In August 1542 three thousand riders followed him along the southern bank of the Tweed. They were making for the easy, dry crossing of the border at the Reddenburn. The big raids were about to resume – and with a vengeance.

Hadden Rig lies to the east of Kelso, one of the gently folding ridges which climb out of the Tweed Valley and up towards the Cheviot Hills. It commands wide views to the north and sits astride an old track running south west through good farming country. Sir Robert Bowes thought it a handy base for his big raid. Only a mile or two inside the frontier and less than a day from his castle at Norham, the site had many advantages. Principally, Hadden Rig was an open place, on high ground, difficult to surprise.

Following the pattern of previous big raids, Bowes divided his forces. While a holding garrison camped on the high ground at Hadden Rig, two substantial sorties were despatched to raid in the Tweed Valley around Kelso. This was fertile farming country and decent pickings could be expected. Led by John Heron of Ford, the Redesdale and Tynedale families formed one group and the Berwick and Norham garrisons made up the other.

James V had sent George Gordon, Earl of Huntly, to do what he could; which turned out to be a great deal. Perhaps with local advice, certainly showing real awareness of the situation, he devised a simple plan. Even though it was always a dangerous tactic, the big raids depended for their success on a division of strength and Huntly focused on this. His riders manoeuvred themselves between Bowes' camp up on the rig and the sorties out in open country. And they attacked them as they returned with their loot.

The Earl of Angus had defected to the English at the time, and he later wrote down what he saw. Like the reivers they were, the Tynedale and Redesdale surnames did not hang about. Seeing that Huntly's attack was succeeding, they gathered together what plunder they could manage and cut and ran for the Cheviot Hills immediately to the south of Hadden. But once they had turned to flee, the English reivers were highly vulnerable, and as often happened, more men were killed when the retreat scattered into a rout.

At some point Lord Home arrived with 400 riders behind him and his sudden presence seems to have turned Hadden Rig from a defeat into a debacle. Bowes, his brother Richard and John Heron of Ford were all captured for ransom and several hundred horsemen were killed. Estimate vary – as they always do in war. Hadden was a comforting victory for the Scots, an encouraging example of good, thoughtful tactics winning out over superior numbers. But in truth it was not significant. Henry VIII had determined to invade Scotland in strength and the fell engines of war were rumbling into place. The Borders was about to suffer its most appalling period of devastation, and Scotland its most humiliating defeat in battle.

At York the Duke of Norfolk and his quartermasters made preparations for the muster of a large army. It was early October and very late in the year to be campaigning, but King Harry would have his way – the Scots were to be brought to their knees and humbled. Many of the 20,000 men who made their way to Norfolk's headquarters were mounted and it was an age-old dictum that cavalry only fought when the grass grew. Quartermasters complained immediately that they were critically short of provisions, especially beer. Even so, the English column eventually clattered out of the old Roman city and filed up Dere Street, the north road, the invasion route to Scotland. By 21st October Norfolk's troops had crossed the Tweed fords, and war had once more burst over the Borders.

After his victory at Hadden Rig, the Earl of Huntly's strength had been bolstered by reinforcments but was still no match for the English in open field. Knowing that such a large invading army could not expect to feed itself by foraging, especially in late October, and that it was forced to carry all it needed, Huntly was content to shadow the Duke of Norfolk's advance. If he could restrict their efforts to find fodder and food, then it could only be a matter of time before the English were forced to withdraw.

Before that day came, though, Norfolk's soldiers were busy. They left a trail of smoke-blackened devastation along the Scottish bank of the lower Tweed. Paxton, Ednam, Stichil, Nenthorn, Smailholm, Roxburgh, Kelso and Kelso Abbey were all ransacked and burnt. The invaders crossed the river, possibly rebuilding Roxburgh bridge (one of the stone piers is still visible) and then fording the Teviot just west of Kelso. The villages of Sprouston, Redden and Hadden were all fired. No attempt was made to control the countryside by anything other than brute force: what Henry VIII intended was systematic destruction. This was a punitive raid to teach the king of Scotland a lesson – but as usual it was Borderers who were forced to learn it.

HIRSELS HEFTED

Many modern Britons have an ignorant eye for farm animals. To us they all look the same, or at least very similar. Border Reivers and Border hill farmers of the twenty-first century knew and know their beasts well, and understand their habits. A hirsel, or small flock of sheep, become hefted to a hillside. In other words they become attached to a particular patch of pasture and do not often stray from it. Observant shepherds understand this mysterious process. Ewes create the heft. Before weaning, lambs stay very close to their mothers and even afterwards they graze with her on the same patches amongst the heather and bracken, often enlarging them. Eventually several generations, essentially families of sheep, have learned to crop a particular area of hillside. They will likely have scraped bields, places where the sheep can shelter from the worst of the winter weather, and where a good shepherd will find them in the deepest snow. Robert Elliot of Carewoodrig used to farm his Galloway cattle and sheep on the back of a pony. It could take him to places inaccessible for a quad bike and could sometimes help the dogs sniff out buried sheep. When Robert brought his pony into its stable after the last gather in 2005, an immense tradition was at last broken.

By the time Norfolk's 20,000 pitched camp at Fairnington, south of St Boswell's, not far from the line of Dere Street, supplies had dwindled alarmingly. If the army retreated to Berwick, the English captains argued, they could be supplied by sea and still sally out into Scottish territory to inflict more damage. If they remained in the Borders countryside, haunted by Huntly and with winter closing in, they could find themselves dangerously weakened. The duke took their advice and after only eight days on Scottish soil, and a swathe of terrible destruction, his soldiers marched downriver to pitch camp under Berwick's walls.

Meanwhile James V had been busy assembling an army. The muster was called to Fala Moor in Midlothian, on Dere Street. Recent historians have reckoned that only 15,000 to 20,000 soldiers came, less than half the number who marched to Flodden 30 years before. That dark memory was still fresh. And when news of Norfolk's retreat to Berwick reached Fala, there were widespread desertions. Perhaps a third of the army melted away.

James V had been a virtual prisoner of the Douglases for much of his young life and his consequent mistrust of the Scottish nobility had led to a general atmosphere of simmering dislike and disunity. Matters were not eased by the king's habit of promoting lesser lairds (who depended absolutely on his patronage) to high office and ignoring those powerful families who believed they had a traditional right to be involved in government. In November 1542 many magnates found excuses for staying at home – some may even have welcomed an English invasion which might remove a troublesome king – and when the royal host moved south to climb up Soutra Hill, it may have numbered only 12,000 to 14,000.

The usual strategy was adopted. With the main English strength lying in the east at Berwick, the Scots would avoid direct confrontation and attack in the west. Given the clear reluctance of the nobility and their captains, this traditional manoeuvre may have been all that was politically possible. Morale was not improved when James V became too ill to lead his army, and his household made its way to Lochmaben Castle to wait upon events. Lord Maxwell was Warden of the Scottish West March, and in the absence of the king, he may have assumed that command of the army would be his. He assumed wrong.

As the Scots threaded their way through the Southern Uplands, English scouts hurried down to Carlisle. The warden, Sir Thomas Wharton, knew how badly outnumbered he would be. A more timid man might have shut himself up inside Carlisle Castle and let North Cumbria burn around him. Others had done exactly that. But when he heard of the Scots' advance, Wharton gave orders to fire the beacons. They should blaze over the hilltops and summon 3,000 riders to their warden, far too few to face the Scots but enough to do some damage. Wharton could not possibly have imagined how much damage.

The invading army had formed itself into two battles or battalions, one based in Langholm, the other in Mortonkirk. They moved quickly south towards the border and in the gathering dusk of 23rd November, their skirmishers attacked the Debatable Land, firing its farm buildings and scattering those Grahams who had been bold enough to stay behind.

With orders to send on latecomers as fast as they could ride, Sir Thomas Wharton galloped north out of Carlisle with only two or three thousand horsemen at his back. He knew that the Scots would have to cross the Esk fords just below Arthuret (now Longtown) and pick a careful way along the edges of the great Solway Moss, a treacherous, shifting stretch of waterland at the mouth of the firth. With his captains, Wharton made for Arthuret Church and the heights above the sacred well of St Michael. From there he could see the sky lit red by the burning farmsteads of the Debatable Land, and in the grey hours of the early morning of 24th November the English riders watched the Scots battallions begin to splash across the Esk and make their way through the moss. If it had been a still October morning, Wharton would have heard men shouting and complaining their way through the chill water. Even though he was vastly outnumbered and his small force incomplete, Wharton saw that this was his moment.

As the Scots floundered across the river, full of winter rain, Sir William Musgrave charged down from Arthuret Heights and tore into the ragged flank of the army. The difficult fords and the moss restricted the ground and did not allow soldiers to turn in formation to face Musgrave's 'prickers'. The tactics of hitting and running, attacking ferociously and then retreating before the Scots could organise themselves began to spread panic. How many were they? Was an English force waiting up on the heights? And then panic was turned into pandemonium by a moment of signal idiocy from the absent James V.

Twenty miles to the north in Lochmaben Castle the king had a rush of blood to the head – an episode all too typical of the headstrong Stewart dynasty. Instead of appointing Lord Maxwell, an experienced Borderer able to demand loyalty, he sent a commission to Oliver Sinclair to take command of the army. Described as 'the king's minion', he had been born into the Sinclair family which held the wealthy earldom of Orkney, but more to the point he was good-looking and the king's favourite. 'Minion' is an odd description and it appears in several accounts of the battle. It did not carry the meaning of 'underling' or 'slave' in the sixteenth century. The word derived from the French 'mignon' and it meant 'sweet' or 'dainty'. Perhaps its repetition was a faint reference to the nature of Oliver Sinclair's relationship with the king, certainly it was not a set of characteristics likely to appeal to a force of hard-bitten soldiers on the point of invading England and who found themselves sore beset by determined Border horsemen. A sweet and dainty general? Perhaps not.

When Sinclair's commission arrived, he was raised up 'on pikes' so that all his captains and the men near him could recognise their new commander. The reaction was immediate. It is said that 'a general murmur and breach of all order ensued'. Little imagination is needed to guess what soldiers had to say when they saw Oliver attempt to take command. There almost certainly followed substantial desertion as the news of James V's madness spread like wildfire. The Scottish army began to implode.

All the while Musgrave's horsemen were attacking and wheeling away – and eventually breaking up the Scottish ranks and getting in amongst them, as reivers loved to do. Extraordinary scenes began to unfold. Most of those in the rear who had not crossed the Esk turned and fled north, others began to surrender en masse. Sometimes three or four Scots would throw down their weapons and surrender to one English rider. The army simply lost all its confidence. No one wanted to die fighting for Oliver Sinclair (including Oliver Sinclair – he surrendered like the others) or the royal idiot who had appointed him. Many were trapped at the Esk fords and did not lift a hand to resist. The list of aristocratic prisoners who would fetch good ransoms is long, and very eloquent about the battle which had become a debacle in moments. Opposite the names of Scottish earls and lairds are their captors, those who could claim the ransoms. In the main these were ordinary English borderers such as Wat's Willie Graham, George Pott, Willie Storey, and Oliver Sinclair found himself the prisoner of one Willie Bell. No doubt they were both as startled as each other.

Sir Thomas Wharton must have been astounded. As he watched from Arthuret Heights and marvelled at how easily the Scots army came apart, he had never seen classic reiver tactics succeed so brilliantly – and against a force many times larger. He did not have the manpower to pursue the Scots who were fleeing north. They fell prey to Scottish reivers, many of them glad of the chance to repay the king for his policy of vigorous suppression. James V joined his retreating remnant, and finally took to his bed in Linlithgow Palace a few days later. He died at the age of only 30, possibly of shame. Willie Bell, Willie Storey and their friends were no doubt amazed to find themselves heroes, and no doubt better pleased to discover that Henry VIII had promised them all 'ready money' for their unexpected prisoners.

ARTHURET

Fords were often the sites of important battles. When an army was forced to cross a substantial river, it immediately found itself in a weak position, its strength temporarily divided in three: a vanguard having crossed, those behind crossing, and those waiting to cross. Fords were predictable, places where generals were forced by nature to go. Solway Moss was not the first battle to be fought at the Esk fords near Longtown in Cumbria. In 573 the pagan king of Carlisle, Gwenddolau, fought the Christian kings of York at Arderydd, or Arthuret, the ancient name for Longtown and still the name of its parish. It is thought that the historical King Arthur fought battles in the north, some of them at fords in north Northumberland, on the River Glen near Wooler and the Rede, near the top of Redesdale. Like the men who won so spectacularly at Solway Moss, it is likely that he and his warband fought on horseback using similar equipment and similar tactics.

The dismal defeat at Solway Moss turned out to be little more than a prelude to even more misery for the Borders. English military capability was untouched by the battle. The ambassador from the court of the Emperor Charles V reckoned that only 700 or 800 of Wharton's riders had actually engaged with the Scots, and of those a mere seven were killed. A shameful statistic, something which helped persuade James V to turn his face to the wall.

With the king's death, the Stewart succession became shaky. The baby who would become Mary, Queen of Scots, was only a week old. Henry VIII moved quickly to take advantage of the uncertainty and betroth the infant to his son, Prince Edward, and a political wrangle began – and ended in the middle of 1543 with the Scots' withdrawal from the match and the resumption of the alliance with France. At one point in the negotiations the English considered a radical approach. They offered the hand of Princess Elizabeth to the son of the Regent of Scotland, the Earl of Arran. The proposed deal was cut and dried. If Arran agreed, he would be made King of Scotland 'beyond the Firth', meaning the Forth–Clyde line. It was an old judgement. After the Agricolan invasions of AD 79, Roman historians believed that if a conquest had to be undertaken at all then southern and central Scotland were the only bits worth having, the north being too wild, infertile and hostile. Despite Arran having royal lineage (he was the grandson of Mary, the sister of James III), the negotiations never moved past speculative talk. But it is worth a moment's pause to reflect on what might have happened if they had. Princess Elizabeth eventually became Queen Bess of Merrie England – and James Hamilton might have become King of Great Britain more than 50 years before James VI did.

Dynastic union was more than an undercurrent. The 1540s saw an aggressive English attempt to force it through in a series of episodes Walter Scott called 'the rough wooing'.

In the west Sir Thomas Wharton was busy extending his influence over much of Dumfriesshire. He encouraged Scottish surnames into feuds with each other. Armstrongs attacked Scotts and Kerrs while Elliots and Nixons raided in the countryside around Jedburgh. The policy was both simple and clever. Wharton supported the lesser surnames in their attacks on the greater, dangling the promise of the extensive lands of the Scotts, Kerrs and Humes as a reward for the likes of the Turnbulls, Pringles, Rutherfords and others. That way powerful and substantial support for the regency from the great Border families would be eroded without any obvious interference from the English king or any of his soldiers.

Wharton and his agents also furthered English policy in southern Scotland by non-violent means. Hundreds of minor lairds and aristocrats took 'assurance of the King of England'. In effect, they took his money. In return for an oath of allegiance to Henry VIII many Borderers were paid what amounted to wages or a pension from the London exchequeur. Some were forced into this arrangement by their feudal superior or their heidsmen and as time went on it became more and more sophisticated. If an assured Scot found himself attacked or robbed by a neighbour who was not a fellow pensioner, or by the Edinburgh government, or even in some accidental way by English action, then he could make something very like an insurance claim. The network spread wide: from Berwickshire and the lower Tweed up to East Lothian and Fife. Considering the frequency and ferocity of English incursion into the Border 'taking assurance of the King of England' must have seemed no more than common sense.

In May 1544 the heavy hand of Henry VIII reached into Scotland once more with the first of the big raids of 'the rough wooing'. Two hundred ships appeared in the Firth of Forth carrying the Earl of Hertford's army and they attacked the port of Leith. Two ships and a valuable store of grain were captured but the army, more than 10,000 strong, failed to breach Edinburgh's city walls and had to content themselves with the looting of Holyrood Palace and the abbey. When the Provost of Edinburgh attempted to negotiate with Hertford, he was met with little more than invective, a speech which ended with a statement of the simple purpose of the expedition. The Earl declared: 'he was sent thither by the King's Highness to take vengeance of their detestable falsehood' (the rejection of the marriage treaty between the infant Mary Queen of Scots and Prince Edward of England), 'to declare and show the force of his Highness' sword to all such as should make any resistence unto his Grace's power'.

The English army turned south from Edinburgh and found the small villages and farmsteads of the Borders much easier prey. When the king commissioned Hertford, his instructions were indeed unequivocal: the Tweed Basin was to be 'tormented and occupied'. Kelso was considered as a base for operations and the immense strength of Roxburgh Castle noted. The summer of 1544 saw a nightmare come to haunt the Borders. The early sixteenth-century history of the area is littered with the language of war and misery, and it is difficult to attach adjectives which a carry sufficient sense of how awful life must have been for the mass of ordinary people. Suffice to say that in a place which had already suffered dreadfully, the worst came that year. As Hertford's men burned, killed, raped and looted, Sir Ralph Eure's troopers rode over the Carter Bar, descended on Jedburgh and burned it. It was the largest town in the Tweed Valley, save Berwick. Here is the report sent by the Earl of Surrey to Henry VIII:

> The town is so completely burned that no garrison, or anyone else, can be lodged there, until it is rebuilt . . . The town was much larger than I thought it was, for there are twice as many houses in it as there are in Berwick, and well built, with many honest and fair houses, sufficient to have lodged a garrison of a thousand horsemen. And there are six good towers there. But the town and the towers are completely destroyed, burned and thrown down.

In the same letter Surrey comments on the Borderers he fought:

> I assure your Grace that I found the Scots, this time, the boldest men, and the hottest that I ever saw in any nation. Throughout the expedition, upon all parts of the army, they continually skirmished.

I never saw the like. If they might assemble 11,000 men like that, instead of only 1,500 or 2,000, it would be a hard encounter to meet them.

The English had also come to visit hellish destruction on even the smallest of places. Ever thorough, Hertford's clerks listed every place on the trail of tears and sent it back to London to show how busy they had been. Exactly 192 towns, villages, farmsteads, towers and bastle houses were burned and razed. At Lessudden (the old name for St Boswell's east end) there existed a cluster of 16 bastle houses making the village more like an armed camp of blockhouses. All were cast down. In his excellent footnotes the historian, George Ridpath, adds to this:

Scots slain four hundred; prisoners taken eight hundred and sixteen; nolt [cattle], ten thousand three hundred and eighty six; sheep, twelve thousand four hundred and ninety two; nags and gelding, two thousand, two hundred and ninety six; goats, two hundred; bolls of corn [a boll was 54 litres], eight hundred and fifty; insight gear [furniture] etc, in indefinite quantity.

Such lists are the litany of rape, the rape of a whole community and countryside. The effect of it all can only be imagined, or at best inferred. The record-keepers of Hertford and his fellow captains show no interest in the fate of those burned out of their houses, unless they were valuable aristocrats. These are no more than the habits of mind of the times. Scots raiding in Northumberland or Cumberland would have behaved no differently. As ever, ordinary people are left to suffer in historical silence. No doubt most fled before the gathering storm, but for a population of around 45,000, where was there to flee to? The summer shielings certainly but Hertford had 10,000 at his command and Eure and others rode with more. There can have been few hiding places – and little respite. The summer of 1544 probably saw only a meagre harvest, anything allowed to ripen being commandeered by English quartermasters.

The wealthy were also brought to the point of destitution. Lord Hume had been robbed so often and so thoroughly that he literally 'had no goods left undestroyed to furnish his castle'. As heidsman of major Border surname, he was not part of the English scheme of assurance and so the Scottish parliament granted him £300 in 1545. Henry VIII desired to torment the Borders, and there is no doubt that he did.

OLD BUITTLE TOWER

Near Dalbeattie, in Dumfries and Galloway, Jeffrey and Janet Burn
live at Old Buittle Tower. At weekends they and their friends
recreate the way of life of Border Reivers, and it is wonderfully
well done. The tower itself has been sensitively restored, there is a
blacksmith's forge, a medieval hall and a kitchen. But best of all are
the ponies. The Galloway Nag being extinct, Jeffrey Burn has
found its nearest relative in the fell ponies which live happily in
his stable barn. In costume and with precisely remade sixteenth-
century saddles and tack, Burn and his 'Borderers' group ride
reiver-style for the visitors who gather in the paddock opposite
the tower. And they are very accomplished horsemen able to
control their ponies in the same way as the reivers did in the
sixteenth century. The saddles are particularly interesting. With
high cantles and pommels, they wedge a rider in and make
impossible to rise in a conventional trotting style. But the ponies
are so well schooled, strong, small and sensitive that the technique
of riding with one or no hands is soon picked up, even by a novice.
Simply laying the reins on a pony's neck will cause it to turn –
immediately. Buittle Tower is fascinating – and the website with all
the details of activities is easy to find.

As autumn began to turn to winter, it appears that the Earl of Hertford
and many of his men returned south. But the raiding continued along
the border. Winter was after all the traditional season amongst local
families. Sir Thomas Wharton and Lord Dacre were joined by the
assured Scots, the Earls of Lennox and Glencairn, in an attack on
Dumfries. Once the town had been fired, the Nith and Annan valleys
were looted and harried.

Over on the east coast, at Coldingham, there was fighting around
the ancient church, once a possession of the Bishop of Durham. It had
been desecrated and garrisoned by invaders. Allied to the English at
Hadden Rig, the Earl of Angus had rejoined the Scottish cause and he
fought bravely. It was said that Angus had been disgusted by the
destruction of his family's tombs at Melrose Abbey and English
attacks on his lands, but it may also have been the relentless destruction which persuaded Archibald Douglas to change sides. How would
a wasteland benefit him and his family – especially when he owned a

great deal of property in its midst? There seemed to be no long-term plan – only fire and sword.

In February 1545 Sir Ralph Eure and Sir Brian Laiton attacked Melrose and its abbey with 5,000 men. The town lay at the centre of Douglas country and the abbey was the last resting-place of Robert the Bruce's heart. Angus reacted quickly but rode out of Edinburgh with only 300 and was unable even to skirmish with the English. Instead he retreated to the higher ground south-west of the Eildon Hills and waited for reinforcements. After Walter Scott of Buccleuch and Norman Leslie, the Master of Rothes in Fife, had brought substantial companies of riders to join him, Angus and his allies laid their plans.

Having looted Melrose, Sir Ralph Eure and Sir Brian Laiton led their 5,000 south towards Jedburgh, down the old straight road, Dere Street. Using all his local knowledge and probably encouraged by Buccleuch to remember his reiver tactics, Angus overtook the plunder-laden English by riding around them. He took care to go quietly, avoiding any contact with the enemy. At Lilliardsedge, about a mile north of the village of Ancrum, he found good ground to set an ambush. No doubt believing that the sheer size of the army was sufficient protection, and believing that Angus had few riders at his back, Eure and Laiton failed to scout their route properly. At a place where the ground was boggy and treacherous on both sides of Dere Street (especially in winter), the Scots hid themselves and waited.

To bait the trap, Angus stationed a small force on the road, probably near where the modern A68 breasts a rise and reveals a stunning view of the Eildons and the middle Tweed Valley, somewhere they could be easily seen. When the English vanguard caught sight of what they assumed was a small party of riders, they gave chase – and were pulled into the ambush. When the Scots erupted from their cover and attacked on three sides, it became quickly clear that in the narrow corridor between the treacherous ground numbers would no longer count. The Borderers who had suffered in the terrible summer of 1544 fought like furies, spitting vengeance at those who had burned their homes, killed their relatives and stolen their cattle. Those Scots in the English ranks (either assured like the Olivers, Rutherfords, Nixons or Crosiers or merely mercenaries) soon saw which way the battle was moving and they tore off their badges of the cross of St George and turned on their comrades. Realising that they could expect no mercy, Eure and Laiton fought to the death, finally falling in the ruck of slaughter at the centre of the battle. Much blood flowed on Ancrum Moor as vengeance was taken.

Much was made of the Scots' victory, not only in Edinburgh but also amongst their allies in France. But in truth it did not represent more than a temporary reverse. Henry VIII had more rough wooing to do and Borderers were about to suffer second summer of terrible torment.

Muster points often have a long history. They have to be places known to all those called to arms, and for centuries prehistoric standing stones, some dating back to 3,000 BC, were often nominated. In the west march, reiving bands and national armies used the Clochmabenstane to rally. It is ancient and stands at the northern terminal of the Solway fords. In the east, the standing stone known as 'the King's Stone', lies not far from the battlefield at Flodden. It was where the Earl of Hertford's raiding army mustered in early September 1545, camping on the flat ground of Crookham Moor in north Northumberland. This time there was a plan, rudimentary, but something more thoughtful than more fire and more sword. There would be an attempt to hold what was overrun. Destruction would continue, certainly, but 1545 would see the establishment of a network of fortresses with garrisons to control the countryside around them. The Borders would become an English pale, a similar arrangement to what had been set up around Dublin by King Henry VII.

Hertford had 12,000 men. Numbers were swollen by mercenaries, some of them exotic like the Spanish arquebusiers, Germans, Frenchmen, Italians, even Greeks. Marching alongside this cosmopolitan force were troops of what the English and Scots considered semi-savages, the Irish 'kernes'. Lightly armed foot soldiers, these men had acquired a fearsome reputation during the Tudor wars in Ireland. With their long hair, their shrill Gaelic war cries and careless courage, the kernes probably terrified many who gathered by the old standing stone at Crookham Moor.

The English army made straight for Kelso – and immediately, and surprisingly met resistance. Heroic, if ill-advised, around a hundred men, including twelve monks, had barricaded themselves into the abbey church. Hertford had the York Herald demand surrender, but when they shouted out of the upper windows that they would not, he brought forward the Spanish arquebusiers. Fixing their blunderbuss-like guns onto tripods, probably just out of range of arrows and missiles, they took careful aim at the fabric of the old church. The intended effect may have been to frighten the defenders into quick submission with these loud, fiery and new-fangled weapons of war. When it failed, the English rolled up their cannon and began to pound and breach the walls. The bombardment drove the defenders into one of the towers of the abbey's double crossing. And as night fell, they had managed to hold on against heavy odds.

KERNES

In the sixteenth century those wishing to become professional soldiers had few opportunities in Tudor England. There was no standing army and only three permanent garrisons (this reduced to two when Calais fell in 1558). Two of these were in the Borders, at Carlisle and Berwick. These towns were defended by soldiers who were paid royal employees, and the English March Wardens often had professional military ambitions. In Celtic Britain the tradition of soldiering for pay was much better developed. In addition to the employment of Gallowglasses, Irish kings used foot soldiers known as 'kernes'. Some companies migrated to mainland Britain where they were greatly feared as savage, almost feral, uncontrolled fighters. They could work themselves up into what was known as a 'rage-fit' before an attack. Europe came to know the Irish kernes in the early seventeenth century when many were forcibly transported to fight in the armies of Gustavus Adolphus in the Thirty Years War. When the plantations began in the north of Ireland, 'wood kernes' or forest bandits became the stuff of nightmares – the wild men of the woods emerging from the shadows to attack the hated new settlements.

Whoever set pickets around the abbey will have heard a sharp word the following morning. A dozen defenders had let down ropes from the tower and slid down into the darkness, somehow finding their way through the English camp to freedom. When daylight came, the bombardment resumed and within hours, the English had broken into Kelso Abbey and killed those left behind.

Perhaps to discourage any more resistance, or to ram home very publicly and obviously his destructive mission once more, Hertford gave orders that the beautiful, cathedral-like church and the monastic precinct around it was to be destroyed. Engineers undermined the walls (as at many medieval monasteries, the foundations were often very shallow) so that much of the nave and the east end with the crossing over the altar was tumbled to the ground. Lead was stripped off the roof and 'all was overthrown'. It took a week for the bulk of the monastic buildings to be levelled, Hertford going to considerable trouble to destroy most of a famous landmark which had stood for centuries. None of the other three Border abbeys suffered as badly as Kelso did.

In 1545 the raider-army appears to have singled out churches. Melrose, Dryburgh and Jedburgh were also wrecked, as were the friaries at Roxburgh and Jedburgh. Once again a detailed list of destruction was compiled: 16 castles, towers and piles (large houses), 5 market towns, 243 villages, 13 mills and 3 hospitals (often used by pilgrims). It must have been heart-breaking to see the bone and sinew of Border life cut away so cruelly. The abbeys and churches had supplied what passed for social services and education in the sixteenth century, the market towns were central to the local economy and many of the 243 villages must have been burned for the second time within a twelvemonth. When the second half of the sixteenth century saw a spiralling rise in reiving – is it any wonder, given the pounding taken by Borderers in the first half?

Sir Robert Bowes, defeated and captured at Hadden Rig, left a very rare comment on the effect of the Hertford Raids on ordinary people. As he rode along Border tracks, he saw that there was no one left to fight, 'save only women, children and impotent creatures, who, nevertheless by night times and holidays work as they may to manure the ground and sow corn . . . so wretchedly can they live and endure the pain that no Englishman can suffer the like'. They had no choice, nowhere else to go.

The year 1546 seemed like a respite. No large-scale incursion loomed from the south, and while English-sponsored raiding flickered on, particularly in the west march where Sir Thomas Wharton continued to be very active, Border horizons saw few plumes of black smoke rising in the summer skies. People crept back to their villages and farms, and ever watchful, tried to grow food and repair their blackened and charred houses.

Some historians have reckoned that the number of Scots taken into assurance rose markedly that year, perhaps as high as 7,000. This seems unlikely, certainly very expensive, but if the total number in English pay, be it in kind or in cash, is counted, then it may be accurate enough. Wharton had hundreds of Scottish reivers riding under his banner, the Armstrongs were especial allies, avid to pay off old scores while in English service. But it could be a dangerous stratagem. As at Ancrum Moor, Border horsemen in it only for the money could change sides in a moment. In early 1548 Sir Thomas led a large Anglo-Scottish force up Nithsdale as far as Drumlanrig deep into Douglas country. His son, Thomas Wharton, rode with him and left a record of what happened. The Earl of Angus ambushed the vanguard and then attacked the main force: 'when the assured Scots with my father perceived the enemy coming, they took or laid hands on any Englishmen in my lord's company. I cannot tell whether my father or what others are taken or slain, but few or none came away'. In fact Sir Thomas did escape and regained the safety of his castle at Carlisle.

RUTTER

James V was curious about his kingdom. In 1540 his fleet sailed right around the Scottish coast, from the Firth of Forth to the Firth of Clyde. Piloted by Alexander Lyndsay, the expedition had scientific as well as political aims. The king not only wanted to see the troublesome Western Isles for himself and exact obedience from the Highland chiefs, he also wanted to collect the materials needed to make an accurate map of the coastline, all of the headlands, islands and inlets. Lyndsay's chart subsequently fell into the hands of English sailors who passed its details on to a French mapmaker, Nicholas de Nicholay. He produced the first recognisable, proportionate and reliable outline of Scotland – and with copies of his map, he accompanied the French fleet which sailed to besiege St Andrews Castle after the murder of Cardinal Beaton in 1546. The map is now known as 'the Nicholay Rutter' after its maker and a corruption of the French word 'routier', meaning 'way finder'. It was part of an 86-page handbook of directions for sailors, the sort of thing skippers used before the era of accurate instruments. Only a dozen copies of the Nicholay Rutter survive and they fetch high prices at auction.

Over the winter of 1546/7 King Henry VIII's health began to fail. He had been an active, dynamic ruler for nearly 40 years. On 28th January 1547, Henry died, leaving his ten-year-old son as Edward

VI. Scots – and none more than Border Scots – must have prayed for a change of royal policy. But after a palace coup had left the Seymour family in the ascendant, there was to be none. Hertford became Duke of Somerset and 'Lord Protector of the Kingdom and Governor of the King's Person'. And all powerful, and determined to bring Scotland and the Borders within his control.

The wording of the oath of assurance grew more elaborate. Those who accepted an English pension were made aware of exactly what they were getting into. They swore 'to serve the King of England, Edward VI, renounce the Bishop of Rome, do all in their power to advance the king's marriage to the Queen of Scotland, take part with all who served the king against his enemies, not assist the said enemies, and obey the Lord Protector, lord lieutenants and Wardens'.

However, the policy of assurance was beginning to crumble. The unrelenting destruction of the big raids had alienated many who had to live amongst their consequences and it began to drive some into the welcoming arms of the French. Aiming to keep Scotland in a catholic Europe and ever angling for a dynastic marriage for their king with the young Mary, Queen of Scots, the French began to pour men and money into Scotland, though not soon enough to save the south from one last visit from its nemesis, Edward Seymour, the new Duke of Somerset.

Preparations for war were put in hand and all summer long provisions laid in and plans made. The Scots waited. A chain of warning beacons was set up on the coastal high points in the east, between St Abb's Head, North Berwick Law, Arthur's Seat, Edinburgh Castle and Binning Crag, above Linlithgow Palace. Lookouts expected to see the sails of an English fleet coasting up from the south. Post horses were stationed in the event that the invasion force was first seen further inland.

Somerset came by both routes. At the end of August 1547, 18,000 troops tramped up the north road to Berwick, and they were shadowed by a fleet of 34 warships, 30 transports with supplies and a single oar-driven galley. The English had come in force – and this time to do more than burn and kill. If a pale was to be created, then strongpoints and garrisons were needed to hold it. At Eyemouth Somerset ordered the construction of a fort at the harbour mouth, and the castle at Dunglass, wisely surrendered by Matthew Hume, was demolished.

Meanwhile the Earl of Arran had successfully mustered a much larger army, perhaps 30,000, possibly even more. As the English approached Edinburgh, the Scots moved east to the line of the River Esk, near where it runs into the sea at Musselburgh. Using the line of the river to his advantage, Arran drew up his battle formations behind it, barring the road to the city. And then, as often seems to have happened, the Scots needlessly abandoned a strong position. Partly because the English fleet found it could reach his lines with a bombardment, and partly because he mistakenly believed Somerset had ordered a retreat, Arran allowed his army to cross the river and charge. Poor communications, an impression that the Earl of Huntly was about to desert and the distraction of the Highlanders by the promise of plunder all combined to disorganise the Scottish army. On both land and sea, Somerset's artillery had a murderous effect, and within a very short time, the battle had turned to a rout.

The day after, the English advanced to Leith to seek provisions from their ships. Somerset had planned a march down Dere Street, up and over Soutra and down into Lauderdale and the middle Tweed – far from the sea and the supporting fleet. Home Castle surrendered three days later and it was quickly stripped of most of its stores and garrisoned by Lord Dudley and 200 men.

From there the invaders moved to the site of the old burgh of Roxburgh, near Kelso, and camped on what is now known as Friar's Haugh. Otherwise detailed records make no mention of the ruins of the old town and it seems that by 1547 it was deserted. Somerset had come because he was anxious to exploit the massive mound of Roxburgh's ancient castle. Long and steep-sided, between the rivers Teviot and Tweed and controlling the crossings of both, it was 'as strong a place ever I saw in Scotland'. So enthusiastic was he that Somerset is said to have stripped off and joined the work gangs repairing the walls. The old fortified area on top of the mound is extensive, and the English engineers proposed to reduce the defences substantially. By digging transverse ditches and using the upcast to form broad, mounded banks, they created a square artillery emplacement out of an oblong medieval castle – which had been very vulnerable to bombardment. After the accidental death of James II below its walls in 1460, Roxburgh had been 'doung to the ground'. Now Somerset had made a modern fort out of the ruins and with its guns in place, given it a commanding presence once more. The outline of the Tudor banks and ditches can still be clearly seen amongst the tangle of fallen trees, nettles, brambles and willowherb which now clutter the magnificent ruin.

ROMAN ROXBURGH

At the west end of Roxburgh Castle's impressive mound there are a series of ditches and banks almost, but not entirely, obliterated by modern deep-ploughing. The mound itself also looks somewhat artificial, perhaps a natural eminence at first but then almost certainly enhanced by the back-breaking labour of mattocks and baskets of earth. The most concrete evidence of Roxburgh's great antiquity lies on the opposite bank of the River Teviot, which runs at the northern foot of the castle mound. In a flat field known as the King's Haugh archaeologists have found hundreds of Roman coins. Some are valuable, such as a gold aureus, but most are the small change of the Empire. Bronze radiates, they date to the late fourth century AD, very late in the life of Roman Britain, especially in the north. More clues as to what was happening at Roxburgh lie in old names. The ancient kinglists for the lost Celtic realms of southern Scotland include several men with Roman or Romanised names. Tacitus and Aeternus may have simply been leaders who took their names as a sign of their conversion to christianity (very closely associated with the Empire) or they may have been Roman or, more likely, Romano-British commanders of cavalry units based at Roxburgh. One of these was Paternus Pesrut, a name combining Latin with Old Welsh. It means 'Paternus with the red cloak', perhaps a serving Roman officer. The ancient name for Roxburgh itself (the present one, derived from 'Hroc's burh', dates from the seventh century AD and the Anglian takeover of southern Scotland) is 'Marchidun'. It means ' the Cavalry Fort'.

Somerset's captains followed his energetic example and the fort was finished in only five or six days. All the while local lairds and heidsmen rode to Roxburgh to make their submissions and to swear the oath of assurance. Kerrs, Douglases, Humes and many others promised the Lord Protector their support and loyalty. Sir Ralph Bulmer was appointed constable of the castle, given a garrison of 500, and then the main body of the army dispersed and its general returned to London.

The English Pale was strengthened and extended. To sit astride the main inland road of Dere Street, a fort was built at Lauder, and to keep a grip on East Lothian, Lord Grey moved to fortify Haddington and make it a base of occupation. A large garrison of 2,500 was based in the town.

Diplomatic talk of dynastic and political union echoed back and forth. Sharp-eyed observers in London will have noticed how sickly the young king Edward VI was and, however tuberculosis was diagnosed, it was understood to be ultimately fatal. But that did not necessarily hinder the notion of union – in any arrangement, England would inevitably be the senior partner. Somerset was in the ascendant, presiding over the flow of history, as it must have seemed to him.

The French were forced to respond. A bargain was struck. If the young Mary, Queen of Scots could be sent to France (thus virtually guaranteeing eventual union between the two royal houses), then an expeditionary force would be sent in the opposite direction. In June 1548 Le Sieur D'Esse landed at Leith with 6,000 troops and almost immediately marched to attack the English at Haddington. After some hard pounding, they found they could not breach the walls and were compelled to organise a blockade to starve the garrison into surrender. Relief came with the Earl of Shrewsbury and a large English army. After lifting the blockade, they marched south to the Borders and ravaged Teviotdale, treating those unable to escape with great cruelty. A company of 3,000 German mercenaries behaved savagely. Le Sieur d'Esse attacked when he could. It was said that when the Scots campaigned alongside the French, they bought English and German prisoners from them so that they could torture and kill them.

All of this marching and counter-marching was extremely expensive and draining, and with the departure of the young Scottish queen to France, England and Somerset's dreams of dynastic union were fading fast. The French began to spend huge sums in Scotland. In 1549 £1 million pounds Scots was poured in. Assured Scots replaced English with French gold (sometimes enjoying both simultaneously) and the political tide began to turn decisively.

Trouble flared elsewhere for Somerset. Far to the south on the invisible border between England and Cornwall, rebellion spilled over. The English Reformation under Henry VIII had at first been only political. Doctrinal change came with the Act of Uniformity in 1549 which abolished the wide diversity of religious observance which had been happily tolerated all over England and Wales. The new Book of Common Prayer was to be in English, the beautiful English of Archbishop Thomas Cranmer, and all of the services formerly said and sung in Latin were to be conducted in that English. The Cornish were outraged, and in East Anglia Robert Kett led a well organised insurgency sparked by the new liturgy, as well as a residual resentment at the dissolution of the monasteries. The latter was crushed by the Earl of Northumberland (his army stiffened by the company of German mercenaries who had terrorised the Borders) and he emerged as a serious rival to Somerset. By October, the Duke had been toppled and sent to the Tower of London accused of treason. With his fall, the policy of Henry VIII towards Scotland and the Borders collapsed. The strongholds of the English Pale were taken piecemeal and by 1551 a treaty between England and Scotland had been agreed and signed.

THE REBELLION OF THE PIOUS

As far from the Borders as it is possible to be in mainland Britain, Cornwall unwittingly interceded in Border history – for the better, and twice. In 1497 Henry VII had been voted heavy taxes by parliament so that he invade Scotland: James IV was unwisely harbouring the pretender and imposter, Perkin Warbeck. Suddenly, in the west a rebellion erupted in Cornwall. Led by the charistmatic Michael Joseph, a blacksmith (known by the Cornish name of 'An Gof'), an army raised in Cornwall marched clear across southern England to Blackheath, outside London, where they were mercilessly crushed by King Henry's army. Dragged upside down on a hurdle through the city, An Gof and his comrade, Thomas Flamanck, suffered the awful death of a traitor. In 1549 Cornwall rose again. This time it was to protest at the new reformed church liturgy in English. Archbishop Cranmer and the London government had forgotten something crucial. In the mid sixteenth century most of the Cornish did not speak English, and interspersed in the old Latin mass, priests had spoken and chanted Cornish to their congregations. They complained that the new service was 'like a Christmas game . . . we will have our old service of Mattins, Mass, Evensong and Procession in Latin as it was before. And so we the Cornish men (whereof certain of us understand no English) utterly refuse this new English.' Somerset was ruthless in suppressing the rebellion, his men draping so-called Popish items like rosaries and censers around the necks of priests and then hanging them from their bell towers and spires.

With Somerset's execution in Janury 1552, the period of the Borders' greatest suffering came to a close. Certainly war would crackle along the frontier more than once after that, but nothing like the devastation of the big raids led by Somerset would be repeated. But his death did not mark the beginning of a happier time of peace and fruitfulness. Far from it. The terrible international conflicts which rolled back and forth were a prelude to the most intense period of reiving, the second half of the sixteenth century. Violence and thievery might be more local, sometimes done by men well known to their victims, but it was violence for all that.

7

Riding Times

Buried deep in the darkness of Tinnisburn Forest, barely discernible in the tangle of brambles, sits a prehistoric monument. A group of small standing stones was raised on the southern slopes of Tinnis Hill around 5,000 years ago. Nearby are two long cairns which may be a little older but are certainly related. Before the vast, green, suffocating blanket of sitka spruce was planted after the Second World War, it might have been possible to understand something of the reasons why our ancestors laboured to erect their monuments on this hillside. Perhaps the views to the south and the Solway were long, perhaps the view of the stones and the cairns from afar was what mattered more. The Old Peoples who lived amongst the Border hills undoubtedly revered those who had gone before them and they may have dragged the stones upright to commemorate their forebears, and also visibly to assert their rights over the land itself.

Place-names sometimes sound faint echoes from a long past, and the little monument stands on the flank of Tinnis Hill, near the Tinnisburn. And it is an old place. 'Tinnis' is the local version of the Welsh word 'dinas' which now means a city but in the first millennium BC described a 'stronghold' or a 'place of refuge'. Near at hand is Tinnis Well, a useful as well as sacred place. Blown by the whistling west wind and carpeted by the sterile forest, Tinnis Hill was a place of power once, a place of forgotten significance.

By the eleventh century, the power had long gone but the significance of the standing stones had not entirely fled. When King William Rufus came north to subdue Cumbria and lay out a plantation town on the old Roman grid at Carlisle in 1092, he established a frontier with the ambitious and expansionist Gaelic kings of Scotland. It ran along the Esk and the Liddel Water. Two generations later it moved decisively south. David I macMalcolm took possession of Cumbria in

1136 and held it until his death, at Carlisle Castle, in 1153. To bind local magnates closer to the Scottish crown, he granted to the Cumbrian Lord of Liddel lands lying to the north, the parishes of Canonbie and Kirkandrews on Esk. After 1153 and Henry II's rapid retrieval of the north-west, the lordship straddled the border, part of it under Scottish jurisdictions, part English.

This sort of split happened elsewhere along the Border line and many great medieval barons held land from both the Scots and English kings. But after the battle at Bannockburn in 1314 and the rise of Robert the Bruce and a vigorous nationalism, such holdings became increasingly awkward. By 1318 the Scots had taken back the parishes of Canonbie and Kirkandrews. Animated dispute followed, and after 1349 the Lords of Liddel assigned their claims to the English crown in order to put more weight behind them. In this way what had been a private disagreement became an issue of national sovereignty. By the fifteenth century the 7,400 acres of the two parishes had become known as 'the Debatable Land'. Its northern boundary began at the standing stones on Tinnis Hill and 12 miles to the south it terminated on the Solway shore between the outfalls of the Esk and the little River Sark.

Over in the eastern Borders there were other debatable areas. On the fertile southern banks of the Tweed longstanding disputes went on over 100 acres at Carham, 300 at Haddenrig and 40 at Wark. In the sixteenth century several efforts at arbitration failed. As late as 1769 the ownership of these 'threiplands' was still unclear. And, surprisingly, the twenty-first-century frontier is by no means a fixture. Near Hadden is a substantial woodland of mixed spruce and birch which might be English – or Scottish.

But the Debatable Land was much the most extensive and valuable place of contention. It is described exactly as that, 'terra contentiosa' in the fifteenth century, and by the early decades of the sixteenth the activities of reivers had converted it into a political as well as a legal problem. An area of uncertain jurisdiction was a god-send for law-breakers on either side of the border, and the best, or rather the worst, of them happened to be near-neighbours.

The northerly segment of the Debatable Land, above the Esk and around the villages of Canonbie and Rowanburn, appears to have fallen securely into the arms of the Armstrongs. A strong tower had been built at Gilnockie (and almost certainly occupied by Black Jock, or Johnnie Armstrong) in the early sixteenth century and other fortified settlements existed nearby. In the south a famous English reiver family was dominant. The Grahams were much feared, called 'viperous', and were so cocksure that they nailed lists of those paying and owing them blackmail on the door of Arthuret Church, near Longtown. At their zenith, they held 13 towers in north and east Cumbria.

These two powerful families and their numerous allies further complicated the question of the Debatable Land. When they occupied it, the Armstrongs had the brute strength to beat off a small English army led by the Warden of the English West March. The Grahams became so ruthless and rapacious that at the beginning of the seventeenth century they found themselves deported from Cumbria and dumped in central Ireland.

Because there was no fixed jusrisdiction, customary law came to decree that there should be no fixed abode in the Debatable Land. Whenever any group looked like settling, their farmsteads were routinely burned and their beasts driven off. March Wardens on both sides did this. But the ban on settlement (and by implication a clear claim of ownership) cannot have been total. The village and priory of Canonbie (hence the canons and the place-name) was well established and other places in the north seem to have gone unchallenged. The reach of the Armstrong base in nearby Liddesdale probably discouraged dispute.

The southern area was different. At the mouth of the Solway much of it was moss, useless, treacherous bogland. As the land rises above the 30-metre contour, it becomes more fertile, more valuable. But it must be significant that south of Canonbie, between the Esk and the Sark, there are still no villages or even hamlets to be found. The area is still something of a blank. Across the Esk from Longtown the Ordnance Survey shows a huge factory covering much of the southern end of the Debatable Land. No name is attached by the mapmakers to this massive and mysterious complex. It is in fact DM Longtown, or Defence Munitions Longtown, and its eerie presence perpetuates the sense of a no-man's land.

THE DEVIL'S PORRIDGE

War continued to dominate the land around the mouth of the Solway even into the twentieth century. Between Longtown and Eastriggs, right across the southern Debatable Land and the Solway Moss, the largest factory in history was built. Nine miles long and two miles wide, it maufactured what Sir Arthur Conan Doyle called 'the Devil's porridge'. In the trenches of the First World War, artillery was dominant, but for the first two years of the fighting, Britain's was dangerously inadequate. High explosive shells were in short supply and the huge factory was quickly set up to make them. A mixture of gun cotton and nitroglycerin, 'the Devil's porridge' was the explosive ingredient in ordnance and 800 tonnes of bullets and shells were being turned out each week by 1917.

The factory was enormously extensive because its buildings needed to stand well apart so that any accidents could be contained. The Longtown, Gretna, Eastriggs site was chosen because of the excellent rail links nearby, its location well to the west and out of range of zeppelin attacks, and the handy source of coal from Canonbie and Sanquhar. At its peak, 30,000 worked in the great factory. Two towns, at Gretna and Eastriggs, were built to house the workers and because many of them were women, a unique women's police force was recruited. With 100 miles of water mains, 130 miles of internal rail track and 30 miles of roads, the scale was vast. And yet very little remains to be seen. Apart from a few enigmatic ruins, the world's largest ever factory has virtually disappeared.

As relations between England and Scotland warmed after the death of Henry VIII negotiations began. First, a treaty was agreed between France and England (with France doing most of the talking for Scotland) and then at Norham more specific issues were discussed and resolved. One of the heads of agreement concerned the Debatable Land. Since the Armstrongs and the Grahams had become more and more established there, diplomats on both sides were anxious to agree something on sovereignty. If it remained anomalous and unresolved more than local trouble might flare.

At first scorched earth was proposed – again. Both surnames were to be burned out. But it was persuasively argued that while such draconian measures might be dramatic, they had never worked in the past, or at least never had any lasting effect. Better surely to seek a peaceful, and cheaper, solution by agreeing on a territorial division. Commissioners were summoned, but apparently the air grew quickly heated when they convened. Before fighting could break out, a professional diplomat, in the shape of the French ambassador, took charge. Approximately where Graham influence collided with the Armstrongs, a straight line was to be drawn from east to west. Simple as that, 'mes amis'.

The Scots Dike (the majority usually confer names, and the majority in this case were English) runs for 4 miles from near the River Sark at a farm called Craw's Knowe. A generous gap round the end was probably left for access. Its eastern terminal is on a height above the River Esk, and again a gap was left. The busy A7 now rumbles through it. The dike itself is an earthen bank, the upcast from two ditches on either side. Around three metres wide and originally standing two and a half metres high, it must have been imposing – and unmistakable. A modern wood completely screens it now. Red sandstone markers were placed on either end and it was agreed that no buildings would be erected near it. One sharp-eyed historian has pointed out that a very similar frontier lies close by: the vallum constructed behind Hadrian's Wall.

SLIPPERY STONE

In the autumn of 2004 a television crew was filming a series about the frontier between England and Scotland. The Scots Dike is one of the most dramatic and important stretches of that frontier but it has no signs leading to it, no information board and no car park at its western end. It just looks like a long strip of woodland. As the film crew fought their way along the overgrown path to find the beginnings of the dike and its ditches, one of the presenters slipped on a large stone. After some scraping around, it was found to be the western terminal marker stone, although the royal arms of Scotland and England which had been carved on either side had long been effaced. But it was certainly what it seemed to be. Later the same day the film crew found that the eastern terminal stone was exactly the same. This was an important archaeological find. But who to contact? The stone had collapsed into the ditch on the English side, but the dike was surely a joint monument. Sadly English Heritage have still to return the phone call and Historic Scotland have shown no interest. Surely this fascinating stretch of the border deserves better. With the explosion of interest in walking, to say nothing of history, its restoration would prove an attraction. The Scots Dike is one of the most substantial and tangible memories from the age of the reivers.

The Scots Dike marked more than a boundary. It also signalled the
end of an era, what had been an indescribably painful time for the
Border country, especially the Scottish side. More trouble certainly
lay ahead in the remainder of the sixteenth century, but no devastating invasion would cross the Tweed or the Esk until the Civil
War brought troops tramping up the north roads. After the labourers had laid the last turf on the banks of the Scots Dike, it
would be local rather than national or international politics which
sparked violence and reprisal in the hills and river valleys. In fact
reiving began to ratchet up to its most frantic pitch in the second
half of the sixteenth century. These would be the years of the 'ever-
riding' surnames, the decades known simply as 'the riding time'.
The foundations, what a modern politician called the 'causes of
crime', and the grim, hard-bitten attitudes of a society which lived
by larceny had been laid in the fire and smoke of the 1520s and
1540s. If not quite every man for himself, it was definitely every
surname for themselves.

And the weather grew worse. More reports of extreme conditions
spatter the historical record, especially in the 1570s and 1590s. A
period of relative peace did not bring a revival in farming, a string of
bad summers and wet winters discouraged cultivation and led to a
more widespread adoption of the less risky business of husbanding
beasts. More herds of hardy cattle and sheep munched the green, well-
watered landscape.

History often seems inevitable in hindsight, but at the time events
might have turned in any direction. Astute Border heidsmen kept a
weather eye on developments in Edinburgh and in London. In the
closing decades of the sixteenth century it became increasingly likely
that James VI of Scotland would become James I of Great Britain and
Ireland. But anything could have happened to prevent that. James
might have died young. Queen Elizabeth might have astonished
everyone by contracting a late marriage and thereby altering the
succession. But the heidsmen knew that the most likely outcome
would involve the erasure of the border by a union of the crowns.
And that would be bad for business.

Through the late 1580s and into the 1590s there was a gathering
realisation that life would change radically – and sooner rather than
later. Borderers must have listened intently for news. But like addicts,
the reiving surnames kept at it, and as the old queen grew older there is
a sense that they went at it harder. Instead of positioning themselves

for change, they grabbed as much as they could before the party ended.

When the Scots Dike was being dug in 1552, most of these considerations lay far in the future. In Newcastle, in the middle of September, the new Deputy Lord Warden General of the English Marches summoned a council. Thomas Wharton had himself been the first appointment made by the Lord Warden General, the Earl of Warwick, John Dudley. It was an astute move. The victor at Solway Moss, Wharton was one of the most experienced, cool, wise and reliable royal officers on the frontier. Warwick's own appointment as Lord Warden General of the Marches was also politic. The garrisons at Carlisle and Berwick and the troops of horsemen stationed around the English border strongholds were the only professional soldiers in England and to gain control of them made Warwick even more powerful.

Edward VI was young, ill and rapidly failing. Only 15 years old, the king suffered attacks of smallpox and measles in 1552, and by the end of the year the deadly symptoms of tuberculosis had been observed. From that time onwards it was not a question of if but rather when the king would die. Warwick was the weightiest player at court and the dying young monarch relied on him to manage the succession and stave off a potential catholic revival led by his sister, Mary. Elevated to the dukedom of Northumberland, Warwick installed his son into the royal line by contracting a marriage with Lady Jane Grey.

The Lord Warden rode north to make his own first-hand assessment of the state of the marches, England's defences and their organisation. The chaos of the 1540s had seen the mechanics of law and order rust with disuse and abuse. Warden courts were convened at Alnwick, Newcastle and Carlisle as the new duke attempted to sort out the mess. He toured the fortifications along the border, stopping at Berwick where expensive new work was beginning. However, the fragility of the king's health discouraged long absences from court and after his summer inspection, the duke hurried south to London.

Wharton was left to get on with it. For reasons of prestige as well as good order, the administration of the marches needed to be shaken up. Wharton was the man to do it. At his council at Newcastle, he welcomed three men on whom he could rely: Lord Eure was to be Warden of the English East Marches, Lord Ogle the Middle and Sir Thomas Dacre the West. In addition the captains of all the strongholds on the frontier were in attendance along with about thirty of the most powerful local noblemen.

It was a lengthy meeting with a substantial agenda, and detailed records of what was decided have survived. The list of measures to discourage reiving and generally maintain good order are eloquent: they have a good deal to say by inference about what was being discouraged.

Most important to Wharton and his officers was information – and its rapid and effective transmission. Undetected raiding, until it reached its target, was a central problem. Watches had been kept before but it was a dreary and thankless business which could easily slip into laxity or worse. The Newcastle council ordered that between 1st October and 16th March watches would be resumed, and properly kept. These winter months were traditionally the time when raiding reached its peak.

River fords were seen as the most important places to set sentinals. And they all had to be watched. Every raiding party, particularly when the winter spates ran, was forced to use them en route to their quarry and on the way back as they drove plundered beasts before them. Two men were assigned to each of the fords over the Tweed and also, crucially, to those on its tributary, the Till. Notoriously deep and treacherous in places, this little river flows south to north and falls into the Tweed east of Cornhill. Its 39 crossing places were painstakingly listed and where it was not practical to set a watch (there are no large settlements along the river which might have supplied men), the ford had to be made unusable. This was done by damming the flow to create as deep a pool as possible where there had been shallows.

Landward passes threading in and through the Cheviot Hills also had to be watched. Equipped with a horn, men were charged to raise the alarm if they saw a party of raiders making their way down from the hills. How exactly they were expected to see them in the winter's dark is less clear. Perhaps ears were more useful than eyes. But the emphasis on the ready availability of good, quick ponies and a sound knowledge of byways and back tracks was probably not misplaced.

THE RAIDERS

One of the very best modern poems about the Border Reivers was written by Will H. Ogilvie. Born at Holefield, near Kelso, he lived a life almost as romantic as his verse. At the end of the nineteenth century, Ogilvie spent 12 years in the Australian outback, his horsemanship much admired by even most hard-bitten of the 'jackaroos', the cow hands on the remote cattle stations. Camped out in the bush, under the stars and with an audience around a campfire, Ogilvie honed his poetic talents – to excellent effect.

Last night a wind from Lammermuir came roaring up the glen
With the tramp of trooping horses and the laugh of reckless men
And struck a mailed hand on the gate and cried in rebel glee
'Come forth, Come forth, my Borderer and ride the March with me!'

I said 'Oh! Wind of Lammermuir, the night's too dark to ride,
And all the men that fill the glen are ghosts of men that died!
The floods are down in Bowmont Burn, the moss is fetlock deep;
Go back, wild Wind of Lammermuir, to Lauderdale – and sleep!'

Our spoke the Wind of Lammermuir, 'We know the road right well,
The road that runs by Kale and Jed across the Carter Fell.
There is no man in all the men in this grey troop of mine
But blind might ride the Borderside from Teviothead to Tyne!'

The horses fretted on their bits and pawed the flints to fire,
The riders swung them to the South full-faced to their desire;
'Come!' said the Wind from Lammermuir, and spoke full scornfully,
'Have ye no pride to mount and ride your father's road with me?'

A roan horse to the gate they led, foam-flecked and travelled far,
A snorting roan that tossed his head and flashed his forehead star;
There came the sound of clashing steel and hoof-tramp up the glen
. . . And two by two we cantered through, a troop of ghostly men!

I know not if the farms we fired are burned to ashes yet!
I know not if the stirks grew tired before the stars were set!
I only know that late last night when Northern winds blew free,
A troop of men rode up the glen and brought a horse for me!

Wharton understood the personal connections and networks constantly at play in Border politics, and he attempted to break the links
between the reiving families on either side of the Cheviots and the
Tweed. No man was permitted even to speak to a 'Scotchman', far less
associate with him. More ambiguously only those individuals known
to the watch were allowed to pass and if any raiders were allowed to
escape without a fight or a chase, then the watchers themselves would
be imprisoned as criminals. As well as deterrents, incentives were
offered. If goods were recovered, there was 'a price of rescue' on offer
with a clear tariff attached. And if there was an argument, various
resorts for settlement are described in some detail. Clearly arguments
regularly sparked.

Further up the social scale, Wharton insisted that wardens, captains
and the other royal officers of the marches had to be very carefully
chosen. Too many local lords had themselves been complicit in raiding
in the past to police it properly in the future. It was decreed that one
man could hold only one appointment and that he should stay 'in the
proper station'. This avoided any sense of these roles being seen as
honorary or ancillary. Whoever was Captain of Berwick stayed in
Berwick, commanded the garrison and did his job – himself.

The 30 noblemen at the Newcastle council were instructed to enclose
more of their land. Old-fashioned open pasture made it much easier for
reivers to operate and it was decided that hedges, or 'quickset', would
inhibit movement. The method was prescribed. Ditches were first to be
dug (five quarters wide [45 inches], six quarters deep [54 inches]), and on
either side quickwood (usually hawthorn, blackthorn, wild rose or crab
apple) was to be planted (at no less than a height of three quarters [27
inches]). Some of these thick sixteenth-century double hedges can still be
seen, and they are formidable barriers. There is a fine run near the farm at
Pressen Hill, not far from Kelso.

Finally, either Etal or Ford castles were to be repaired in order to
provide a residence for the Deputy Warden of the East March.
Wharton himself would be based at Alnwick. These government jobs
were no longer the prerogative of local lords but hands-on jobs for
professionals.

While a virtual state of undeclared war had obtained throughout
the 1540s, the cross-border truce days had, not surprisingly, fallen
into abeyance. Many complaints were long outstanding. A renovated
set of procedures was proposed at Wharton's council. Those living in
England who had been robbed or suffered in some other way at the

hands of Scots were to report complaints to their local wardens. They in turn would submit them at the next cross-border meeting where a jury of six Scots and six Englishmen would adjudicate. If they found a complaint justified, it was filed or 'fouled', and at the next meeting the guilty was bound to be produced. When it worked, it worked well.

In 1553 all manner of disputes appear to have been settled peacefully at truce days. Grazing rights were reinstated and compensation paid by those who had abused them. A fishing on the English side of the Tweed was returned to its rightful (Scottish) owner, stolen sheep were restored and the crime of tresspass clarified. The small change of Border justice was being exchanged once more.

Sir Robert Bowes, a wily old warrior, noted another traditional – and more immediate – response to theft: 'men may lawfully follow their goods either with a sleuth hound on the trod thereof, or else by such other means as they can best devise'. This was the pursuit well known as the 'hot trod', or hot trail. Those who had just seen their beast or goods, or both, stolen had the right to raise a posse and to follow hot upon the heels of the theives. Even if the latter made it over the border, a hot trod could be lawfully pursued in either direction. In fact Wharton set out a list of punishments for those neighbours who did not join in. The horseman leading a pursuit was said to have carried a burning peat on the end of his lance to lead the way and signify to all that a trod was in progress – but this sounds unfeasibly theatrical, a piece of highly unlikely romance. What is sure is that trods were often run. If a posse could not be rallied on the night of the robbery, or the theft not discovered until morning, then for six days after that a cold trod was permitted. Borderers were well used to taking the law into their own hands, and here was an institution which encouraged them to do exactly that, legally. Rewards or rescue money also supplied an incentive.

ON THE BOUND ROAD

Border towns like Selkirk, Hawick, Langholm and Lauder like to think of their common ridings as the oldest and most senior. But they are not. The central notion behind these annual events is to patrol the marches, the boundaries of the towns' common land. Encroachment from neighbouring landowners needed to be checked and vital customary rights maintained and asserted. This is exactly what was being done on the Berwick Bounds as early as

1438. Selkirk has the earliest records in the Scottish Borders and they go back only to the early sixteenth century. In 1438 the enclave around Berwick on the north side of the Tweed was agreed and the burgesses of the town immediately began to patrol what became known as the Bound Road. The major difference between the ancient perambulations which set out from the Border towns and those at Berwick is that its marches were also an international frontier. This made for more vigilance, and by 1550 the Captain of Berwick and the Marshall of the garrison (an office still filled every year) rode at the head of a troop of light cavalry. By 1604 ditches had been dug and marker stones set up. Some can still be seen. On the Coroner's Meadow, on the banks of the Tweed, an old-fashioned horse race, around a long course, is held as an assembled crowd roars on the riders and takes a little refreshment. Berwick's sister-city of Casey in Australia also rides its bounds each year in direct – and flattering – imitation and the Hotspur Trophy is awarded to the Champion Rider.

As ever English records have survived in relative abundance, and were in any case probably better kept than the Scots'. No equivalent refreshment of the Border laws seems to have taken place in Scotland. Indeed, with the assassination of Walter Scott of Buccleuch by the feuding Kerrs in the streets of Edinburgh in 1552, it seemed like grim business as usual. But the Queen Dowager, Mary of Guise, did manage to agree a practical measure with the Governor, the Earl of Arran. Border lawlessnes might be at least partly cured by a long holiday. The Kerrs and their allies, the Humes, were told to muster 500 of their most warlike horsemen and lead them into the service of the King of France in continental Europe. Perhaps they might never come back.

At the same time as Wharton was at Newcastle attempting to work out how to forestall and deter Scottish reivers from crossing the border, a man from Haddington was causing all sorts of trouble only a few yards from the castle, at St Nicholas Parish Church. John Knox had, astonishingly, survived two years' brutal imprisonment as a slave on a French galley. At one of the most dramatic incidents in the early phase of the Scottish reformation, the siege of St Andrews Castle, he had been captured and sent to what was reckoned to be certain death at the oars of a French ship. But Knox was released, found safe haven in Edward VI's determinedly protestant England and was accepted at St Nicholas in Newcastle as a lecturer, a preacher paid a stipend. From the pulpit he thundered so effectively against the Roman pope and all his works that thousands came to listen. Most were fellow Scots and John Dudley, the Duke of Northumberland, worried at such large gatherings of the very people Wharton was trying to control. The bishopric of Rochester in Kent was vacant and just at the point when the duke had begun to persuade all concerned that Knox was the best candidate, Edward VI died and sent the process immediately into reverse. The accession of his catholic sister, Mary, sent Knox fleeing out of the country and ultimately north to Scotland in 1555 as the reforming movement was gathering momentum. It was Rochester's loss.

One of Wharton's most pressing problems was the apparent seamlessness of disputes in the Borders. Few incidents, raids, reprisals, trials or simple enmities stood by themselves. There was usually a history attached, and this made reform and a decisive break with the past very difficult. At Newcastle the Deputy Warden General had insisted that particular care be taken over the appointment of royal officers. Far too frequently the local nobility, who expected to be given these jobs by right, were so entangled in the disputes they were expected to resolve that the workings of border justice, when they worked at all, had become impossibly labyrinthine. The years 1552 and 1553 were not easy for Wharton as he wrestled with the problems of asserting royal policy over local politics.

Cuthbert Musgrave would probably have shrugged his shoulders and got on with it. Very early on a July morning in 1552, as he climbed into the saddle, that was exactly what he was doing, getting on with it. Musgrave was Captain of Harbottle Castle, the stronghold guarding the southern end of Clennel Street, where the old road wound down from the Cheviots into the fertile fields of Upper Coquetdale and the Northumberland plain below. Five hundred riders had mustered under Musgrave's command and as he and his deputy, John Hall, led the huge raiding party north-west into the summer hills, there was no attempt at stealth. How could there be with five hundred men in the saddle on a July morning?

From later recriminations and defences, it looks as though Cuthbert Musgrave was out on legitimate business, believing that he had Wharton's commission to ride in strength up over Clennel Street and down into the Bowmont Valley and Scotland beyond it. The

English troopers made good time and by ten o'clock they had reached the villages of Yetholm and Kirk Yetholm. Sheep and cattle were briskly rounded up, many of them belonging to George Kerr of Gateshaw. His tower still stands near Morebattle, at the foot of the Kale Water valley. The livestock may have been Kerr's property, or it may not. Musgrave's men lifted a huge number: 3,500 sheep and 500 cows, and it seems likely that this well-reported incident was consequent on something unreported. Perhaps there had been a raid on the English side? When the Scottish warden complained, Lord Grey, the English deputy, refused to concede that anything illegal had taken place. Given the openness and scale of the Musgrave expedition, it looks very much as though the Captain of Harbottle Castle was going about the business of righting a prior wrong. In his opinion.

Some blatant chicanery did routinely take place – and was perpetrated by royal officers. Norham Castle looks across the Tweed at Scotland at a place where the river bends away northwards. There are deep pools where salmon feed and the fishing is reliable. Snaking out into the current are long breakwaters made from big stones known locally as 'yiddies'. They are very old indeed. Yiddies were probably first made by prehistoric hunter-gatherers to help create areas of slack water where fish could bask, away from the effort of constantly swimming against the strong currents. They also took fishermen away from the bank into the midstream where they could cast their nets cleanly, not risking fouling them on bushes and trees on the bank. The ancient pools all have names and opposite Norham Castle is the Halywell fishing, likely to have originally been the property of a nearby religious house, perhaps the Cistercian nunnery at Coldstream. By 1553 the Hume family owned it but their claim was hotly contested by Richard Bowes, the Captain of Norham Castle.

Bowes countered with his own assertion that Norham Castle had rented the Halywell from the Humes for many years. It was a convenient source of good food for the garrison. When Hume's men picked their way carefully out on the yiddies to cast their nets, they came within bowshot of the castle walls. It appears that the Captain had been ordering his men to fire on the fishermen. The dispute became so serious that the long-suffering French ambassador was summoned once more to arbitrate, and he found in favour of Hume. This bad-tempered little incident showed how sour cross-border relations could be, and how petty. The horrors of the 1540s had mercifully passed but the memory would take a long time to fade.

It also shows how royal officers were by no means above bending the law and legal process to their advantage. If Wharton was aiming to free the English frontier administration from all the corruptions and brokerage of the past, then to do that properly, the law had to be relied on. But if matters became strained over a few pounds of fresh salmon at Norham, the Deputy Lord Warden General had much bigger problems upriver at Wark. The English Captain of the castle was due at a Truce Day on 24th August 1553 to be held at the time-honoured trysting place near Kelso, right on the border at the Reddenburn. He saddled up early and with 120 men at his back rode hard up the side road to Hadden, where he had business to deal with. Bloody business, as it turned out, for the Captain and his men laid hands on Patrick Jameson and John Davidson and killed them.

The murder took place in the morning, only two hours before the Truce Day began at Reddenburn, a few hundred yards from Hadden. On the face of it, it was an incendiary act. Friends and relatives of the two victims were gathering at the Reddenburn where large groups of heavily armed Englishmen and Scots would face each other. However, if any reaction flared into violence, it was not reported. Which is very surprising. It may have been another case of offence and reprisal. There had been serious outbreaks of fighting at Truce Days on infinitely less inflammatory pretexts.

PRIORESS HOPPRINGLE

High religious office tended to stay in the hands of the aristocracy, often the family who were principal benefactors of a church, monastery or nunnery. In 1505 Isabella Hoppringle took over from her aunt, Elizabeth, as Prioress of the wealthy and important nunnery at Coldstream. March Wardens often met there and truce days were occasionally held. Everything changed on 22nd August 1513 when Prioress Hoppringle watched part of a huge Scottish army splash across the Tweed at the Coldstream fords, hard by the convent walls. When battle was joined at Flodden, only 3 miles away, the nuns could hear the roar of the cannon and the tumult of shouts, screams and war cries as men hacked at each other. When George Hume of Wedderburn was persuaded to leave the battle-field, being the sole heir to the family estates, Prioress Hoppringle (the name was later shortened to Pringle) rebuked him and he went back to the fighting, and to his death. The day after the slaughter, the nuns and their servants drove carts to Flodden to pick up the dead for burial, probably only the aristocratic dead. Two years later the Prioress gave sanctuary to Queen Margaret Tudor, James IV's widow and the Queen Mother. It was an astute gesture. Throughout the time of the English invasions of the 1520s and 1530s, the Queen Mother repeatedly wrote to the commanders of the English forces (often she knew them personally) asking them to spare Coldstream's nunnery, which they did. When Isabella Hoppringle died in 1537, her beloved priory did not outlive her for long. In the wake of the Reformation it ceased to exist. But in the 1860s traces of the graveyard were found (while digging for a gasometer), the place where Prioress Hoppringle had had some of the fallen at Flodden buried.

The way in which these regular border meetings was organised was formal, and the rigidity and predictability of the ritual was designed to reduce tensions. Truce Days were essential for any possibility of international justice working effectively. At the traditional trysting places along the border (most meetings seem to have been held at the Reddenburn, Cocklaw, at the top of Clennel Street, Redeswire on the Carter Bar, Kershopefoot in Liddesdale and at the Lochmabenstane near Gretna) the wardens and their parties of riders came together. These parties could be very large, sometimes more than a thousand men on each side and since the express purpose of the meetings was to discuss and settle grievances, the atmosphere could be volatile.

When Truce Days were held, the ground chosen was usually open. At the Reddenburn, the small stream which marks the frontier, before it joins the Tweed, has carved out a shallow declivity. The ground on either bank rises to form two ridges which face each other, more or less. When wardens and their men approached the trysting place by the side of the burn, they would halt on the ridges, presumably out of bowshot. Each side took time to appraise the other. No doubt men looked along the opposite ranks to see if either accused or accusors had turned up. And numbers mattered in any potentially explosive situation. If one group overwhelmed the other, then the smaller might be glad of the opportunity to retreat.

After a time it was the English warden, by tradition, who rode forward and crossed the burn into Scotland accompanied by a few of his lieutenants. He would ask of the Scots warden that the peace be kept until the following sunrise (or longer if the weight of business demanded more time). This was important because it allowed men time to get safely home. When it was agreed to uphold the peace, and hold the Truce Day, then both wardens held up their hands as a signal for the two groups of riders to come together. At the Reddenburn there is a flattish stretch of haughland by the Tweed and that was probably where the wardens got down to business.

The preliminary always first on the agenda was the appointment of a jury to hear and decide on cases or complaints. Using an elegant formula, the English side chose six Scottish jurors and the Scots chose the six Englishmen who would sit in balanced judgement with them. Some fine calculations must have been routinely made. Perjury had always been a problem and in 1553 a tariff of punishments was formulated. The most severe was not a fine or imprisonment but something many Borderers feared more. If a man was found guilty of lying under oath then his word would never be believed again and no testimony, promise or surety would be admitted or given any weight. It was a potentially profound humiliation in a society where honour of a visceral sort did operate, and where to be branded a liar was deeply shaming. As Geordie Burn confessed to Robert Carey, honour was something to be ruthlessly upheld, since he 'had spent his life taking deep revenge for slight offences'.

Major insults were often exchanged at Truce Days. The custom of 'bauchling and reproaching' raised the temperature as the men of one side literally pointed accusing fingers at someone in the ranks opposite. By blowing horns, name-calling and pointing lances at a man they reckoned to be guilty of an offence – even before any judicial process had had a chance to get underway – they could turn the already difficult atmosphere of a meeting into an impossible one. Fighting often broke out and wardens had to force themselves into the melée 'to stand together and make a quietness about them'.

In 1553 bauchling and reproaching was sensibly banned at Truce Days unless prior permission had been sought and granted by both the English and Scottish wardens, and if any broke the ban they were to be arrested by their own warden and handed over to the other side. Perhaps it worked occasionally.

James V's widow, Mary of Guise, became increasingly powerful in Scotland during the minority and then absence of her daughter, Mary, Queen of Scots. By 1554 the Queen Dowager had replaced the Earl of Arran as Regent, and a year later she was active in measures to deal with lawlessness in the Borders. On the castle mount at Roxburgh the fort built so quickly by Protector Somerset in 1547 was to be refurbished at the substantial cost of £20,000 and used as a base for government forces. Mary herself had probably visited the impressive old stronghold, for later in the summer of 1555 she held a council at Duns. A straightforward proposal to improve the policing of the border on the Scottish side was made. Like Lord Wharton, Mary's advisers wanted to disentangle frontier administration from local politics, and instead of depending on part-time soldiers and riders owing their allegiance to local lairds and heidsmen, they planned to employ mercenaries. These men would depend on central government and have no connection with the Kerrs, the Humes, the Scotts, Armstrongs or any of the other leading reiving and landowning surnames, who of course vigorously objected, particularly since it became clear that the cash to pay the mercenaries would come from taxation levied directly on them. The proposal was not adopted and strife and dissent continued to spark.

In the summer of 1555 there were two meetings at the Reddenburn and it appears that the numbers attending were growing tremendously large – never a good sign. At the Truce Day of 28 June an astonishing 2,000 turned up with the English March Warden, 1,000 complaints of trespass were made against the Scots in one march alone. This was not a matter of the illegal incursion into England of individuals, in the sense that we understand trespass now. The problem was that Scots were, allegedly, grazing their beasts on English ground (this is what might have been behind Cuthbert Musgrave's expedition to Yetholm) without permission. So that all the complaints could be properly heard, a double Truce Day was arranged at Norham, one session to take place at Norham Church, the other across the border at Ladykirk.

One of Mary of Guise' most active supporters in the Borders was Patrick Hepburn, Earl of Bothwell. Having inherited a wealthy patrimony, and a handily placed castle at Crichton near Pathhead, he allied himself with the catholic Regent but was himself a protestant. Bothwell attended the Truce Days at the Reddenburn and later mounted expeditions to Liddesdale to quell the wild Armstrongs. But as the Rev. George Ridpath drily remarked in his *Border History* of 1848, 'the banditti had the advantage in two rencounters'. Nevertheless Bothwell was influential in the government of Mary of Guise, one of the few Scots to matter as the embrace of catholic France grew tighter, even suffocating, in the Scotland of the late 1550s. Most of the strategically important castles were garrisoned by French troops under their own commanders, and they of course did nothing but pursue the political interests of France.

Henri d'Oysel sailed to Leith to become Mary of Guise' chief military adviser, and in effective charge of French forces in Scotland. Although Edward VI's sister, the new Queen Mary of England, was a devout catholic and had married Philip II of Spain, this did not help create friendly relations across the border. In the balance of European power politics the match placed England against France, and as ever the French were anxious to use Scotland to force a threat if not a war on two fronts.

In 1557 d'Oysel rode south in strength to Eyemouth where, despite the provisions of the Treaty of Norham expressly forbidding it, he began to build a modern fortress on the headland, the northern wing of the harbour mouth. With the expertise of Italian engineers, defensive ditches and banks were thrown across the narrow neck of the peninsula. Two broad bastions were added and a state-of-the-art artillery fort created – only 6 miles north of Berwick and 4 from the English border. It was a deliberate provocation and the Berwick garrison tried to disrupt the work. D'Oysel's men beat off their attacks, but the episode did galvanise the London government. Mary Tudor ordered Sir Robert Lee to Berwick to begin work on building modern defences which could withstand artillery bombardments.

While these international tensions did not spill over into outright war, there was a constant state of alert along the border. Nicholas Ridley, Bishop of London, reflected on what life was like:

> In Tynedale, where I was born, I have known my countrymen watch night and day in their harness, such as they had, that is in their jacks, and their spears in their hands . . . And so doing, although at every such bickerings some of them spent [lost] their lives, yet by such means, like pretty men, they defended their country.

As the political temperature rose, Thomas Wharton's reforms began to wilt. The big raids resumed. The Scots crossed the Tweed in numbers and forayed in Northumberland, the English under Henry Percy penetrated Berwickshire and reived 4,000 cows, some nags and took a few prisoners. More marching, raiding, counter-marching and skirmishing followed, but when Henri d'Oysel brought the Scottish nobility and their soldiers to muster for a full-blown invasion, they would have none of it. At Flodden a Scots army had fought and died for French interests and the bitterness still festered on.

In November 1558 Mary Tudor died and was succeeded by her half-sister, Princess Elizabeth. A martyr-burning catholic had been replaced by a protestant conciliator anxious to see peace settled with Scotland. The diplomatic game changed quickly; French influence north of the border suddenly seemed even more problematic. Mary of Guise still held the reins of power and her daughter, Mary, Queen of Scots, had married Francis, the Dauphin of France, in April 1558. Dynastic union looked very possible because the marriage settlement agreed that in the event of Mary's death, Francis should become King of Scotland. But the growth of Scottish protestantism, followed by the accession of Elizabeth, made that outcome anything but certain. When Henri II died in July 1559 and Francis II and his Scottish Queen succeeded to the throne of France, arguably the most powerful in Europe, the pieces all moved again and history was poised to take any number of directions.

PLAY THE MAN

Unusually, a scion of a famous reiving surname became a bishop, and ultimately a martyr for his protestant beliefs. After an education at Newcastle and Cambridge, Nicholas Ridley became Bishop of London and contributed importantly to the liturgical revolution which created the Church of England. When the catholic Queen Mary came to power he was arrested, removed from his bishopric and put on trial at Oxford. A skilful and brave defence against catholic interrogation made no difference, and with Hugh Latimer, former Bishop of Worcester, Ridley was condemned to the hideous death of a heretic. When brought out into Broad Street and faced with his pyre, his nerve broke and the terrified man began to weep and shake uncontrollably. At his side, Latimer is said to have whispered consolation; 'Be of good comfort, Master Ridley, and play the man. We shall this day light such a candle by God's grace in England, as I trust shall never be put out.'

And it promptly did, taking an unexpected turn. Within 18 months of his accession, King Francis died from an ear infection. He was only 17 years old, and in contrast to what had been agreed for Scotland, Mary did not succeed him as sovereign of France.

In fact it became increasingly clear that Mary was left with no substantial role in her adopted country and that it was highly likely she would return to Scotland to begin her personal rule. The political picture was developing yet another layer of complexity. Since the burning of Patrick Hamilton outside St Salvator's Chapel in St Andrews in 1528 the Scottish reformation had stuttered, appearing by turns inevitable, impossible and often leaderless. Between Hamilton's death and 1558, twenty-one had suffered the awful fate of the martyr/heretic and many of the important figures in the reformist movement fled Scotland, or were removed, like John Knox. The brutal strategy of 'the rough wooing' in the 1540s had discouraged many from a closer relationship with England and the new faith. Meanwhile catholic France had poured men and money into Scotland.

While the Regent, Mary of Guise, was in France in 1558 attending her daughter's marriage to the Dauphin, catholic zealots arrested Walter Mylne. Accused of preaching protestantism in Dysart in west Fife, he was taken prisoner to St Andrews, tried for heresy, and after his refusal to recant, was condemned to death at the stake. Mylne was 82. There was widespread revulsion at the sentence. At first an executioner could not be found to carry out the gruesome ritual on the old man. But when the ashes were at last swept away and the smoke cleared, politics in Scotland had shifted again. Mylne would be the last martyr.

Protestantism flourished in the towns where better-off supporters kept 'privy kirks' in their homes. Preachers held the reformed communion in small rooms with families and their friends. Privy kirks were not routinely suppressed but discretion on both sides had kept Scotland from the worst excesses. In 1557 a faction of the nobility felt strong enough to combine formally as 'the Lords of the Congregation' and their avowed aim was the establishment of the reformed church. While Mary of Guise retained power and French garrisons controlled the country, the Lords' had to bide their time, but Walter Mylne's death seemed to quicken the pace. John Knox returned in 1559 and preached with great passion at Perth and St Andrews. Rioting followed and some churches were vandalised, especially those with ornate interiors.

As ever, political alignments ran alongside religious convictions. After the accession of Elizabeth to the English throne in 1558, her support for Scottish protestantism and the Lords of the Congregation gathered momentum. While Francis II lived and the marriage settlement with Mary held out the real possibility of dynastic union with France – to say nothing of their claims on the English throne – England could do nothing. But despite the events of the 1540s, support inside Scotland grew for Elizabeth. Protestants increasingly looked as if they wanted Scotland to retain its independence while catholics seemed to be ready to acquiesce in the nation becoming part of an enlarged French kingdom, little more than a principality.

Knox of course played hard on these connections, claiming that Mary of Guise was a much reviled Regent acting mainly in the interests of her native France. In 1560 the surprising sight of an English army arriving in Scotland to support the protestant cause brought the situation to a head. Discouraging rather than defeating French forces outright, the English intervention cleared a way forward for the Lords of the Congregation. Mary of Guise conveniently and unexpectedly died at the height of the crisis and a solution was forced on the French. By the terms of the Treaty of Edinburgh, Scotland was to be free of occupation by foreign troops. In August 1560 parliament met and, in effect, set out the legal basis for the Scottish Reformation. The mass was banned, the reformed confession of faith (written by John Knox) installed and papal jurisdiction removed. Scotland was no longer a catholic nation, at least officially.

In rural areas such as the Borders change happened only slowly, and was sometimes even humane. At Kelso Abbey the brothers were allowed to continue to live in the conventual buildings and enjoy some of the revenues of the old church until 1587 when 'the haill monkis of the abbay of Kelso ar decessit'. The pattern of change was patchy. By 1574 Scotland's 1080 parishes had almost all been taken over by protestant ministers or readers (there was an initial lack of men ordained in the reformed faith), but in the 1580s a third of the nobility still held to the catholic church. The proportion of heidsmen who had not changed allegiance was probably higher.

The domestic effects of the Reformation are difficult to detect in the Borders. No doubt some families were split, others indifferent. But the general political consequences were certainly beneficial. When the Treaty of Edinburgh removed foreign soldiers, it also reduced by many degrees the likelihood of cross border conflict. After the reigns of Edward VI and Mary I, Elizabeth found the royal treasury much depleted. Stability, she correctly judged, would produce prosperity and revenue for the crown, which was also what her subjects desired. Her policies allowed peace to descend over the borderlands.

But it was to be a guarded peace. Orders were issued for the massive defence works at Berwick to be carried on, troops of horsemen were stationed along the frontier and cash was made available to pay and feed them adequately. Remarkably, Lord Dacre received the queen's thanks for a foray he had made into the Scottish west march in the winter of 1559/60, but was also advised that it would have been more politic to have done nothing. The Scots were not to be provoked, and instead watchfulness was the word from London. On each side of the border garrisons were brought up to full complement and Lord Wharton's advice for proper administration of the English marches was to be followed. Elizabeth wrote to the Lords of the Congregation that there was not 'a better place betwixt the realms than ever was heard of in any time'. Not for long.

Soon after her return to Scotland, Queen Mary gave her half-brother, Lord James Stewart, a difficult commission. By whatever means were to hand he was charged to pacify the borders – and they were the usual brutal means. Levies were raised, and at Jedburgh the usual suspects rounded up and twenty of these banditti summarily hanged. Forty more were dragged off to Edinburgh to stand trial. At Kelso Lord James met Lord Grey, Warden of the English East March, and Sir John Forster, Warden of the English Middle March. They agreed to cooperate as best they could.

Forster and Grey were related and both leading men from powerful Northumberland surnames. Like the Scots, their loyalty was to family first and nation or crown second. Elizabeth I's civil servants had no illusions about this, and unlike the Scots, far fewer natives were appointed to the wardenries. Neutral southerners with no prior attachments were usually preferred. But Sir John Forster was exceptional in other ways. Making his debut appearance as Warden of the English Middle March in 1558, he held the office, off and on, for nearly 40 years. Living to an immense age, probably 101, Old Sir John was at the centre of Border politics for the whole of the second half of the sixteenth century. He was clearly a rogue, what might now be generously termed a pragmatist, in the period when reiving spread like an epidemic. But Forster was also attractive: clever, unscrupulous, kind, a spade-caller, and fiercely loyal, he might be described as the epitome of the age, a reiver's reiver.

Forsters were to be found mostly along the eastern marches, holding lands and tenancies north of Coquetdale, particularly around Aln-wick, Bamburgh and Belford, and the rolling farmland fringing the North Sea coast. Sir John was wealthy – and generous. With his long-standing mistress, Isabel Sheppard, he had several children whom he readily owned as his own, giving them the Forster surname. Nicholas Forster was much favoured and he appears in later records as a considerable landowner. With his long-suffering wife, Forster seems to have had two daughters, Grace and Juliana. Both married into the Northumbrian gentry, spreading family connections ever wider.

Since the rebellions of the late fifteenth century and because of their adherence to the old catholic faith, the Percy earls of Northumberland had suffered the stain of royal mistrust. Elizabeth I would tolerate them as great barons, but not allow them to recover their ancient power in the north which might make them even greater barons. Sir John Forster was an implacable and constant enemy of the Percys and at feud with their supporters, the likes of the Collingwoods who also held lands in north Northumberland. In the 1560s these tensions festered – and then burst into flames when rebellion broke. In 1569 Thomas Percy joined Charles Neville, Earl of Westmorland in what came to be known as the Rising of the Northern Earls. They were catholics and outraged at the execution of Henry Howard, Duke of Norfolk.

Late in the year, badly organised, panicked into precipitate action by the discovery of their plot, the rebels nevertheless looked dangerous – as a catalyst. The reiving families of Tynedale and Redesdale saddled up to join Percy's insurgents, and for a few weeks it seemed as though substantial support from southern Scotland's catholic surnames might ride over the border.

Sir John Forster was a puritan, at least in name, and he moved smartly to blunt the rebels' momentum. Taking Alnwick and Wark-worth castles back into royal hands, he also sent riders to block the hill trails and prevent more from joining Percy and Neville. Then he occupied the walled city of Newcastle. Word went out to the Forster network of alliances and connections, and rallying riders to him, Sir John skirmished and harried rebel forces. There was news of an army mustering at York for the crown, and more mobilisation in the south. Percy and Neville faltered, lost confidence and the Rising of the Northern Earls began to disintegrate. With Forster giving chase, the rebels fled into Liddesdale, in desperation trusting the Armstrongs to protect them.

Much relieved and ready to be grateful if not generous (she was famously penny-pinching). Elizabeth I summoned the triumphant Sir John to London so that she could thank him personally. The episode was the making of Forster and it was to forgive many transgressions, keeping him in office almost to the end of the century. The queen outlived him by a year.

Deal-making rather than rigid adherence to the law came to characterise the administration of the English middle march. Forster turned many blind eyes – when he was Captain of Bamburgh Castle, he allowed smugglers to unload contraband below the walls – but whenever anyone was awarded a favour, another will have been expected in return. Operating at the centre of a web of interlocking loyalties, Forster was more like a mafia godfather around whom the world seemed to turn rather than a royal official. 'He possessed all in Northumberland,' complained those excluded from the penumbra of patronage. It was an exaggeration, but only a slight one.

March Wardens were expected to communicate with the civil servants in London, their paymasters (Forster once boasted that he was wealthy enough and didn't need the money). The fact that they did so regularly is the main reason why English records are comparatively full. Forster's preferred approach was simple: he wrote frequently with good news. The border was quiet, all was well, thievery contained. Even more quietly the warden dealt with business in his own way, by constant brokerage, favour for favour, punishment meted out when obligations were not met. The question of lawbreaking was less important but Forster kept order of a sort. By 1568 his enemies had seen through the deceptions and complained to London directly, saying that the border was far from quiet, that the warden had done nothing about Scottish raiding, that he had too many Scottish friends and repeatedly failed to raise contentious issues at Truce Days. The Rising of the Northern Earls piled up credit at court in the nick of time.

BOOK HANDS AND CHARTER HANDS

Handwriting in the sixteenth century took two forms. Before the invention of printing (and for some time afterwards – in fact some bibliophiles would not have printed books in their libraries and commisioned manuscript versions), book hand was used for the copying of formal, important texts, like bibles. This involved what we might call lettering rather than writing. Several strokes could be used to make a letter, wide margins were often left, illuminations persisted and all was done on durable vellum. For less permanent work clerks or scriveners wrote a more cursive script, that is, one stroke of the pen was enough to form a letter and sometimes a whole line. The March Wardens used scriveners to compile reports to London in a charter or cursive hand. Often they developed idiosyncrasies which made forgery difficult. These could be highly original abbreviations, almost a code, or even consistent and deliberate mistakes. sixteenth-century charter hands can be very difficult to read because many were written at great speed, as though from dictation. When he was in a rage, it might have been difficult to keep up with Old Sir John Forster.

There was more where that came from. On 23rd January 1570 Lord James Stewart, by that time Earl of Moray and Regent of Scotland after his half-sister's abdication, was riding through the streets of Linlithgow. An assassin shot him out of the saddle and bleeding uncontrollably from a stomach wound, he died a few hours later. Lord James had managed to hold the Scottish Borders in check, but his sudden removal had an immediate effect. The day after, a huge raid was mounted by two of the largest surnames. Led by the catholic Kerrs of Ferniehurst and the Scotts of Buccleuch, it was run in support of Mary, Queen of Scots and the usual motives were spiced by politics. In addition to plunder, the Border lords intended severe provocation. After a diversion to burn the treacherous Hector of Harelaw's house in Liddesdale, they rode over the border to create havoc, hoping to let loose the dogs of war with England, to goad Elizabeth beyond endurance. Westmorland rode with the reivers, perhaps reflecting on how direct and uncomplicated their approach was – compared with his own dithering lack of resolve a few weeks earlier. They burned stores of corn at Mindrum and later raided as far south as Morpeth.

In February the Kerrs and Scotts rallied their men again in the cause of their catholic queen and aimed to link up with Leonard, Lord Dacre, and a small army of English sympathisers in east Cumbria. They had mustered under the ingenious pretext of banding together to protect the countryside against the Scottish raids. This conflagration promised to be even more dangerous than the rebellion of Percy and Neville.

Queen Elizabeth's cousin, Lord Hunsdon, had been appointed Warden of the English East March, and with Sir John Forster and his men, he rode quickly to Hexham. Before Dacre could be reinforced by the Scots, the wardens hurried on west. They met him south of Brampton on the banks of the River Gelt. And although outnumbered, Hunsdon and Forster's men had the better of a fierce little fight and drove Dacre and his riders into a panicky retreat. The queen was evidently delighted at the news, sending thanks to her wardens and her great gratitude and favour ensuring that Forster could continue to do as he pleased in the middle march.

A Truce Day was set for 7th July 1575 at the Carter Bar, the scene of an event which came to be known as the Raid of the Redeswire, the border name of the place where the River Rede rises. The border line runs down from the Carter Fell (now following the edge of a large forestry plantation on the Scottish side) and crosses the A68 on a small plateau. It is the watershed of the Carter Burn which runs north into the Jed Water and also of the Rede, which runs south. The view into Scotland is panoramic, the whole of the middle Tweed Valley unfolds to the three Eildon Hills far in the distance. Visitors who turn their gaze south see only moorland stretching down into England, the busy road running through a wide area of bleak hill country before it reaches the fertile green of the Northumberland plain.

The Redeswire is always given as the location of the Truce Day of July 1575, but it is incorrect. The meeting is commemorated by a stone set up on the north-facing slopes of the Carter Bar ridge, at least 200 yards into Scotland, above the watershed of the Jed. The reason for this is traditional. Truce Days were always held just to the north of the border because 'the Scots did always send their ambassadors into England to seek for peace after a war'. And the English ought to be prepared to cross into Scotland to parley. That sounds unlikely, like a later rationalisation by an English historian. But it might have vaguely mirrored the formulaic preliminaries to a Truce Day. The Scots warden usually rode into England to agree the peace with the English warden, and perhaps a habit developed of an equivalent recrossing of the line into Scotland for the meeting itself. Correct form was always important and occasionally had been the subject of argument when Truce Days were first held.

However all that may be, it appears that in 1575 there had been some awkwardness in protocol. The Scottish Warden of the Middle March, Sir William Kerr of Cessford, was for some unstated reason unable to attend. Perhaps he was ill. His deputy, Sir John Carmichael, also Keeper of Liddesdale, came to the Redeswire in his place. For England, Old Sir John Forster, the Warden of the English Middle March appeared and his deputy, Sir George Heron of Ford, accompanied him. There had been difficulty at a previous meeting between Carmichael and Heron and it may be that Forster himself turned up to sort things out. At the extraordinary age of 74, the ride up the steep and winding valley of the Rede would have been a business for Forster, and perhaps he only climbed onto his pony on that summer morning because he had to. The meeting also seems to have been unusually well attended, and that only happened when there were important complaints to be settled, issues affecting many families. The ballad composed afterwards noted the arrival of 'five hundred Fenwicks in a flock', but the attractions of alliteration might have triumphed over accuracy.

At first matters went forward as they should. Complaints were called from the roll by the clerks and dealt with. Then the case of the man recorded as Farnstein (this is very likely to have been a scribal error for Falstone, or Harry Robson of Falstone) came up. Old Sir John could not produce the accused as he was bound, and promised faithfully to bring him to the next meeting. Perhaps Farnstein/Falstone had also failed to appear at the last warden meeting, the one where Heron and Carmichael had argued. In any case the no-show at the Redeswire was not good enough for Carmichael. The temperature rose, maybe drink had been taken. Insults were traded. Drawing himself up to his full stature, Forster pulled rank on the young Scot. He had been the Queen's Warden for nearly twenty years and Carmichael was a mere deputy and knew nothing of the Border! The old man no doubt grew red in the face as he went on to cast more than aspersions on his parentage. The Scots rebuked Sir John: 'Fye Fye! Comparison, comparison.' And then the angry tumult suddenly got completely out of hand. The Tynedale contingent, including the flock of Fenwicks, loosed a volley of arrows; some of Carmichael's men were killed and wounded, and the Scots were driven down the slope, where they met the men of Jedburgh, late arrivals at the Truce Day. No truce being observed, and much reinforced the Scots fought back, killed Sir George Heron along with a handful of others and took Forster and a few English notables prisoner. While they were at it, the party rode down into Redesdale and reived 300 head of cattle.

It was all very embarrassing. The Scottish Regent, the Earl of

Morton, had the prisoners quickly released (the Scots claimed, probably truthfully, that they had only taken prisoners to protect them from a worse fate) and packed them off home with gifts. John Carmichael was offered as a hostage into England, and then released 'with honour'. A commission of inquiry was convened. The likely instigator of the fracas, grumpy Old Sir John, was interrogated at Berwick where it was made clear to him how furious Elizabeth I was. An entirely unnecessary diplomatic fuss at a time when relations between England and Scotland were delicately poised. Lord Killigrew, the queen's ambassador, reported that 'the English warden was not so clean in this matter as he could wish'.

Like himself, Forster's way of doing things was ageing, becoming obsolete. He had come across Carmichael, who was not a Borderer and owned no land in the area, who sought justice and good order more than personal advantage, and they clashed over a case whose details have long vanished from the record. But for some lost reason it particularly mattered to Forster and he resented the persistent, even dogged, interest of Carmichael. It was nothing to do with him! Old Sir John would fix it. Some historians have even gone so far as to suggest that the Farnstein/Falstone case was about to reveal something particularly incriminating about Forster and that he deliberately goaded Carmichael and his men into violence as a cover-up, and perhaps a way of having the Scots Deputy Warden removed. The significance of the Raid of the Redeswire, as it came to be known, was not military or even diplomatic. It signalled the beginnings of a long end for an old way of doing business across the border.

Forster's credit with Queen Elizabeth had not yet run out. She remembered his courage in the face of rebellion in 1569 and 1570 and left him in place as warden, with promises of better behaviour. Henry Hastings, Lord Huntingdon, had become president of the Council of the North and he kept a critical eye on Old Sir John, occasionally calling for his resignation. Well into his eighties, the warden increasingly suffered from what his enemies bluntly termed 'imbecility and weakness', but the ancient warrior had grown into an icon, buttressed by a supporting group of aides and family members, tightly woven into local loyalties by a seamless web of connections and obligations. In addition Forster was a puritan, of a sort, and Huntingdon's candidate to replace him as warden was Sir Cuthbert Collingwood, a catholic and former supporter of the Percy family. Both sides regularly wrote to London complaining about the other.

The feud came to a head in 1587 when Collingwood and Huntingdon's accusations were considered so numerous and plausible by the privy council as to merit investigation. Sir John was obliged to step down but he must have allowed himself a wry smile when he learned that his friend, Lord Hunsdon, the queen's cousin, was to replace him and make a report on his alleged crimes. The old man had been particularly censured for having too many Scottish friends, but it was Forster's preferred means of preventing even more trouble. If a working understanding, a modus vivendi, with the Kerrs, the Burns, the Elliots and other reiving surnames could be found then the ever-present threat of warfare would be averted. If the price for relative peace was a culture of raid and counter-raid, then it was worth paying.

Hunsdon's report to the privy council was unequivocal:

> I find that mere malice [has been] prosecuted by Sir Cuthbert
> Collingwood of long time, and furthered and maintained by my
> Lord of Huntingdon. There is no man [Forster] so perfect and
> having so many great matters to do in so great a wardenry, and
> having to deal with so many perverse and malicious people as in this
> country

Sir John was duly reinstated in 1588 but the task grew ever more thankless, and a very old man by the 1590s it seems that he found it impossible to carry on as raiding intensified and ran out of even his control.

Lord Huntingdon kept up the pressure, and by 1595 he succeeded at last in having Forster dismissed from the Wardenship of the English Middle March. He had been shameless in his unconcealed understandings with the Scottish surnames – the criminal activities he had ignored 'would fill a large book'. He had allowed, it was claimed, more than forty Scots who deserved the gallows to go free. But the charges would not come to anything – he knew for certain that none would testify against him. A mafia-style omerta seems to have locked down any evidence. Here is the old godfather's reply to his accusers:

> I am accompted a negligent officer, an oppressor, a man inclined to
> private gain and lucre, a destroyer and not a maintainer of the
> Borders, a bearer with Scots and their actions, and a maintainer of
> them against my native countrymen . . . God forbid that any one of
> them could be proved against me!

Despite outfacing his opponents, Sir John found himself suffering the indignity of house arrest under the jursidiction of the Bishop of Durham. His replacement as warden, Lord Ralph Eure, was forced to endure a torrid baptism. With little or no local loyalty to back him, and the undying antipathy of the Forster faction to contend with, he found himself virtually powerless to deal with Scottish raiding. Like most politicians coming into office, he blamed the past: 'Sir John has ruined this country.' But he also understood why he himself was so ineffectual: 'there is no gentleman of worth in Northumberland not near of kin or allied to Sir John Forster'.

In the Border country of the 1590s resentments did not die, they simply matured, and even though Sir John was in his late nineties, those bearing grudges were determined on revenge. In October 1597 a troop of Scottish riders came for him. Arriving under cover of darkness below the walls of Bamburgh Castle, they broke in and found the stair leading up to Forster's private apartments. As they scrambled up, Lady Forster came out onto the landing to see what the noise was, ran inside and got the door shut and bolted in the nick of time.

In 1602 the old warrior died in his bed. More than a hundred years old, he had seen it all, and done most of it himself. Sir Robert Carey had followed the hapless Lord Eure into the English middle march and he left a measured judgement on Sir John Forster:

> [He] had been an active and valiant man, and had done great good service . . . [but] grew old, at length to that weakness by reason of his age, that the borderers, knowing it, grew insolent, and by reason of their many excursions and open roads [raids], the inhabitants of the march were much weakened and impoverished.

Lord Hunsdon had affectionately reckoned Old Sir John 'the fittest man for his time'. And it was true. For all his corruption, Forster remains an impressive figure, a long-lived paradigm for the story of the border in the second half of the sixteenth century, in many ways the worst of times. He was a quintessential reiver lord.

DEEP DNA

Several websites now offer loggers-on impressive services to help trace their DNA. Tests are easy to take, all they involve is spitting into a sample container (apparently not after having drunk a cup of coffee) and sending it through the post to analysts. Newcastle University prefers blood, and in particular they are looking for the descendants of Border Reivers to carry on a long tradition and spill some – their own. At the Border History Fair held at Hexham on 2nd December 2006, many people with the right qualifications came forward. These included being able to trace all four grand-parents to the same area, either in Northumberland, North Cumbria, County Durham or the Scottish Borders. It also helped if subjects had reiver surnames such as Fenwick, Robson or Milburn. The Head of the Institute of Human Genetics at Newcastle University is Professor John Burn, a prime candidate who meets all of the criteria, although why he would actively seek a genetic link with the likes of Geordie Burn is less clear. And apart from sharing the same DNA, it would be entertaining to work out the precise connection between Old Sir John Forster and the delicate English novelist, E.M. Forster.

When Sir John's long career was only beginning, international politics pulled Borderers in various competing directions. Mary, Queen of Scots was a committed catholic and a focus for all those who continued to worship in the old faith in both England as well as Scotland. By itself that set her in opposition to the protestant Elizabeth I, who also worried over Mary's strong connections with catholic monarchs in continental Europe. The French-speaking young Queen of Scots had very recently been one herself. Further complications were added by Mary's profound wish and ambition to be named as the heir to the throne of England.

Because Elizabeth believed that Mary would ultimately prove hostile (no matter that they initially exchanged an elaborately affec-tionate correspondence, and hoped very much to meet and talk, although they never quite did), she was determined that her northern frontier would be well organised and well guarded. The new fortifica-tions at Berwick continued to rise, soaking up vast sums from the London exchequeur. Henry, Lord Scrope of Bolton, was appointed Warden of the West March and instructed to summon a commission to sort out the administration of the border, just as Thomas Wharton had done a decade before. It was also in Mary of Scotland's direct interest to show herself at least as effective a sovereign as Elizabeth if she wished to succeed her, and her wardens cooperated in the commission. Meetings were held at Carlisle and Dumfries in 1563 with Scrope, Sir John Forster and Lord John Maxwell in attendance. The agenda shed more light on the condition of law and order – and life – on the border.

With the recent resolution of the matter of the Debatable Land, more confusion over jurisdiction was not to be tolerated. Severe confiscations would punish any Scots or English (the deliberations make it clear that it was mainly Scots involved) who pastured their cattle in 'the opposite realm'. A time limit of six hours was set by the commission. Inside that period, no offence was deemed to have taken place, but over it, then the beasts would be forfeit, seized by the landowner whose pasture they were illegally grazing. The Cheviot ranges and the lower lying valleys and watersheds were open, unfenced country in the sixteenth century and cows and sheep had no idea where the border was. Therefore it made sense to allow shepherds time to turn straying beasts back to their own pasture.

Problems arose when the border was persistently ignored and Scots in particular were in the habit of attempting to establish customary rights to pasture which lay in England. One of the many complaints against Old Sir John Forster was that he turned a blind eye to this practice in the English middle march. Scots were apparently going so far as to build summer shielings in England.

Over in the west, the Grahams also drove their animals to grazings over the border, but in the other direction. After many years of doing this without hindrance, they were appalled when the Maxwells cited the laws of 1563 and seized their flocks and herds. In 1580 the Grahams fell foul again when they bought land in Scotland and simply moved over the border and settled down to sow and grow corn. There existed a general prohibition of cross-border cultivation – but the complaints about the Grahams seem like an extreme application of the law. But then they were Grahams.

Scrope, Maxwell, Forster and their clerks spent much effort on the problem of 'overswearing'. This was the sixteenth-century equivalent of an exaggerated insurance claim. When beasts had been reived and a complaint subsequently made to a warden, injured parties had got into the habit of overswearing. That is, they greatly inflated the value of what they had lost so that when fines were levied and compensation paid, they did very nicely thank you. Amongst farmers of the twenty-first century, this cultural habit may not have entirely died out. Back in 1596 Lord Scrope wrote to London with the extraordinary calculation that Borderers often claimed twenty times the value of goods lost. Some compensating increase was acceptable but this had become ridiculous. No doubt many imaginative scams were running – in both directions.

The commissioners of 1563 wished to hold Truce Days once a month, so heavy was the press of business. This proved impractical, but certain simple and draconian measures did at least clarify the legal picture and force the pace of justice. When a man committed the same offence three times, he was to be summarily executed. No doubt many were guilty, but how many answered with their lives is less certain. An unconscious note of irony ends the deliberations of the warden meetings of 1563. All should know and understand the content of what had been agreed, that is, the new laws made since the last period of 'amity and perpetual peace'.

That 1564 was considered a peaceful year on the border says much about the state of civil order. It was not as if an age of amity and perpetual peace had dawned, more that the year seems to have seen slightly less raiding and killing than usual.

The ever-canny Elizabeth I continued to strengthen her hand. After the death of Lord Grey, towards the end of 1563, she sent Francis Russell, Earl of Bedford, north to take over the wardenship of the east march. He was also made Governor of Berwick, a title with a decided colonial ring to it. On 27th March the earl arrived in the town and was much vexed to find the defences in a weak and vulnerable state, and the garrison little better, lacking in organisation. A census of 1565 counted more than 2,000 soldiers, labourers and tradesmen working at Berwick, and Russell immediately set about tightening up administration. As a second in command, he appointed a High Marshall, a Treasurer, a Chief Porter (to control traffic in and out) and a Master of the Ordnance. To set an example, Russell took his turn at doing sentry duty along the walls.

The Scots were also active, but in a very different way. In the west march the bloodfeud between the Elliots and the Scotts sparked into life. Led by Martin Elliot of Braidley, near Hermitage Castle, a party of 300 raiders made their way up Carewoodrig, over Mosspaul and descended on Scott territory around Hawick. Black smoke billowed into the air. Flooding into Liddesdale in great strength, the Scotts quickly retaliated, lifting many cattle and killing both Elliots and their close allies, the Crosers. Ill-matched, and almost overwhelmed by superior numbers, Martin Elliot was forced to play politics. Contacting Lord Scrope at Carlisle, he offered to deliver Hermitage Castle into English control and sought the protection of Elizabeth I. The Elliots would even change their nationality and become Englishmen. Scrope sensibly declined both suggestions, but he did agree to support the Elliots with cash, and if they needed occasionally to escape the Scotts by crossing the border, the warden would turn a blind eye. For all the surface talk of amity and perpetual peace, the privy council were happy quietly and ruthlessly to encourage mayhem in the Scottish borders. Sir John Forster, as usual, understood the situation better than most: 'the longer such conditions continue . . . the better quiet we shall be', meaning it was much preferable to see the Scots fighting amongst themselves than raiding over the border.

Despite the number of bloodfeuds (almost 40 were festering at that time on the middle and east marches), there is an increasing sense of raiding being seen as international rather than internecine. It may be an impression formed by the nature of the sources, but the Scots seemed to be directing their raids more towards England and vice-versa.

Feuds were different. Usually carried on amongst neighbours of the same nationality, they tended to be local affairs. In Northumberland the Herons feuded with the Carrs over the ownership of Ford Castle, and were said to wish to 'overthrow each other rather than face the enemy', and the Forsters were at odds with the Muschamps and with the Greys. By 1560 Lord Grey, Francis Russells's predecessor in the English east march, was complaining that everyday life was coloured by continual feuding: 'there is daily armour and weapon used both to the church, the market and the field, as in time of war: as no man here minds to deal in the matter, it is needful that some be sent from the Queen and Council to make an end hereof'.

Some brave, or foolhardy, people occasionally took matters into their own hands and intervened. When Bernard Gilpin was preaching at Rothbury Parish Church in Coquetdale in 1566, he noticed the Heron family in the congregation, fully armed, and also the Lisles and Ellerkers – with whom they were at feud. Paying little attention to the service, both sides glared at each other and appeared to be moving closer. Swords were drawn and then sheathed. When they were drawn a second time, Gilpin halted the service and his sermon, and he:

came down from the pulpit, and stepping to the ringleaders of either faction, first of all he appeased the tumult. Next he laboured to establish peace between them, but he could not prevail in that: only they promised to keep the peace unbroken so long as Mr Gilpin should remain in the church.

When it became clear that that was as much as he could achieve, Gilpin climbed back into his pulpit 'and spent the rest of the alloted time which remained in disgracing that barbarous and bloody custom of theirs'.

The commissioners of 1563 at Dumfries and Carlisle were anxious to revive and clarify the old practice of hot trod, which encouraged the immediate pursuit of stolen goods and thieves even if it involved crossing the border. One of the difficulties was an understandable fear of feud. Many law-abiding farmers relieved of their beasts believed that reprisals would follow any successful hot trod, or indeed a Cold Trod. It was simply not worth the risk, better to seek redress through the wardenries, or accept the loss. In this way feuding in an increasingly fearful society greatly hindered the administration of justice.

At Berwick the new defences spoke loudly of the possibility of war between Scotland and England. No one had ever seen such massive walls, and the ruthlessness which had demolished many houses on the north and eastern sides of the town to create open fields of fire underlined how seriously Elizabeth took that possibility. Even the medieval castle of Berwick, where Edward I had listened to claimants for the throne of Scotland in the 1290s, had been left outside the perimeter.

Nevertheless, diplomacy tried to keep pace with construction (to say nothing of the funding of the feuding Elliots in the west) and Francis Russell was directed to convene a meeting at Berwick to discuss the pressing matter of dynastic politics. Elizabeth was strongly suggesting her favourite, Robert Dudley, Earl of Leicester, as a suitable match for Mary, Queen of Scots, but as a rival queen, she felt that his rank was inferior, 'unequal and dishonourable', as one nineteenth-century historian remarked. For three days Russell, Randolph, the English ambassador in Edinburgh, and Lord James Stewart, Earl of Moray and William Maitland of Lethington, Mary's Secretary of State discussed the matter and arrived at no conclusion. Eight months later the young queen arrived at her own and married Henry Stewart, Lord Darnley, a sufficiently distant cousin. He was 21 years old, possessed of the Stewart good looks, the Stewart arrogance and the Stewart recklessness. Through his mother, he was also the eldest male descendant of Henry VII's eldest daughter which gave him as powerful a claim on Elizabeth's throne as Mary's.

The Darnley marriage hardened attitudes – on both sides of the border. Mary's half-brother, James, Earl of Moray, felt compelled to rise in the armed rebellion known as 'the Chaseabout Raid'. Battle was never joined and after only a few weeks, Moray was isolated. Most of the major surnames in the south, the Maxwells, both branches of the Kerrs and the Humes remained loyal to Mary. By September Moray was in Dumfries pleading for English support. Elizabeth sent £1,000 and the Earl of Bedford gave £500 on his own account. The English ambassador, Thomas Randolph, advised the privy council to maintain their subsidy to the Elliots so that they continued to raid the Humes in the east march 'and kept them at home'. Substantial bands of reivers began to ride again, and in the west march the Maxwell/Johnstone feud found some pretext or other to flare up into renewed bitterness.

THE CHEVIOT, THE LAMBS AND THE BLEAK, BLEAK HILLS

Hardiness was and remains the basic quality of those sheep bred for meat in the Border hills. Lincoln rams and some Leicester bloodlines were used in the eighteenth century to improve the breed and generally produce larger animals. But it is their ability to live out on the windy hills and high valleys all year round which is reckoned to make their meat so dense and flavourful. Hay is only dropped for them when the snow is deepest and even the most determined ewe cannot scrape her way down to the bitter winter grass. Hill lambs mature late, having seen at least one winter, and the grazing they live on is entirely natural, with all its herbs and different varieties of grass, the very definition of organic. The older ewes are often sold to lower-lying farms where the climate is kinder and a longer productive life is possible.

Work at Berwick accelerated and the Earl of Bedford was encouraged both to promote discord, but quietly, over the border and also to hold his garrison in a state of readiness. The moment for action came when two of the Berwick captains led 800 riders to pillage the nearby villages of Chirnside and Edington, and to lift stock and take prisoners. The exchange of protests and protestations of innocence and misunderstanding which followed the raid was a classic passage of sixteenth-century frontier diplomacy.

When Mary, Queen of Scots' council complained and asked Elizabeth to reprimand Bedford for such a flagrant breach, they received a reply which was convoluted in its reasoning but, given the fondness of Borderers for punch and counter-punch, not altogether implausible. The English claimed that they had only attacked Chirnside because they themselves had been ambushed by a party of Scots some time beforehand. These Scots had captured a few Englishmen, who themselves were attempting to take prisoner other Scots (or possibly the same Scots who ambushed them in the first place) who had been robbing both Scots and English on either side of the border. So the expedition was not an unprovoked attack but rather a rescue attempt. And anyway there were only 400 riders in the party, not 800. In a master-stroke of po-faced hypocrisy, Elizabeth ordered Bedford to make sure the laws were respected and complaints properly heard. So there.

Despite all the diplomatic froth, 1565 saw the general atmosphere darken. Maxwell was attending to the state of his fortresses in the west, and James Hepburn, the Earl of Bothwell, had command of a troop of horsemen and was attempting to subdue the English-backed Elliots in Liddesdale, though with only mixed success. A year later Little Jock Elliot was to deal a hefty blow to Bothwell's prestige.

As part of their marriage settlement, Mary insisted that her young husband be recognised as 'Henry, King of Scots'. It all seems to have quickly gone to his head, and there were reports of near-insufferable swagger and arrogance. Darnley and Mary had been married by catholic rite, and although he had come to Scotland religiously neutral, the new king embraced the old faith when he attended mass at Christmas 1565. It was said that afterwards he strutted along Edinburgh's High Street announcing that with his reconversion all Scotland had come back to catholicism. Reaction to this found scandalous expression in the murder of Mary's Italian secretary, David Riccio, by a band of protestant lords. The fact that Darnley's was one of the daggers left in the corpse shows inconsistency at the very least and also substantial dashes of jealousy and rashness. At court and around Edinburgh the hotheaded King Henry was rapidly finding himself an excluded, almost irrelevant figure.

Nevertheless he did serve one vital dynastic purpose. Darnley fathered a son on his queen and in June 1566 the baby who would become James VI and I was born. Three months later Mary led a judicial expedition to deal with the ever-present problems of the Borders. Levies were summoned to muster at Melrose on 8th October, and from there the queen rode with her small army to Jedburgh. Assizes were put in session for six days. Apparently the trend was for offenders to be heavily fined – if they had the cash. The historian, Robert Lindsay of Pitscottie, reported that 'poor men were hanged and rich men were hanged by their purses'.

At some point during the assizes, Queen Mary heard that Bothwell had been attacked by Little Jock Elliot of the Park, and then carried in a litter, badly, maybe fatally wounded, back to Hermitage Castle. No doubt against all advice, to say nothing of common sense, Mary set out to ride from Jedburgh, through dangerous Elliot country, to Hermitage and back – in a day. It is not an easy journey from Hawick up the valley of the Slitrig to the bleak high pass over Whitrope and down into Liddesdale, and the fact that Mary could not be dissuaded from making it speaks of the play of powerful emotions. The round trip was nearly 50 miles on horseback, no mean physical feat for a fit man and a hardy, surefooted pony, and a tremendous challenge for a slight, 24-year-old woman only four months after giving birth to her first child. No other explanation for this rashness fits so well as the simple likelihood that the queen had fallen madly in love with Bothwell. Memorably described as 'a man sold to all wickedness', he was just that, a man, a vital, brave and dynamic man, and not a preening boy or a sickly French prince.

After spending only two hours with the wounded earl at Hermitage, Mary climbed wearily back into the saddle for the long journey back to Jedburgh. It was 16th October, a short autumn day. And it may have been that in the gathering gloaming, her little grey pony missed its footing and threw the queen headlong into a marsh. Probably soaked through, Mary and her escort trudged back to Jedburgh. The house where she lodged still stands; it had been lent by the Kerrs of Ferniehurst.

The day after her return, the queen fell gravely ill, possibly having contracted pneumonia as a result of her soaking. Fevered, fainting, Mary believed that her last hours and days had come, and when the illness allowed, she began to make her peace. For her nobility, or 'governors', unity was what mattered above all:

> You know that by the division of governors, provinces and regions
> are troubled and molested, and contrariwise, by agreement and

unity, they are stabilised, pacified and advanced. Therefore above all things, I require you to have charity, concord and love amongst yourselves.

To du Croc, the French ambassador, she asked:

Commend me to the king, your master: tell him I hope he will protect my dear son, and also that he will grant one year of my dowry, after my death, to pay my debts and reward my faithful servants: but above all, tell the Queen-Mother that I heartily ask her forgiveness for the offences I may have either done, or have been supposed to have committed against her.

Despite her conviction that the end would soon come, Mary's illness reached its crisis after six days and her doctors were optimistic: 'Her Majesty has been sick these six days past, and this night had some dwams of swooning, which puts men in some fear. Nevertheless we see no tokens of death.'

On 25th October the Earl of Bothwell was brought to Jedburgh after an uncomfortable journey on a horse-litter from Hermitage Castle. Lord Darnley arrived three days later when the queen was almost recovered but he was not well received by the earls and lords attending her, and indeed he may not have been permitted to see his sick wife. In any event King Henry stayed only one night, not lodging in the same house, but with Lord Hume in the High Street. The presence of his rival, the cause of all the alarm, cannot have made for conviviality, but all was clearly well with Mary by 30 October, when a messenger was dispatched to Edinburgh to buy and bring red silk, black taffeta and black velvet to make a new gown. She had survived but the business of bringing justice to the Borders had almost cost Mary her life. The remainder of her reign would turn out to be brief and the rest of her life nothing but a deepening disappointment, and she was sometimes heard during her long imprisonment to remark that she wished she had died in Jedburgh.

BUSTLE AT THE BASTLE

When Mary, Queen of Scots stayed in Jedburgh in 1566, she and her entourage of ladies took over a large house owned by the Kerrs of Ferniehurst. It had survived the terrible destruction of the English raids of the 1540s and been much added to since. Originally a near-indestructible bastle house, it was heightened, climbing to four storeys, although the windows remained sensibly and defensibly small. The staircase supports the theory of the left-handed Kerrs since it has the rope/handrail on that side. Rather as happens before modern royal visits, a new toilet was installed for the queen's use, and for her ladies. At Jedburgh Mary was attended exclusively by her identically named body servants, the famous Four Marys: Mary Seaton, Mary Beaton, Mary Fleming and Mary Livingston. Confusing. In 1987 the house was refurbished and opened to visitors. For some reason it was timed to coincide with the 400th anniversary of Mary's execution.

Fully recovered, the queen led her retinue eastwards to visit Hume Castle, and from there on to Berwick and Eyemouth. The frontier around the town encloses a substantial pale, a tract of good farmland sufficiently large to feed at least some of the garrison, and it is marked by the Bound Road. There Sir John Forster met Queen Mary, probably at Mordington Bridge, on the old road from Duns. Bothwell rode with her and Lord Hume and Walter Kerr of Cessford had 500 men in attendance. They made their way down to Halidon Hill, the site of the Scots' dreadful defeat at the hands of Edward III's archers in 1333 and a place where they could see the town of Berwick and its splendid new walls. Any sense of historical irony was not recorded. The Master of the Ordnance fired a volley from his cannon in salute, but as the queen dismounted she was kicked by Sir John's pony, and while managing to conduct a meeting on cross-border business, she grew very uncomfortable. In fact the pain and bruising were so severe that Mary was forced to abandon the planned visit to Eyemouth and retrace her steps to Hume Castle to rest for two days. Clearly the Borders was not a lucky place for her majesty.

As raiding grew into an ever more constant sore in the second half of the sixteenth century, ill luck struck many. At the end of a winding track in the high country on the southern flanks of the Ettrick Valley lies the remote farm of Dodhead. Walter Scott made it famous because he preserved and 'improved' a ballad which told the unlucky tale of the laird, 'Jamie Telfer o' the Fair Dodheid'. The people named in its verses were real and they set the action probably in the 1570s, possibly as late as the 1590s. It tells the sorry tale of the victim of a raid into Scotland, and tells it with verve – and even a happy ending. The Captain of the fort at Bewcastle, a government officer, raided the farm and lifted all of Telfer's cattle:

> There's nothing left in the fair Dodhead,
> But a greeting wife and bairnies three,
> And six poor calves stand in the stall.
> A routing loud for their minnie.

Even the least of the Border lairds had connections they could call upon in extremis, and Jamie immediately rode over the hills to Stobs in the Slitrig Valley, below Hawick. But Gibbie Elliot refused to join the hot trod after Bewcastle, telling Telfer that he should seek help from those to whom he paid blackmail. There are suspicious echoes of the Elliot links with the English March Wardens and their generous subsidies, and the local politics of the Elliot/Scott feud persuaded the persistent Jamie to ride down to Teviotdale. At Branxholm, Buccleuch promised to raise 'the water', meaning all of his people who lived by Teviot Water.

> Go warn the water, broad and wide,
> Go warn it soon and hastily!
> They that will not ride for Telfer's cows,
> Let them never look in the face o' me.

> Warn Wat o' Harden and his sons,
> With them will Borthwick Water ride,
> Warn Goldilands and Allanhaugh,
> And Gilmanscleuch, and Commonside.

The intended route of the hot trod was made clear by Walter Scott of Buccleuch's instructions. After mustering a party at Branxholm, Telfer and the Scotts planned to ride up Teviotdale to the watershed at Mosspaul, and then up over Carewoodrig and down into Liddesdale:

> Ride by the gate at Priesthaughswire
> And warn the Currors o' the Lee;
> As you come down the Hermitage Slack,
> Warn doughty Willie o' Gorrenberry.

But they caught them up much sooner than Buccleuch believed they would, coming on the Captain of Bewcastle and his stolen cattle making a weary way up the narrow pass carved by the Frostlie Burn. It was a classic example of fast-moving pursuers overtaking a party of thieves ponderous with too much plunder. It often happened, and was the reason why a hot trod was encouraged. Telfer and the Scotts first tried talking, but negotiations quickly failed. 'Set on!' shouted young Willie Scott and a furious fight ensued along the banks of the little burn:

> Then to it they went with heart and hand,
> The blows fell thick as bickering hail,
> And many a horse ran masterless,
> And many a comely cheek was pale.

First into the thick of the fray, Willie Scott was killed, and his kinsman (perhaps even his natural father), Auld Wat of Harden, was enraged. All the Scotts roared for revenge, led into the ruck of the fighting by the barrel-chested, bull-like old warrior:

> But he's taken off his good steel cap,
> And thrice he's waved it in the air;
> The Dinlay snow was never more white
> Than the lyart locks o' Harden's hair.

> 'Revenge! Revenge!' Auld Wat did cry,
> 'Fye lads, lay on them cruelly!
> We'll never see Teviotside again
> Until Willie's death revenged shall be.'

> O, many a horse ran masterless,
> The splintered lances flew on high,
> But before they won the Kershope Ford,
> The Scotts had gotten the victory.

Jamie Telfer had his cows back, but the cost had been heavy. As well as young Willie Scott, thirty of the Bewcastle troopers had been killed, and although in its triumph the ballad does not name them, more Scotts probably fell by the Frostlie Burn. The Captain of Bewcastle had been taken prisoner – and perhaps he might prove useful.

There was a price to be extracted for all that blood, and Auld Wat rallied his surname to him. In what might have been a pre-arranged plan, and what would certainly have supplied a motive, the pursuers turned into raiders and made their way down into Liddesdale. Their target was Stonegarthside Hall, an impressive house which still stands by the roadside south of Kershopefoot. It belonged to the Captain of Bewcastle and the Scotts intended to return the compliment by lifting his cows. Auld Wat probably reckoned to manage all without a fight, enough Scott blood had been spilled that day, by offering the captured captain in exchange for his beasts.

Recorded in a ballad much repeated and probably more than a little altered (in fact there is a version in which the Elliots did ride to help Dodheid – and it is true that Sir Walter Scott sometimes inserted the Scotts into unwarranted starring roles), the tale of Jamie Telfer o' the Fair Dodheid nevertheless carries the marks of authenticity. It feels as though it was composed soon after the event when memory was fresh and the details reliable. It was the small change of life on the frontier, a routine raid and counter-raid, conducted in part under the walls of Hermitage Castle and in the jurisdiction of the Keeper of Liddesdale.

In 1567 the Earl of Bothwell was not at Hermitage, but in Edinburgh, and although historians have argued the facts endlessly, it appears that he was involved in plotting the death of King Henry Darnley. At Jedburgh and elsewhere it was said that Mary, Queen of Scots had made it clear that she could no longer stand the sight of her feckless husband and in fact longed to be rid of him. Divorce was possible but that option might have compromised the legitimacy of her precious son and heir, Prince James. That left only one other course of action, but in the dark recesses of hatred, passion and boundless ambition, who knows if the queen said more?

In any event, gunpowder changed the political landscape spectacularly. In February 1567 Darnley's house at Kirk o' Field, which lay just outside the Flodden wall to the south of Edinburgh, was blown up. The strangled corpse of the young king was found in the garden. Who did it? Whatever the evidence and the actual truth of the matter, the Earl of Bothwell was widely suspected. Due process was required. The death of a king, albeit one only in name, had occurred and someone had to stand trial. Bothwell appeared in front of a jury on 12th April, and a well-armed troop of riders hung around near at hand to make sure the correct verdict was arrived at. It was. And the growing scandal began to gather momentum.

When Mary took the next step, even if it was with Bothwell's hand on her neck, by marrying him on 15th May, matters had gone beyond repair. The couple had lost the support of most of the nobility. Darnley had been a joke and his removal almost tolerable, but Bothwell as Mary's husband and potentially king-consort could be dangerous. And appearances were important. Mary had profoundly stained the institution of monarchy by seeming to have encouraged the murder of her husband, and then becoming the wife, willing or not, of the man suspected of that murder. Public opinion ran strongly against the queen and her lover, and her government of Scotland began to wobble.

FÊTE ACCOMPLI

The baptism of the infant James VI was marked by the staging of the first Renaissance fête ever seen in Britain. On the esplanade of Stirling Castle a wooden fort was built and defended in a mock siege. As fireworks crackled and flashed, 'wild Highland men' and other agents of anarchy (surprisingly, no Border Reivers are reported) were beaten back by Mary, Queen of Scots' valiant garrison. The fête was based on spectacles seen by the queen, and specifically on the lavish entertainments mounted on the French/Spanish border by the young French king, Charles IX in 1564-5. Like these, the Stirling extravaganza was intended to symbolise the power and durability of the Stewart dynasty while stressing the need for religious tolerance and friendship between England and Scotland. As in the French celebrations, a political message was made unmissable and explicit. The following was composed by Patrick Adamson, a Protestant minister.

Our leader has transposed Mars ablaze with civil war into peace in our time . . .

A powerful young woman, whose race was from the lofty blood of kings, controls by her rule the warlike Scots . . .

The importance of kingship is eternal; it will be in the power of the Stewart family; the crown of Mary awaits her grandsons . . .

The fates will grant you to extend the territory of your realm, until the Britons, having finished with war, will learn at last to unite in one kingdom.

Chased by Lord Hume and 800 riders, Mary and Bothwell fled from Edinburgh, first to Borthwick Castle in Midlothian and then to Dunbar. On 15th June the crisis came to a head when the Confederate Lords, the coalition formed to oppose the queen, met her forces in battle order at Carberry, south of Musselburgh. After a day of talking rather than fighting, Bothwell was granted a safe conduct into exile (he died in Denmark) and Mary was taken into the custody of the lords. When she reached Edinburgh, the mob chanted, 'Burn the whore! Burn the whore!'

There was to be a dramatic escape from the castle on Loch Leven and a losing battle to fight at Langside near Glasgow, but compromise at Carberry signalled the effective end of the reign of Mary, Queen of Scots. She abdicated in favour of her son in July 1567 and the little boy was crowned James VI at Stirling a few days later.

Meanwhile it was business as usual in the Borders. Turmoil at the heart of central government always encouraged the reiving families to saddle up, and as the autumn and winter of 1567 came on, they rode hard and often for plunder.

James Stewart, Earl of Moray, was named Regent again and he quickly determined to stamp on disorder in the south. A central difficulty faced by many large and well-advertised judicial expeditions was that the really hardened elements often ignored summons to appear before the court. In October 1567, Moray quietly gathered a small force with Lords Lindsay and Hume and the Earl of Morton, and suddenly descended on Hawick, hoping to surprise Liddesdale men in the town. The intelligence was good and 40 reivers were captured. Some were drowned in the pools where the Slitrig meets the Teviot, others were taken for trial in Edinburgh.

A year later, Moray was in the marches again, this time with 6,000 men in the west, making sure that Queen Mary's Maxwell supporters did not stir. On the English side Lord Hunsdon, lately made Warden of the East March, was dishing out summary justice to Teviotdale reivers, and with Sir John Forster he cooperated with Moray in keeping the Borders quiet.

Under house arrest in England, moved from Carlisle to Bolton Castle, Mary remained a focus for the catholic cause. Supporters proposed a marriage to the catholic Duke of Norfolk (with a clause insisting that Prince James would be betrothed to Norfolk's daughter), but it was pie in the political sky. To no one's surprise, Elizabeth frowned at the idea. Within months Norfolk found himself in the

Tower of London, indicted for alleged treason and certain recusancy. His execution shocked the predominantly catholic northern aristocracy and his brother-in-law, Charles Neville, Earl of Westmorland, began to ponder the removal of his queen, her replacement with Mary and the restoration of the old faith.

BRING BACK BOTHWELL

After the debacle at Carberry, James Hepburn, Earl of Bothwell, fled, ultimately to Denmark. Captured in 1567, he was imprisoned in grim conditions at Dragsholm Castle on the island of Zeeland. Apparently he spent the rest of his life chained to a stake half his height. This may have been a means of restraining him because it is said that Bothwell went mad. Cause and effect are difficult to disentangle. After ten years in the dungeon, Hepburn died and, surprisingly, his body was mummified and now lies in Faravejle Church, near Dragsholm. Tourists are encouraged to visit the last resting place of 'a Scottish king'. Bothwell's direct descendant, Captain Sir Alastair Buchan-Hepburn, is campaigning to have the body returned to Scotland. The Danes are unwilling – for the strange reason that they believe the mummy may not be the earl. Buchan-Hepburn has offered to have his DNA compared with it, and if there is a match, which there should be if it is indeed Bothwell, then it should be brought back to Scotland. Perhaps the Danes will relent.

Thomas Percy, Earl of Northumberland, had approached Lord Scrope, Warden of the English West March, when he had the Scottish queen temporarily in his custody at Carlisle Castle. He attempted to persuade him that protocol would be served if she was released into his keeping. Percy had remained a catholic, not thought reliable by Elizabeth I and Scrope wisely declined his kind offer. And so when the Earl of Westmorland looked for support in his rebellious plans, he did not have to look far.

With the help of highly talented and utterly loyal civil servants such as Thomas Cromwell, Robert Cecil and Francis Walsingham, the Tudors had built up an efficient, centralised administration which could be run from London. A vital function was the gathering of intelligence and its use in formulating policy. Walsingham and Cecil, men who depended entirely on Elizabeth I for their status and advancement and were not powerful hereditary landowners, created a network of informants whose tentacles reached into every corner of England – and many in Scotland, Wales and Ireland. In 1569 it was only a matter of time before London got wind of Westmorland and Northumberland's treasonable talk. Subsequent events showed considerable incompetence, and it seems likely that in formulating plans proper secrecy and discretion were not observed. The earls had been in touch with the Spanish for help, and written to the Duke of Alva, Governor of the Netherlands.

When Elizabeth sent word to Westmorland and Northumberland, summoning them to appear at court in Windsor, they flapped into a panic, believing that royal spies had discovered their plot. They probably had sniffed something, but Westmorland flew into precipitate – and pointless – activity. It was said that it took threats and cajolements to stir Northumberland into rebellion. No coherent plan of campaign appeared to exist, and when it quickly became clear that help was not on its way from the Spanish Netherlands (a fleet was expected at Hartlepool) or from catholic sympathisers amongst the Border heidsmen, the earls panicked even more and began to think of flight rather than victory. With Sir John Forster standing firm, having retaken the castles at Alnwick and Warkworth (without a fight) and fortified Newcastle, and the Regent Moray recently arrived in the Borders with soldiers at his command, options and time began to run out.

At Hexham the rebel army disintegrated and Westmorland and Northumberland ran for it. Their support now only a personal bodyguard of forty or so faithful men, the earls and Lady Anne, Countess of Northumberland, fled for shelter to Naworth, the house of Leonard Dacre, a local catholic lord. His door remained firmly shut, and at midnight on 20th December, in desperation, they took the only course remaining and rode into the nest of thieves and outlaws that was Liddesdale.

It was a headlong descent. Charles Neville, Thomas Percy and his wife, Lady Anne, were now entirely at the mercy of men like Jock o' the Side Armstrong and Black James Ormiston, one of the killers hired to stab David Riccio to death. Hoping that the rising would succeed, Mary, Queen of Scots had written to catholic sympathisers amongst the Border surnames, and so the arrival of the earls in Liddesdale was not exactly a surprise, even if the circumstances were certainly a disappointment. But Ormiston and Armstrong were ruthless reivers, thieves for whom everything – and everyone – had a price.

Through her agents Elizabeth I let it be known that she was willing to pay handsomely for the traitors, while on the Scottish side, the Regent Moray was similarly disposed, anxious not to offend England. Black Ormiston and Jock Armstrong must have rubbed their hands in glee at the thought of a lucrative auction. Sleeping on the earthen floors of what they certainly thought of as miserable, verminous, freezing hovels, changing their expensive and conspicuous clothes for the rough cloth of ordinary people, the earls and their countess no doubt looked at each other and pondered the high price of rebellion.

The Regent Moray wasted no time. Messages were got through the winter weather to the mercurial Martin Elliot of Braidley. He rode with three hundred to deliver an ultimatum to Black Ormiston. The earls could not stay in Scotland, their presence was a political embarrassment. They were to be gone in a day – or else. Ormiston acted immediately and moved the fugitives down the Liddel Water to Harelaw, the tower of Hector Armstrong. It lay only half a mile from the border. Westmorland and Northumberland had been stripped of all they owned. Countess Anne had been left behind in Liddesdale, her value as a captive probably the only thing keeping her from greater indignities at the grubby hands of Jock o' the Side and his crew of unwashed ruffians. The lady was a famous beauty, and will have no doubt been a sore temptation.

At Harelaw, Hector Armstrong managed somehow to detach Northumberland from Westmorland and those men who had stayed with him. Despite Armstrong 'having obligations' to the earl, he promptly sold him for cash to the agents of the Regent Moray. Westmorland attempted a rescue but Thomas Percy was hurried away to prison in the castle of Loch Leven, no doubt more secure than when it failed to hold Queen Mary.

Meanwhile the catholic Kerrs of Ferniehurst had saddled their ponies. Riding down into Liddesdale, they released Lady Anne and the feckless Earl of Westmorland and took them back to the comfort of warm firesides, clean clothes and some deference to their rank. Sir Thomas Kerr did not trouble to conceal his guests. When an English spy talked his way into Ferniehurst, he casually came across the Earl of Westmorland out walking, apparently unconcerned about security or that persons unknown to him might approach. Such laxness would soon cost Kerr dear.

The rebels were also looked after by the Scotts of Buccleuch at Branxholm before making their miserable way into exile in Flanders. Surprisingly the Border heidsmen appear to have acted solely out of fellow feeling for those who clung to the old faith. After a failed, shambolic attempt at rebellion in the north of England, there could be absolutely nothing in it politically for them, but their support showed how easy it was for powerful Borderers to ignore government policy and act independently. The English were sore displeased, and here is Lord Hunsdon's letter of 9 January to the Regent Moray:

> That notwithstanding his grace's direct proclamations against receiving or aiding the queen's rebels anywhere in Scotland, yet the Earl of Westmorland and others were openly kept in Ferniehurst, and some others of them at Branxholm with Buccleuch, others of them with Bedrule, Andrew Kerr, and the Sheriff of Teviotdale. And upon Thursday night last, the Countess of Northumberland was brought by Ferniehurst towards Hume Castle, and was forced to stay by the way at Roxburgh, by the soreness of the weather (being a great storm), so as it was eight o' clock on Friday morning ere she came to Hume . . . The Regent well knew that the queen could not take this well at their hands, especially at Lord Hume's . . . and she [may] make him repent his folly.

A letter to the Earl of Leicester ends the sorry tale of the Rising of the Northern Earls with a footnote on the fate of Lady Anne:

> The Countess of Northumberland retired out of Scotland for very penury, being miserably treated there, and forced for her safety to move from friend to friend without rest, fearing always to be spoiled by these barbarous people.

Hunsdon's letter to Moray was imporant for more than political reasons. Unusually it mentions the weather; but then the weather in the 1570s was itself unusual. The great storm which delayed the Countess of Northumberland at Roxburgh was only one of many in that rainy and windswept decade. Elizabeth I's efforts to bring the rebel earls to justice were much hampered by severe weather in Yorkshire, and the Earl of Sussex was forced to delay his expedition into Scotland. Three years later 'a tempest' lasting more than a week washed away part of Berwick's circuit of medieval walls. In 1587 what was described as 'stormy and contagious weather' did at least have the effect of discouraging raiding for a few weeks. It must have been bad. The year after that the Spanish Armada famously suffered in terrible conditions around the coasts of Britain.

There are not many reports noting the weather in the late sixteenth century, but that fact in itself makes a concentration of them at the beginning of the 1570s all the more significant. It was also the period when the last and most intense period of reiving began, and these two facts cannot be a coincidence.

THE DEEP MIDWINTER

Perhaps one of the most popular winter scenes ever painted and reproduced on endless Christmas cards, Peter Breughel the Elder's *Hunters in the Snow* is more than a great work of art. It is also a historical document. The year it appeared, 1565, was the worst winter anyone could remember. Right across northern Europe the snow lay deep and crisp and even – for months. What Breughel's painting recorded was the dawn of a new phase in the little ice age. In the Alps glaciers creaked and groaned once more. Many moved down to the edges of the high valleys, overwhelming villages, scraping over and enveloping pasture, laying down sheets of thick ice on the fields. Near Chamonix, deep in the western ranges of the Alps, shepherds watched in horror as the huge 'mer de glace', the ice sea, slid even faster down the slopes of the Mont Blanc massif. Grinding down the mountain side, it seemed that the long-dormant glacier would obliterate all in its path. Priests brought out the images of saints and whole communities knelt in the snow to pray for God's help in stopping the river of ice. And it worked. The weather warmed enough to convert the glacier into a raging torrent – damaging, but disposable.

After the failure of Leonard Dacre's rebellion in early 1570 and the murder of the pro-English Regent Moray, Elizabeth I determined to suppress support for Mary, Queen of Scots, the catholic faith and the ever-present possibility of foreign invasion. And if the Scottish central government could not keep the Borders and the likes of Kerr of Cessford and Scott of Buccleuch under control, then she would do it herself. Commissioned by the queen to raise a punitive expeditionary force, the Earl of Sussex began his muster. Despite the weather, he managed to scrape together 1,000 horse and 3,000 foot soldiers. They would be augmented as he rode north. When news of the invasion spread – and it was no less than that, an invasion of Scotland by English troops – the Scots reacted. Cessford and Buccleuch sought a truce, which was rejected out of hand, ordinary Borderers 'threshed their corn [so that they could take it with them in sacks]', fled with their cattle and unthatched their houses, and in the west the catholic Maxwells began their own muster. No one knew it at the time, but the 1570 English invasions were not one more episode in an endlessly repeating pattern. This would be the last of them.

Moray's death at the hands of a sniper gave Elizabeth sufficient an excuse. The young James VI was being kept safe in Stirling Castle by its constables, the Eskine family. But over the rest of Scotland government was less secure. The regency passed to the catholic Earl of Lennox, Matthew Stewart, the father of the unfortunate Henry, Lord Darnley. Evidently Lennox was devoted to his wife, his chief counsellor and encouragement. On Moray's death, Elizabeth promoted Lennox enthusiastically for the regency but sought insurance for his good behaviour by keeping his beloved countess under house arrest in England. None of this mattered for very long, since in 1571 he was attacked in the streets of Edinburgh by a supporter of Mary, Queen of Scots and stabbed to death. The Earl of Mar stepped gingerly into Lennox' shoes. After two assassinations in quick succession, the regency was clearly a dangerous commission – and so it continued to prove. Mar lasted no time at all, succumbing, it was widely believed, to poison in 1573.

All of these fatal rounds of musical chairs were music indeed to the ears of the reivers. Kerr of Cessford and Scott of Buccleuch went largely unpunished by any of these short-lived administrations – but not by Elizabeth I. In April 1570 the Earl of Sussex' army tramped out of Berwick, and keeping to the southern bank of the Tweed, they crossed by 'the dry march' at the Reddenburn, near Kelso. At first, the force of 5,000 or so seemed to be moving fast, avoiding the obvious target of Kelso, pausing only to burn a Scott tower near Eckford and a Kerr stronghold near Crailing. At Jedburgh, where the provost and baillies were sound supporters of the young king and the protestant faith, Sussex made rendezvous with Old Sir John Forster who had led the men of the middle march over the Cheviot tops and down the narrow valley of the Jed. Once these two had met and made plans, systematic destruction began.

Z

There is frequent confusion and indeed some mystery about the occasional inclusion of a silent 'z' in Scottish words and names. Menzies, Kailzie and several more. Tailzie, for example, has a puzzling pronunciation. The French fashionable at the Scottish court of the first half of the sixteenth century seems to be the linguistic culprit. The 'z' appears in Scots borrowings to help render the double 'l' or 'yi' sound in French words. So 'tailzie', meaning entail, has the alternative spelling of 'tailyie' and it comes from the French 'taille' which freely translates as 'arrangement'. Sir Menzies Campbell, the Liberal politician, correctly calls himself 'Mingis', although, distressingly, the English tended to pronounce the silent 'z', especially when there existed a chain of newsagents of the same name. When at Jedburgh Mary, Queen of Scots sent to Edinburgh for 'abulziements', she probably asked her ladies to order 'habillements'. S'il vous plait.

An early target was the Scott town of Hawick. But when the English closed in, they could see a plume of smoke billowing on the western horizon. By the time their scouts breasted the ridge above the Teviot at Cavers, it looked as though the town was ablaze. The more experienced soldiers had an inkling of what had happened. Having had enough warning, the townspeople had pulled the thatch down off their roofs, piled it up in the streets and set fire to it. This removed the handiest means for pillaging soldiers to burn their houses. All that remained were rows of wood and stone skeletons – which would take some trouble to light, hopefully more trouble than Sussex' men had time for.

All the inhabitants had gone, taking every beast and scrap of food with them into the hill country around Hawick. Instead of starting them, the English soldiers were forced to put out the fires and to eat what small rations they had brought with them. All of the larger goods, furniture and the like, had been crammed into Drumlanrig's Tower at the west end of the High Street, by the bridge over the Slitrig. No mention is made of the stronghold being stormed. After decades of invasion, it seems that Borderers were at last becoming skilled at minimising the mess.

Teviotdale had a harder time. Farms were not easily defended and much and many will have perished in the flames. Ferniehurst Castle was badly knocked about but the English sappers failed to bring down all of its walls with gunpowder. Tunnelling was used instead, and with some effect. The rest of the Kerr country down towards Kelso was wasted, Sussex's men leaving 'never a house or tower unburnt'. Cessford and Lord Hume came to the English camp to plead for clemency, but when both declined to give hostages or to betray the rebels they had harboured, they were sent packing. Battered by artillery deployed on the heights to the north east, Hume Castle surrendered and was garrisoned by an English force.

At the same time, the Warden of the English West March, Lord Scrope, was moving through Dumfriesshire, burning as he went. United for once, Lord Maxwell and James Johnstone attacked a small force commanded by Simon Musgrave and very nearly gave them a hiding. Scrope rode hard from Cummertrees with reinforcements, arriving just in time to turn the battle. He had the help, almost inevitably, of Liddesdale Armstrongs and no doubt they extracted a good price from the English warden as well as settling some old scores in Dumfriesshire.

Elizabeth I's strategy worked well. During the shaky years of Moray, Lennox and Mar, her wardens rode often across the border, forcing the catholic heidsmen like Scott, Maxwell, Hume and Kerr to stay at home and defend their property as best they could. She allowed them no opportunity to unite with sympathetic lords in the centre and north of Scotland, and lend their considerable military muscle to Mary's cause. By the end of 1570, they had all made their peace with the English queen, pledging to become supporters of the young James VI. The game was up for the Earl of Westmorland, and from Aberdeen he took ship for Flanders, the Spanish, and political oblivion.

For the first few winter months of 1571 the Borders was quiet. Even though it was the favoured season for raiding, hoofbeats were rarely heard on the hill trails after darkness. Part of the reason was a series of devastating storms, one of which washed away several arches of Berwick Old Bridge. Civil war flickered in Scotland, but the Border surnames were rarely involved. James Douglas, Earl of Morton, began to establish himself as Regent, and he wisely took a pro-English position. One of his earliest actions was to sell the captive Earl of Northumberland to Lord Hunsdon, Warden of the English East March, for £2,000. The miserable prisoner was kept at Berwick, behind the newly completed walls. No attempt was made at a rescue, and a few weeks later, the earl climbed onto a scaffold at York and laid his neck on the headsman's block.

In 1573 the Regent Morton led several judicial expeditions to the Borders, and he appeared satisfied with their outcomes. But through inexperience, his officers seemed unaware of how little was actually achieved. Those accused of stealing sheep and cattle had become adept at passing them on quickly to 'privy friends' and thereby removing evidence. At least Morton's men caught up with Black James Ormiston, the betrayer of the rebel earls, and although his fate was not recorded, it may be imagined.

The Regent's diplomatic skills were tested by the Raid of the Redeswire in 1575. A firework rather than a conflagration, it nevertheless required careful handling. Most embarrassing was the killing of Sir George Heron of Ford, Deputy Warden of the English Middle March. After quickly releasing all the prisoners taken by the Scots up on the Carter Bar, Morton attempted some charm by sending gifts of hawks to influential courtiers. Some said that they had been given 'live hawks for dead Herons'.

Between 1575 and 1581 the Borders seems to have lain quiet. Either that, or the reporting of complaints was declining. In any event the Regent Morton exerted himself and maintained 'the amity' with England at almost all cost, and there was no reason for armies to cross the Tweed or the Cheviot tops. Reivers did but the number of reported incidents appears to have remained constant for the latter half of the 1570s.

James VI was growing up, and having spent much of his youth at Stirling Castle in the capable but unloving care of the Countess of Mar, he probably craved both freedom and some colour in his dull life. The promise of both arrived in 1579. Esme Stuart, Sieur d'Aubigny, landed in Scotland. Good-looking, dashing, sophisticated, ambitious, almost certainly gay, and catholic, he was an incendiary mixture of possibilities, few of them good. Barely 14 years old, highly impressionable, James was dazzled and seems to have fallen in love. The earldom of Lennox was in the possession of the Bishop of Caithness, but the king quickly persuaded his great-uncle to resign it in favour of Esme, who was after all a Stuart and a distant kinsman. Overnight d'Aubigny became very powerful at court.

Throughout 1580 the Earl of Morton tried to hang onto his office, but as seemed likely from the outset, beauty proved stronger than a big political beast. Morton had imported a new-fangled French contraption which dropped a heavily weighted and very sharp blade on a man's neck and sliced it clean off. It was a prototype guillotine known as 'the Maiden'. In 1581 the charge that Morton was deeply implicated in the murder of Henry Lord Darnley was trumped up, and the Maiden was erected on a scaffold in Edinburgh and used to part Morton's head from his body.

Esme was created Duke of Lennox, but his catholic leanings and his overweening influence on the infatuated young king were too much for native protestant aristocrats to bear. Amongst the charges were that the king's favourite had not only condoned but actually encouraged the Border surnames to raid into England and thereby inflame the international situation. Catholicism was thought to be baiting Elizabethan protestantism as the reivers lifted English cows, although most of them almost certainly could not have cared less about the wider context. Maxwell, the Ferniehurst Kerrs and the Humes were Esme's main supporters. In 1582 a coup was led by William Ruthven, Earl of Gowrie, the king was abducted, and forced to sign an order banishing his beloved Esme to France. The Duke of Lennox died a year later.

Meanwhile Gowrie had imprisoned the young king at Huntingtower, his castle near Perth, so that government according to the true religion could be taken forward. But in June 1583, while in St Andrews, James VI escaped, and after rallying support to him, he rounded on his traitorous captor. It seems that the Maiden was trundled out once more to 'kiss' Gowrie's outstretched neck.

King James was proving a canny politician, and he used the fact that his closeness to Esme Stuart had alarmed more than the protestant Scottish lords. The French dangled the possibility of a catholic alliance (and a generous pension for the cash-strapped monarchy), leaving Elizabeth I uncertain about which way Scotland would turn. Her concern was such that her chief minister, Francis Walsingham, arrived in Edinburgh in August for talks. Part of his commission appears to have been appraisal. His queen had never set eyes on James and she wanted some idea of his character and abilities. To the profound annoyance of the pro-catholic Earl of Arran and other powerful courtiers, Walsingham insisted on meeting the young king alone, but he found little immediate satisfaction on Border affairs, reporting that the reivers were, in his view, being used to annoy England rather than raiding on their own initiative. By the winter of 1583 disorder was growing and the surnames were to be 'set neither by prince nor warden'. Truce Days were not held with any regularity and the Tynedale families in particular rode into Scotland to carry off what they could.

STEWART BEAUTY

The atmosphere around Mary, Queen of Scots is fascinating. Many monarchs were and are esteemed beautiful as a matter of routine royal flattery, but Mary's arrival in Edinburgh appears to have caused high excitement, even a sensation because she was thought to be very beautiful. Standards have fluctuated wildly over time, for both genders, and it is difficult to judge from her portraits (also routinely flattering, although rather anaemic and characterless to our eyes), but the young queen seems to have been a looker – and got into a great trouble because of it. Many of her extended family were also lookers. Esme, Sieur d'Aubigny, was hailed as 'a fascinating Frenchman', and thought very handsome. 'La Belle Stuart', Frances Theresa, Duchess of Richmond and Lennox was described by Samuel Pepys as ' the greatest beauty' he had ever seen. She married family, a distant cousin, Charles Stuart, handsome grandson of Esme. She was said to have posed for the drawing of 'Britannia' which adorned British coins until very recently. And of course the Stewarts supplied the only heir to the throne ever to be popularly distinguished for good looks, Bonnie Prince Charlie.

When Anglo-Scottish relations were strained or simply uneasy, the heidsmen usually showed less inhibition, raiding whenever the opportunity arose and more disdainful of such forces of law and order as were operational. Contemporaries called this downward spiral 'decaie'. Especially on the Scottish side the warden system worked only intermittently. For those Truce Days that were held a massive backlog of crimes and complaints piled up. More were urgently needed to release it.

For midsummer 1585 on the middle marches another Truce Day was at last set. With their retinues and all interested parties (and there were many), the wardens arranged to ride up to the border ridge amongst the highest of the Cheviot Hills. Thousands appear to have mustered and filed up into the eastern ranges, following the 'Hexpethgate' (a version of 'Ermspeth' or Clennel Street). Old Sir John

Forster no doubt straightened his back and spurred his pony on when he saw the Scots gathering on the saddle between the high Windy Gyle and its neighbouring hill, the Butt Roads. Following the ritual, the old man rode forward into Scotland to meet the warden, Sir Thomas Kerr of Ferniehurst. They knew each other well. Proclamation was made that none would incite another 'by word, deed or look' and the two sides came together at this the most spectacular of all the trysting places on the frontier. From the highest point on ancient Clennel Street long views can be seen on all sides – to the east the massive hump of Cheviot itself rises with its two cairns guarding the ravine of the Henhole.

At first all went according to custom. Bills were exchanged and, given the great backlog, priority was probably given to the most important and urgent. What happened next is a matter of dispute and conjecture. Old Sir John wrote two very different accounts of the affair for Francis Walsingham, one following the other in only three days.

At first Forster claimed in a letter dated 28th July from his house at Alnwick that 'it chanced a sudden accident and tumult to arise amongst the rascals of Scotland and England about a little pilfering among themselves'. His son-in-law, Sir Francis Russell, had become involved and 'now rose and went aside from us, with his own men, and there being in talk with a gentleman, was suddenly shot with a gun and slain'. Before the Truce Day could boil up into a small battle, as it had at the Redeswire ten years before, Forster wrote that he and Kerr, his fellow warden, 'stood together and made a quietness'.

Three days after that version, Forster supplied Walsingham with a second. This was countersigned by 32 Northumbrian lords who had been with their warden at the meeting. What had really happened, said Forster, was much different. Led by Kerr of Ferniehurst, the Scots had evidently marched to the Truce Day on Clennel Street in battle order, flags flying and drums beating. Sir Francis Russell had been shot when the flagrant truce-breakers had charged the astonished English ranks. It had been 'a premeditated matter, devised before', wrote the warden.

What really really happened is that the needs of international politics almost certainly intervened in the three days between the first, and likely truthful, account and the second. The shooting of Russell probably had been an accident, a moment of hot-headedness. Mention was made of an argument over a pair of spurs, money owing, and a young Englishman called Wanless being accused. Forster's subsequent tale of what amounted to a Scottish army appearing over the ridge at the Windy Gyle is simply not plausible. Up on those blasted wastes it is very difficult to conceal thousands of men with flags and drums. It was also claimed that the Kerrs had come with the express purpose of killing Russell – but according to Forster himself, there was no certainty that the intended victim would be there. Attending 'for particular causes of his own', Russell had actually come to the Truce Day against his warden's advice. And a whole army to kill one man? Unlikely.

However, it suited Elizabeth and Walsingam to have the affair inflated into an international incident. The notion that the catholic-sympathising Kerr of Ferniehurst, probably in cahoots with the Earl of Arran, had attacked and killed a notable English lord helped them discourage James VI from following bad advice, as they saw it. The mayhem at the Windy Gyle seems like a good example of an old-fashioned Border scuffle being turned to the purposes of the London government.

The year 1585 also saw the Johnstone/Maxwell feud burst into flames once again. When Morton had found himself facing the blade of the Maiden in 1581, John, Lord Maxwell, rubbed his hands. He had been promised the forfeited earldom, and from soon after the date of the execution, he styled himself Morton, thereby confusing generations of historians. Ambition achieved, he began to behave less like the Warden of the Scottish West March and more like the reivers he was charged to suppress. Gathering a band which included Armstrongs, Grahams, and many broken men, he raided deep into the Ettrick Forest. When Morton/Maxwell refused to come to Edinburgh to answer for his crimes, he was deprived of the wardenry. It passed to James Johnstone of Dunskellie – and it proved a poisoned chalice.

A government force sent to help Johnstone was ambushed by Robert Maxwell, Morton's brother, at Crawfordmuir and slaughtered. The Johnstone tower at Lochwood was burned, along with 300 houses, and more than 3,000 beasts were lifted. James Johnstone attacked Dumfries twice and was only turned back by the dreadful weather of the 1580s. After a more successful series of murderous raids along the Nith, a group of Maxwell widows made a remarkable journey to Edinburgh. Taking the bloodied shirts of their dead husbands, they attempted to persuade the king and his council to act against the Johnstones, but they were refused an audience. The outraged women took to the High Street where they showed the gory sarks to the appalled citizenry. After the Edinburgh mob loudly demanded action, James VI was forced to order Morton/Maxwell (warden again by this time) to arrest James Johnstone of Dunskellie. It was the first step on the road to Dryfe Sands, perhaps the most vicious battle ever fought in the Borders.

By 1585 the English and Scottish sovereigns had convinced themselves and each other that their interests were best served by a peace treaty. The Border at first saw fewer raids, and the wardens called for Truce Days. Then trouble broke out suddenly from Liddesdale and also in Northumberland. It seemed that the situation was highly volatile, not following its usual pattern.

What might have detonated a war twenty, or even ten, years before passed almost without incident in 1587. On 8th February at Fotheringhay Castle Mary, Queen of Scots was at last beheaded for treason. After almost twenty years of imprisonment, apparently endless entanglements in catholic plots, and for continuing to serve as a willing focus for dissent in England as well as the rest of Britain, Mary went to the executioner's block. Her cousin, Elizabeth I, was ten years older and may have believed that the captive queen would outlive her to cause mayhem with what she dearly wished would be an orderly succession. The pretext, carefully managed by Walsingham and his network of spies, was the Babington plot, a feeble business involving only a dozen participants which aimed to free Mary and dispose of Elizabeth simultaneously.

When news of Mary's death reached Scotland, nothing much happened. James VI probably did not mourn the mother he had never known (although he made some show of irritation by refusing to see Elizabeth's messenger), and her removal certainly served to buttress his own position. Incessant rainstorms soaked the Borders in February and March 1587, making the burns and rivers into roaring and impassable spates. No one could even consider driving stolen cattle – or even riding out in darkness – in conditions like those.

Old Sir John Forster thought his march very quiet, and he took time to make his way to Newcastle to deal with accusations of misconduct and corruption. His enemies, Collingwood and Huntington, were attempting to have him removed from the wardenship. It was said later that 'he trusted all to a drunken, bastard son', probably Nicholas Forster. But from other sources, it seems that Sir John's description of a peaceful border was not a tactic to demonstrate his competence but an accurate assessment – at any rate for the winter months.

More wet and windy weather in the summer and autumn of 1586 had flattened the grain harvest so badly that the traditional 'hungry months' of May, June and July, when stores from the year before were running out, were worse than usual. On these long early summer days, much against the grain, raiding rose to new levels. Horsemen must have been forced to scour the hill pasture looking for herds and flocks sent out summering. They were desperate. In Forster's middle march the peace was shattered as 37 raids were counted at that time and the complaints listed 700 cows, 400 sheep, 80 nags and 30 prisoners taken. Lord Hunsdon was so taken aback by this unseasonal outbreak that he suspected that the Scottish reiving surnames might have been party to a deliberate distraction. James VI was being courted by Spain with an offer of wages for 30,000 soldiers for three years, a huge sum for a king mired in penury. But James knew that the great prize was England, and these diplomatic rumblings were probably designed to persuade Elizabeth I to commit to him as her heir.

John, Lord Maxwell, had difficulty committing to anything except his own surname's cause and his catholicism. After his brutal defeat of the Johnstones and reinstatement as Warden of the Scottish West March, he began to behave like an independent reiver-king, answerable to no one. Mustering a substantial band of riders, he again terrorised eastern Dumfriesshire and fortified a network of castles. But his contrariness caught up with him, and although the Johnstones were defeated, Maxwell found himself imprisoned for his faith and then driven into exile. Spain was his immediate destination. Returning to Dumfriesshire in 1588, he set about raising support for the coming invasion, the arrival of the Spanish Armada, known as 'the Enterprise of England'. Logistically it made good sense. A large fleet might sidestep English defences in the Channel and sail up through the Irish Sea to make landfall at the Solway ports, where Maxwell and his small army might make them most welcome.

Suddenly the Borders was more than the scene of internecine squabbles. James VI hurried south to Dumfries, took the Maxwell castles at Langholm, Lochmaben and Caerlaverock and after a chase, captured the rebel himself. Amazingly, Maxwell talked his way out of the hangman's rope, and by the early 1590s was once again warden.

Feuding in the Borders was so much a constant feature of life that little notice seems to have been taken of it. Out of sight, out of mind. When it spilled over into the streets of Edinburgh and claimed the lives of titled lords, that was different and the king became directly involved. Sir Robert Kerr of Cessford attacked and killed William Kerr of Ancrum. The reasons read like the usual genealogical tit-for-tat. Ancrum was a relative and a supporter of the Ferniehurst Kerrs, who were more or less at feud with the Cessford Kerrs for much of the sixteenth century. Because the Ferniehurst heir was only a little boy, his affairs were being managed by Ancrum, who had accused and secured the conviction of one of Cessford's men for raiding into England. Instead of bringing the complaint to the Warden of the Middle March, none other than Sir Thomas Kerr of Cessford, he took it to Edinburgh to be heard. So Cessford killed him. It all made sense at the time, and as always seemed possible with the families who held the Scottish wardenries, Cessford escaped, made himself scarce for a while, and after a great deal of contrition and compensation to the Ancrum Kerrs, he evetually got away with it.

Throughout the second half of the sixteenth century the differences between Scots and English wardens grew starker. Elizabeth I and her counsellors had retained a tight grip on appointments and tended to prefer men who had few, if any, local interests. Sir John Forster was the exception. On the Scottish side, the wardenships were more or less hereditary, sometimes alternating between two powerful families, such as the Maxwells and the Johnstones. They used the office to contend for control of the area. From 1557 the Humes were Wardens of the Scottish East March and their neighbours, except for one year when Sir Thomas Kerr of Ferniehurst held office, were an unbroken line of Cessford Kerrs in charge of the middle march. Despite his colourful criminal record, Sir Robert Kerr acted as deputy to his father from 1590 and probably took over in 1594.

These differences were important – and the source of much cross-border conflict in the 1590s. Robert Kerr rarely hesitated to mount raids, pursue feuds or murder an adversary. If these acts characterised the behaviour of the three principal officers of the law in the Borders, then it follows that there was no law at all. Or at least none that might be recognised as such.

What did exist was a broad code of behaviour and an understanding of certain customary rights. Criminal societies are not necessarily anarchic: in order to function, they need some norms or standards. These were well demonstrated in one of the most famous, and dashing, incidents in reiver history, the rescue of Kinmont Willie Armstrong in 1596.

Through the rainswept darkness of the night of 13th April, Walter Scott of Buccleuch led a party of 80 raiders from Langholm to Carlisle. It was an elite force, the best and most daring men he could find.

Having swum their ponies across the swirling spate of the River Eden, they approached the glowering battlements in total silence, signalling directions to each other, looking for a small postern gate in the west wall. It would be locked from the inside, but Buccleuch's men quietly levered out the stone into which the bolt had been shot and crept like foxes into the courtyard of the castle. Guided by a sympathetic serving-lass, six of the raiders found Kinmont Willie's lodging, got him down and out through the postern, onto a spare pony and away into the mirk of the enveloping night. No one laid a hand on them and no pursuit dared to cross the swollen river. It was a brilliant coup, meticulously planned, perfectly executed, a stinging embarrassment to Lord Scrope, the English warden, and also one of the last great raids over the border.

Its immediate cause was the illegal capture of Armstrong at a Truce Day a month before, but the origins of the rescue stretch a long way back into the sixteenth century, and they can be seen as a paradigm for the development of the unique criminal society of the Border Reivers.

KINMONT CANVAS

In March 2006 Bonhams of London offered for sale at auction an interesting painting. By Richard Beavis, a Victorian artist, it purports to illustrate a moment in the rescue of Kinmont Willie from Carlisle Castle in 1596. Yet it looks more like a leisurely evening hack. Two steel-bonneted riders lead a cavalcade of similarly clad horsemen. The leaders, presumably Walter Scott of Buccleuch and one of his lieutenants, appear to be chatting and their horses walking, even dawdling. Beside them a hound strolls as if out for a walk, looking at the anonymous landscape. The only figure who shows any sense of urgency rides beside the column, wearing a rakish plumed hat (more seventeenth than sixteenth century – as are all the riders. They wear breastplates over shirts with wide lacy collars. Perhaps they were particularly well-dressed reivers who shared the same tailor) instead of a steel bonnet, he seems a little older and more portly than his companions, a little like the 'Laughing Cavalier'. The hat is different so that part of a head of white hair might be revealed, and this offers a clue to his identity. Auld Wat of Harden was noted for his 'lyart' locks, or grey hair, as well as his girth. The painting was sold for more than £7,000.

Like Old Sir John Forster, Willie Armstrong lived a long time, rode forays for more than 50 years and saw many things. At the time of the raid on Carlisle Castle, it seems likely that he was 66 years old, born in 1530, when the outrageous executions took place at Carlenrig kirkyard. Along with Black Jock, Kinmont's grandfather, Ill Will Armstrong, was hanged from a 'growand tree'. The incident must have influenced the attitudes of the little boy, at the very least inculcating an almost genetic mistrust and distaste for authority. Ever independent-minded, the Armstrongs sided wherever their interests were best served and accepted pensions from Henry VIII as 'assured Scots'. Genealogists who have traced Kinmont's branch of the family tree believe that as a 12-year-old, he fought at the battle of Solway Moss – on the English side. In 1547 the boy rode with his father, Ill Will's Sandy, and 300 others to help Thomas Carleton take the Johnstone tower at Lochwood.

For three generations Kinmont Willie rode and raided the border on either side, family far more important than nationality. In 1581 he mustered 400 men and led a daylight foray down to Haydon Bridge on the South Tyne, and a year later was in North Tynedale lifting cattle, sheep, goats and horses. The first Lord Scrope of Bolton, father and predecessor of the warden in 1596, complained that justice would never be done because Armstrong and the Scottish warden were so often in each other's company. Maxwell was very unlikely to uphold any complaints against his friend for raiding into England.

Meanwhile Kinmont cemented other relationships. Having married the daughter of his neighbour, Hutcheon Graham, he arranged for his sister's betrothal to his wife's brother. Their daughter later became the wife of another Thomas Carleton, Deputy Warden of the English West March, and Constable of Carlisle Castle. A family connection which was to prove extremely useful.

When James VI came to Dumfries at the head of a small army to deal with the Maxwells, their ally, Kinmont Willie, suggested a classic Armstrong tactic. To avoid an unequal confrontation and likely capture, the Maxwells were led into that impregnable fortress, the Tarras Moss. It was a wise move. When the Maxwells were restored to the wardenship, the Armstrongs returned into favour with the Scottish king.

Over the border, brooding behind the walls of Carlisle Castle, Lord Scrope was growing old, bitter and testily impatient with the fact that Kinmont could ignore the law with regularity and impunity. Whenever a plan was formulated or an opportunity presented itself to capture him, the target seemed to melt away into the hills like a will o' the wisp. The reason was more prosaic – his son-in-law, Thomas Carleton, always leaked information in sufficient time. The old warden died in 1592, disappointed that one of the greatest reivers on the border had eluded him.

Thomas, Lord Scrope, succeeded to his father's office, determined to do better. In 1593 Kinmont, Will Elliot of Larriston and the Armstrong Laird of Mangerton ran a big daylight raid into Tynedale and drove nearly 3,000 beasts back to Liddesdale. Having received intelligence on the reivers' movements (after the raid), young Scrope instructed Carleton to set an ambush. Once again Kinmont and his associates vanished, and instead Thomas captured two English reivers – who managed to escape before they could be got to Carlisle. Furious, Scrope removed Carleton from the deputy wardenship.

Having made an enemy at his back, Scrope then proceeded to make another over the border. Instead of contacting his fellow law officer, Walter Scott of Buccleuch, the Keeper of Liddesdale, the English warden wrote directly to James VI. He asked the king to appoint 'an officer over against him to provide for quietness till the evil of the winter [i.e. the raiding season] be past'. Buccleuch was incensed.

Truce Days had been held only very irregularly, and the backlog of complaints must have been substantial. On 17th March 1596 at Kershopefoot in Liddesdale a rare meeting was set. Well attended, with a few hundred riders on each side, its business was done at the Tourneyholme, a flat field on the Scottish side of the Kershope Burn, where it runs into the Liddel Water. Neither Buccleuch nor Scrope attended, complaints being dealt with by Robert Scott of the Haining, his deputy, and Salkeld, the English deputy. Presumably because there were matters of interest to him on the agenda, Kinmont Willie came to Kershopefoot. In his sixties, hugely experienced, he would have known almost everyone there and was related to many.

After the meeting and while the Truce Day immunities were still in force, Willie rode home by the banks of the Liddel. What happened next goes to the very heart of the whole matter – but it was and is hotly disputed. It seems likely that a large party of English riders were making their way along the opposite bank. That stretch of the Liddel is not too wide and conversation across it would easily have been possible. Perhaps Willie insulted someone, perhaps the name-calling became heated, but it could all certainly have come to nothing. The

Truce Day immunity and the river would surely keep the English and the Armstrongs apart. They did not. Tempers frayed and snapped. The English riders splashed across, laid hands on Kinmont Willie and took him prisoner to Carlisle Castle. A tremendous diplomatic row began almost immediately.

Lord Scrope had been away when Kinmont arrived at his castle, but on his return, he could and should have cleared up the mess by releasing the old reiver without delay. Instead, however, he saw that at last he had his father's old adversary in custody. Let him stew for a while. Over the border Buccleuch acted with some restraint and wrote to Salkeld demanding that Kinmont be set free. No answer. Then a letter over Salkeld's head to Lord Scrope. No answer. Finally Buccleuch went over Scrope's head and wrote to Sir Robert Bowes, Elizabeth I's ambassador at the court of James VI. This time there was action. Apparently Bowes wrote to Scrope in the strongest terms, insisting that the prisoner be released ('enlarged') before matters got out of hand. This was a delicate time. The English queen was now very old and might die at any moment. If there was to be a smooth handover of power, incidents like this would not be helpful.

After the rescue, in his efforts at self-justification, Lord Scrope claimed that he wrote to Buccleuch saying that Kinmont had somehow broken the terms of the truce, that he was a notorious criminal who in any case deserved incarceration and that he offered to ask King James and Sir Robert Bowes to arbitrate in the dispute. If he did, no evidence of any of these approaches has survived.

All attempts at diplomacy having failed, Buccleuch felt that personal insult had been added to a flagrant breach of the law, and as a man of honour, albeit somewhat dubious, he had to act.

Carlisle Castle was one of the strongest in the north, and the last thing Lord Scrope would expect was an assault – which is precisely what was being planned. Not a frontal assault with all cannons blazing, but an assault made by a reiver, a leader well practised in all the arts necessary – speed, surprise, deception and sheer daring. All that Buccleuch needed lay to hand. This was not a dispute between England and Scotland, as it has sometimes been portrayed, or even between Scrope and Buccleuch. Rather, it was a contest between the old reiver society and conventional government forces of law and order and although no one who took part could know it, a contest between the past and the future. Kinmont Willie Armstrong was the quintessential representative of the unique criminal society of the sixteenth-century Border country, and it would rise up in one last glorious raid to break him out of the clutches of the London government.

On 7th April Thomas and his brother, Lance Carleton, met Andrew Graham, Kinmont's brother-in-law and two of his men. They rode to a rendezvous at Archerbeck, not far from Canonbie, where Buccleuch, his kinsman, Auld Wat of Harden and Gilbert Elliot of Liddesdale were waiting. From the very outset the raid on Carlisle Castle involved both Scots and English, all reivers to their blood and bone, combined against an outsider who had broken their code. It was an alliance which mirrored Kinmont's own web of contacts. Family and not nationality brought the conspirators together. Each had his own reasons, the Carletons in particular, for wishing to see Warden Scrope done down, and each brought the different elements essential for the success of any raid on his squat, dour but very secure castle.

Buccleuch argued for a small, experienced, elite force. Between them the western surnames could raise four or five thousand riders but no matter how large an army galloped up to Carlisle's walls, they did not have the equipment or know-how to break them down. Better to go with only 80 or so – the best of the Scotts, Wat of Harden as a vastly seasoned, unflappable lieutenant, a contingent of Elliots and there was no doubt that Kinmont's four sons could not be kept at home. That was enough. Surprise and stealth would be impossible if more came.

The Grahams would organise security. The raid would cross that part of the Debatable Land controlled by the surname, and they needed to keep it quiet, no blundering into other raiding parties, no possibility of a chance observer galloping to Carlisle to raise the alarm. In order to gain entry to the castle itself, Ebby's Sandy Graham had the necessary skills. Most important was the precise route to be taken once Kinmont Willie had been rescued. In places with good cover, ambushes needed to be set to trap any pursuers, and Willie Kang Irvine, a go-between trusted by Buccleuch, would let the Johnstones and his own surname know where. Scaling ladders were stored at Morton Rigg, Kinmont's own tower. It lay only ten miles from Carlisle and on the route the raiders planned to follow. Finally the Carletons agreed to look after intelligence. Evidently Armstrong was being held in a house in the lower courtyard of the castle, one of several built against the west wall. Next to it was an old postern gate which opened directly to the outside, and crucially, offered a way in which did not involve passing through any of the gates into the walled city of Carlisle. An Elizabethan map shows the arrangement very clearly. It was perfect.

After four hours of detailed discussion, the date was set. The raid would run on the night of Sunday 13th April, and the rendezvous arranged for the day before at Langholm Races. The crowds, the betting and the general hubbub would provide good cover for the muster. Secrecy was vital and to delay any longer, urged the Carletons, would be to risk discovery.

The day dawned, squally and wet as it often can be in spring in the Borders, and Willie Kang Irvine had come to Langholm to ensure that all was ready to go forward. Buccleuch ate with Hutcheon Graham at the castle, which stood immediately adjacent to the racecourse. When gloaming at last began to gather, the raiders saddled their ponies and slipped quietly out of the town on the Carlisle road.

Ever fearful of interception, Buccleuch took care to dispose his small force in military order. A screen of scouts swept the country in front of them, often moving off the road to look for ambushes. Right behind was a support group of about 40 riders. Then came Buccleuch and the handful who would break into the castle and find Kinmont. Pack horses carried ladders, crowbars and other gear. All were followed by a watchful rearguard.

While there was still a little light in the sky, the party splashed across the Esk, probably avoiding the fords at Longtown (where they might be seen), preferring the crossing lower down, near the outfall into the Solway. From then on it was vital to ride in silence: no warning whatsoever must be given. It was raining and very windy, and while that was uncomfortable, the bad weather might keep the curious indoors. Buccleuch wanted to approach Carlisle from the north so that his party would be hidden behind Stanwix Bank. In 1596 the River Eden ran in two channels on either side of the Sands, an island sometimes used for horse-racing and a good bridging point. The plan was to avoid it and make for a point on the riverbank a few hundred yards to the west, where the Eden turned out of sight of any sentries on the bridge. This crossing-point would also deliver the raiders directly below the battlements of the castle, to a piece of ground known as the Sauceries Flat.

But the Eden had to be negotiated first, and that would take some good horsemanship and some brave ponies. After a night of rain it may have been flooding: 'It happened to be very dark in the hindnight (after midnight) and a little misty.' Good cover but dangerous.

Soaked but safely over, the party divided on the Sauceries. Most took a position by the west wall, lances couched, where they could discourage any who sallied out of the Irish Gate and attempted to intervene. Buccleuch led perhaps six or eight up to the postern. Ebby's Sandy Graham set to work with crowbar and chisel to remove the stone by the gate which acted as the keeper for its bolt. It was a technique sometimes used to break into peel towers.

Once inside the lower courtyard Buccleuch might have expected resistance from the sentries, but there was none. In a lame excuse, Lord Scrope later claimed that the watch had either been driven inside by the rainstorm or they had fallen asleep. Or they had been bought by Thomas and Lance Carleton. In any case Kinmont was quickly found and shoved out through the postern, onto a pony and then into the Eden's freezing water for a soaking. Despite the hullaballoo described in 'The Ballad of Kinmont Willie' with all the bells of Carlisle ringing, there appears to have been no pursuit. Perhaps the operation went so smoothly it was not discovered until morning, perhaps none of the sleepy guards fancied a ducking in the midnight river, perhaps too many of the Carleton's coins jingled in their pockets.

A great deal is known of the detail of this incident because of the recriminations afterwards. Lord Scrope extracted information from the Grahams and others, and to placate an enraged Elizabeth I, Buccleuch was eventually forced to make statements about who did what. Despite the excuses and assurances, the raid was emblematic, a carefully planned, immaculately executed example of the craft of the reiver. All of those criminal skills were seamlessly employed as border society of the 1590s ignored nationality and combined to right what it saw as a wrong and defeat the forces of legitimate central government.

But at the moment of perhaps its greatest and most famous triumph, the world of the reivers was fading, and most of the men who rode through the storm to Carlisle sensed it. Elizabeth I was well into her sixties and it had been understood for some time that James of Scotland would succeed as king of a united Britain. That meant no border between separate jurisdictions, no ability to play off one sovereign and their representatives against another, and the more astute of the heidsmen began to turn their minds to the future.

Robert Carey called the last years of the border 'a stirring world', and he was witness to most of its signal events. The seventh son of Lord Hunsdon (said by many to be half-brother to Queen Elizabeth), he trained as a soldier and gained experience as a courtier and diplomat. In 1593 Thomas, Lord Scrope, appointed Carey as his deputy in place of Thomas Carleton, and the young man may have been in Carlisle Castle on the night Kinmont Willie slipped out of the postern gate.

Despite Carleton's well-earned reputation for duplicity and a likely resentment of his successor, he had occasion to give Carey some excellent advice. The new deputy warden was anxious to give the impression of diligence and also to assert his authority. When he learned of the flight of two murderers (they had killed a church minister) and their being harboured in a Graham tower, a troop of 25 was ordered to saddle up. Riding out of the castle in the early hours of the morning, Carey planned a surprise attack. Thomas Carleton came along – and it was just as well.

When the troop reached their target, they found the tower securely barred against them, 'and I could see a boy riding from the house as fast as his horse would carry him'. Carleton understood immediately what was about to happen: 'He will be in Scotland inside this half hour, and he has gone to let them know you are here, and to what end you have come, and the small number you have with you, and that if they make haste, on a sudden they may surprise us, and do with us what they please.' Carey reacted well and did something similar very quickly, a rider being sent the five miles to Carlisle to bring reinforcements.

After a time 400 Scottish riders cantered into view and halted some distance away. With his reinforcements, the deputy warden could probably have made a contest of it, but the Scots holed up in the tower had offered to negotiate and Carey prudently sent a messenger over to the Scots to ask them to withdraw. Which they did, no doubt to considerable relief – on both sides.

Lord Hunsdon died in 1596 after half a lifetime's service on the border and his son took over as Warden of the English East March. It was a plum job. Carey found himself in charge of not only north Northumberland but also the garrison at Berwick. For a professional soldier, it was a rare opportunity to command fellow professionals.

But Carey's satisfaction was short-lived. Because of the dismissal of Old Sir John Forster from the middle march and his replacement with the unhappy Lord Eure, a vacancy occured. Eure departed gratefully, and Carey was moved into the much more difficult job. And while he might have been flattered at such trust in a relatively young man, his memoir complains at how inconvenient it all was. The unfortunate Peregrine Bertie took charge of Berwick and the east march.

At least Robert was able to dodge what turned out to be an unusual, difficult and persistent problem, something the wardens well not well equipped to deal with. Pirates known as 'Dunkirkers' were attacking shipping off the Northumberland coast. Their fleet was large, with 24 substantial galleons, and their prey was crucial to the local economy. Off Berwick Roads they prowled, lying in wait for the corn and supply ships which plied in and out of the harbour, and further down the coast, they captured the colliers which ran coal from the Tyneside pits down to London. Such everyday, bulk cargoes might not at first seem attractive to pirates, but apparently the Dunkirkers drove the captured corn and coal ships to dock in European ports where they auctioned the contents, the crew and their craft.

The pirates returned in 1600 and again in 1601 when Peregrine Bertie manned and armed a warship at his own expense to deal with them. Fishermen had been complaining that they could not leave harbour. Some had been caught, stripped of their clothes and cast ashore to watch their boats being ransacked and sometimes sunk. Even more pressing for Bertie was the fact that the victualling ships supplying Berwick's garrison could not get through, the voyage having become much too risky. It all seemed to overwhelm the warden and, complaining about the Borders, Borderers, and Border weather, Peregrine Bertie caught a bad cold while waiting for the wind on his warship in Berwick Roads. On 25th June 1601, he died.

Suddenly border government on the English side began to look like the sort of family affair it had long been in Scotland. In the west Thomas Lord Scrope had taken over from his father, and in the east Robert Carey's brother, John, became warden. They all knew that their appointments were temporary, lasting only as long as their old queen lived. And astute as ever, Robert Carey reckoned that Elizabeth's death would not be long in coming.

In his entry for 1603, the historian, D.L.W. Tough wrote: 'There really is no more Border history.' In an important sense, he was right. That was the year the political border disappeared. When Robert Carey attended court in London in the winter of 1603, he sensed that Elizabeth had lost the will to go on and sought the release of death. And so he hung on, waiting upon events, and pondering a plan.

Philadelphia Carey, Robert's sister, was one of the old queen's body servants. When Elizabeth took to her bed and sent away Robert Cecil and her other advisers and courtiers, only she and her female companions stayed in the royal presence. It was only a matter of time. Meanwhile Robert organised a relay of good horses to be posted at intervals along the great north road from London to Edinburgh. If he was to hope for favour and preferment at the coming court of King James VI and I, it would do him much good to be the first to give the new King of Great Britain the news he had been waiting for all his life. Official royal messengers would take at least four days, maybe five in bad weather, to make the 400-mile journey. Carey believed he could do it much faster, in two or perhaps three days. He knew the road well. For a wager, he had once walked from London to Edinburgh.

When Elizabeth died in the early morning of 24th March, Philadelphia cut her coronation ring from the queen's puffy finger and rushed down to the courtyard where her brother waited. James VI would need a token that Carey's news was reliable. Hell for leather, he rode out of London on a clear spring day, kicking his first horse on while the rider was not yet tired. Doncaster was reached by nightfall, and then Northumberland by the following evening. Having slept at his house at Widdrington, Carey, no doubt still sore, saddled up, expecting to reach Edinburgh well before darkness fell, but on the road his horse spooked and threw him, somewhere south of Norham, and adding injury to insult, it accidentally kicked him in the head. The wound was bad, progress much slowed but Carey rode on doggedly through the gloaming along the East Lothian coast road, reaching Edinburgh late that night.

When he clattered into the cobbled courtyard of Holyrood Palace, Carey demanded that the king be woken. Bloodied down one side of his face, his cloak and boots caked in mud, the messenger knelt by James' bedside, gave him Elizabeth's coronation ring and acknowledged him as his king, the new King of England and Scotland. From that moment, there really was to be no more Border history; the days of the reivers were over.

Envoi

The end was brutal, and brief. It took only seven years for the new government of Great Britain to dismantle reiving society. As if to stiffen James I and VI's resolve, the Grahams, the Armstrongs and the Elliots took the death of Elizabeth I as their cue for an outbreak of concentrated, almost frenzied, foraying. In what became known as 'Ill Week', 5,000 cattle were lifted in Cumbria, and one band rode as far south as Penrith before reining in their ponies. It seemed like a reflex, a last tearaway gallop before the inevitable. As the Bishop of Carlisle watched from the ramparts of the castle, Hutcheon Graham led a company of reivers through the meadows by the River Eden. His men took their time, not troubling to conceal themselves. Perhaps they looked up at the bishop and made whatever gesture was the sixteenth-century equivalent of sticking up two fingers.

Even before he reached London, the new king left none of the heidsmen in any doubt about what was coming. When James' triumphant progress through his new kingdom reached Newcastle in April 1603, he paused from the celebrations to turn a withering westward eye on the reiving families:

> To his messengers, sheriffs and others, the late marches and borders
> of the two realms of England and Scotland are now the heart of the
> country. Proclamation is to be made against all rebels and disorderly
> persons that no supply be given them, their wives or their bairns,
> and that they be prosecuted with fire and sword.

From London, a few weeks later, a firm deadline was laid down, and the outset of a new era marked with the giving of a new name. The excesses of Ill Week were also noted:

Requiring all who were guilty of the foul and insolent outrages lately committed in the Borders to submit themselves to his mercy before 20th June – under penalty of being excluded from it forever . . . [the king] prohibited the name of Borders any longer to be used, substituting in its place Middle Shires. He ordered all places of strength in those parts to be demolished except the habitation of noblemen and barons; their iron yetts to be converted into plough irons and their inhabitants to betake themselves to agriculture and other works of peace.

Having erased the border line from the map in fact as well as name, and removed all means of avoidance or escape, the king and his counsellors set about enacting a series of measures which would solve a long-standing and profound irritation. There is a distinct impression that James himself had given the problem of the Borders a great deal of thought as he waited for Elizabeth of England to die.

He also had the example of the Highlands to draw on. At the same time as the suppression of the Border Reivers began, James was looking north, to his kingdom's other substantial locus of marginal disorder, the remote territories of the semi-independent Highland and Island clans. In 1608 royal agents tricked and abducted many of the important chiefs and held them as hostages for the good behaviour of their people. The Gaelic language was discouraged as 'one of the principal causes of the continuance of barbarity and incivility', and the elder sons of the chiefs were to be educated in English and in the Lowlands.

Compared with the Statutes of Iona, the treatment of the reivers was summary and savage. The March Wardenries and all of the march laws were first abolished: Borderers would be subject to the same laws as everyone else. In 1603 Lord Hume was appointed as Lieutenant of all the Scottish Marches and Sir George Clifford, Earl of Cumberland, held a matching commission for the English side. Both were supported by deputies who were professional soldiers, respectively Sir William Cranston and Sir Henry Leigh. The hangings began almost immediately.

Methods were not complicated. Known thieves were rounded up, charges trumped up or old ones cited and revived, and hundreds were executed without any or much legal preamble. It was the grisly beginning of what came to called Jethart Justice, a practice of hanging first and – maybe – asking questions later. Mass executions took place in Dumfries, Jedburgh and Carlisle. Hume himself witnessed '140 of the nimblest and most powerful thieves in all the Borders' choke to death on the end of a rope. Not sufficiently nimble to dodge a determined government offensive, the heidsmen could see that this was no routine purge. It was Judgement Day and history was moving.

Walter Scott considered absence a wise course and he mustered 2,000 riders, taking them off to fight in the 'Belgic Wars', the Dutch struggle for independence from Spain. When he returned, Buccleuch did not hesitate to join Hume and he turned on his own surname, those who had loyally ridden behind him to Carlisle Castle in 1596, and any others who appeared to resist.

In 1605 a Border Commission was set up in Carlisle Castle. Five Scots lairds and five English adjudicated on cases, but it seems that whenever Clifford, Leigh, Hume or Cranston or any of their officers referred a case, the same instructions were always issued – hang them.

As Scott and the other, more astute heidsmen lined up on the side of law and order, they were much motivated by the mechanism of dispossession. Whenever an alleged reiver was executed, his lands came up for grabs – and many large estates were grabbed after 1603. Some families were nevertheless unrepentant, too far gone in reputation and inclination. The Grahams were heavily persecuted, many were deported to Ireland, to settle in the landlocked county of Roscommon. Few stayed. The Armstrongs suffered badly, and it must be significant that no substantial aristocratic family bearing either of these feared and powerful names has survived in the Borders.

By 1610 the world had changed. Sporadic raiding still sometimes flickered on a winter's night, but society had moved on. Men were no longer permitted to go about armed, ponies worth more than £30 Scots were forbidden, saddles were to be replaced by work harness, well known thieves did not strut the streets of Hexham or Hawick – even iron gates were to be beaten into ploughshares. While the last sounds like a classical rhetorical flourish, there was nothing allusory about the effects of the Border Commission. In only seven years enough reivers had been hanged, deported or ennobled to alter radically what had been a thoroughly uncontrollable criminal society.

It was a savage and sad end to many old songs. The ballads romanticised the reivers impossibly, almost obliterating the grim historical truth, the killing, 'the deep revenge for slight offences', the rapes, the greed and the pain inflicted. But for all that it is not an entirely unattractive story. In addition to their manifold faults, the reivers had some virtues – or at least some humanity. Stowlugs Armstrong, Nebless Clem Crosier and Davey Bangtail Armstrong had a stoic humour about them, and the nicknames seem to bring them all closer. They were not a fanfare of big names and titles, but a collection of much more modest men and women. Ordinary people do not do what Willie Kang Irvine or Lancie Carleton did, but their otherwise everyday lives are somehow more accessible and not at all remote. They may have been thieves and blackmailers but their characters are pungent, alive, and oddly more attractive than the stiff formalities of kings, queens, bishops and aristocrats who usually people the pages of history.

The reivers also showed unmistakable dash and bravery, routinely risking their necks and sometimes even acting out of more than an immediate self-interest. In their disregard for central authority, constantly cocking a snook, the riding families readily find modern supporters, those who might condemn their actions but cheer on their independent cheek. Most of all they were tough, hard-riding and as durable as the windy hills they knew so well.

When the police action began in 1603, it became quickly clear that some surnames would certainly suffer while others might prosper if they switched loyalty from family to the state. The Grahams and the Armstrongs got nothing, the Elliots and the Johnstones and some of the upland Tynedale and Redesdale families very little. Such dour unwillingness to change seems somehow more admirable than all that jostling and jockeying done by the Kerrs, the Humes and the Scotts. At least the Grahams and the Armstrongs were unflinchingly consistent, unrepentant Border Reivers to the soles of their riding boots. No better than they should have been.

Family counted for everything in the reiving centuries, and in an alienated, fragmented urban world, that is also attractive. 'My name is Little Jock Elliot' was more than a boast, it described a way of life. It has almost all gone now, the riding surnames are only a unique and fascinating memory. The reivers have melted into the moonlit landscape, their grey shapes fading into the darkness of the past. But the names have endured, and Borderers have made other, better marks on history. All of these ancient qualities of bravery, dash, cheek and independent strength of will and mind seemed to coalesce in the greatest foray ever run. Neil Armstrong rode the moonlight like none of his reiving ancestors when he reached out and touched it.

Appendix 1

The Border Ballads

Despite much alteration, licence and the poetic needs of metre and rhyme, the Border Ballads are not ahistorical pieces of fancy. They offer atmosphere, emotion, a sense of how people thought 500 years ago and also what they believed at that time. Beliefs and attitudes inform motivation and that is what makes them integral to any understanding of our history. Here is a selection of five famous ballads. Some describe real events, with flamboyance, while others sing of the raids and the raiders.

(All ballads from *Minstrelsy of the Scottish Border*.)

The Battle of Otterburn

It fell about the Lammas tide,
When the muir-men win their hay,
The doughty Douglas bound him to ride
Into England, to drive a prey.

He chose the Gordons and the Graemes,
With them the Lindesays, light and gay;
But the Jardines wald not with him ride,
And they rue it to this day.

And he has burn'd the dales of Tyne,
And part of Bambroughshire:
And three good towers on Roxbergh fells,
He left them all on fire.

And he march'd up to Newcastle,
And rode it round about;
'O wha's the lord of this castle,
Or wha's the lady o't?'

But up spake proud Lord Percy, then,
And O but he spake hie!
'I am the lord of this castle,
My wife's the lady gay.'

'If thour't the lord of this castle,
Sae weel it pleases me!
For, ere I cross the border fells,
The tane of us shall die.'

He took a lang spear in his hand,
Shod with the metal free,
And for to meet the Douglas there,
He rode right furiouslie.

But O how pale his lady look'd,
Frae aff the castle wa',
When down, before the Scottish spear,
She saw proud Percy fa'.

'Had we twa been upon the green,
And never an eye to see,
I wad hae had you, flesh and fell;
But your sword sall gae wi' me.'

'But gae ye up to Otterbourne,
And wait there dayis three;
And, if I come not ere three dayis end,
A fause knight ca' ye me.'

'The Otterbourne's a bonnie burn;
'Tis pleasant there to be;
But there is nought at Otterbourne,
To feed my men and me.

The deer rins wild on hill and dale,
The birds fly wild from tree to tree;
But there is neither bread nor kale,
To fend my men and me.

Yet I will stay at Otterbourne,
Where you shall welcome be;
And, if ye come not at three dayis end,
A fause lord I'll ca' thee.'

'Thither will I come,' proud Percy said,
'By the might of Our Ladye!' –
'There will I bide thee,' said the Douglas
'My trowth I plight to thee.'

They lighted high on Otterbourne,
Upon the bent sae brown;
They lighted high on Otterbourne,
And threw their pallions down.

And he that had a bonnie boy,
Sent out his horse to grass;
And he that had not a bonnie boy,
His ain servant he was.

But up then spake a little page,
Before the peep of dawn-
'O waken ye, waken ye, my good lord,
For Percy's hard at hand.'

'Ye lie, ye lie, ye liar loud!
Sae loud I hear yr lie:
For Percy had not men yestreen,
To dight my men and me.

But I hae dream'd a dreary dream,
Beyond the Isle of Skye;
I saw a dead man win a fight,
And I think that man was I.'

He belted on his good braid sword,
And to the field he ran;
But he forgot the helmet good,
That should have kept his brain.

When Percy wi' the Douglas met,
I wat he was fu' fain!
They swakked their swords, till sair they swat,
And the blood ran down like rain.

But Percy with his good broad sword,
That could so sharply wound,
Has wounded Douglas on the brow,
Till he fell to the ground.

Then he call'd on his little foot-page,
And said – Run speedilie,
And fetch my ain dear sister's son,
Sir Hugh Montgomery.

'My nephew good,' the Douglas said,
'What recks the death of ane!
Last night I dream'd a dreary dream,
And I ken the day's thy ain.

My wound is deep; I fain would sleep;
Take thou the vanguard of the three,
And hide me by the braken bush,
That grows on yonder lilye lee.

O bury me by the braken bush,
Beneath the blooming brier;
Let never living mortal ken,
That ere a kindly Scot lies here.'

He lifted up that noble lord,
Wi the saut tear in his e'e;
He hid him in the braken bush,
That his merrie men might not see.

The moon was clear, the day drew near,
The spears in flinders flew,
But mony a gallant Englishman,
Ere day the Scotsmen slew.

The Gordons good, in English blood,
They steep'd their hose and shoon;
The Lindsays flew like fire about,
Till all the fray was done.

The Percy and Montgomery met,
That either of other were fain;
They swapped swords, and they twa swat,
And aye the blude ran down between.

'Yield thee, O yield thee, Percy!' he said,
'Or else I vow I'll lay thee low!'
'To whom shall I yield,' said Earl Percy,
'Now that I see it must be so?'

'Thou shall not yield to lord nor loun,
Nor yet shalt thou yield tome;
But yield thee to the braken bush,
That grows upon yon lilye lee!'

'I will not yield to a braken bush,
Nor yet will I yield to a brier;
But I would yield to Earl Douglas,
Or Sir Hugh the Montgomery, if he were here.'

As soon as he knew it was Montgomery,
He struck his sword's point in the gronde;
And the Montgomery was a courteous knight,
And quickly took him by the honde.

This deed was done at Otterbourne,
About the breaking of the day;
Earl Douglas was buried at the braken bush,
And the Percy led captive away.

Dick o' the Cow

Now Liddesdale has layen lang in,
There is na riding there at a';
The horses are a' grown sae lither fat,
They downa stir out o' the sta'.

Fair Johnie Armstrang to Willie did say –
'Billy, a riding we will gae;
England and us have been lang at feid;
Ablins we'll light on some bootie.'

Then they are come on to Hatton Ha';
They rade that proper place about;
But the laird he was the wiser man,
For he had left nae gear without.

For he had left nae gear to steal,
Except sax sheep upon a lee:
Quo' Johnie – 'I'd rather in England die,
Ere thir sax sheep gae to Liddesdale wi' me.'

'But how ca' they the man we last met,
Billie, as we cam owre the know?'
'That same he is an innocent fule,
And men they call him Dick o' the Cow.'

'That fule has three as good kye o' his ain,
As there are in a' Cumberland, billie,' quo' he:
'Betide me life, betide me death,
These kye shall go to Liddesdale wi' me.'

Then they have come on to the pure fule's house,
And they hae broken his wa's sae wide;
They have loosed out Dick o' the Cow's three kye,
And ta'en three co'erlets frae his wife's bed.

Then on the morn when the day was light,
The shouts and cries rase loud and hie:
'O haud thy tongue, my wife,' he says,
'And o' thy crying let me be!

O haud thy tongue, my wife,' he says,
'And o' thy crying let me be;
And aye where thou hast lost ae cow,
In gude suith I shall bring thee three.'

Now Dickie's gane to the gude Lord Scroope,
And I wat a dreirie fule was he;
'Now haud thy tongue, my fule,' he says,
'For I may not stand to jest wi' thee.'

'Shame fa' your jesting, my lord!' quo' Dickie,
'For nae sic jesting grees wi' me;
Liddesdale's been in my house last night,
And they hae awa my three kye frae me.

But I may nae langer in Cumberland dwell,
To be your puir fule and your leal,
Unless you gie me leave, my lord,
To gae to Liddesdale and steal.'

'I gie thee leave, my fule!' he says;'Thou speakest against
my honour and me,
Unless thou gie me thy trowth and thy hand,
Thou'lt steal frae nane but whae sta' frae thee.'

'There is my trowth, and my right hand!
My head shall hang on Haribee,
I'll ne'er cross Carlisle sands again,
If I steal frae a man but whae sta' frae me.'

Dickie's ta'en leave o' lord and master;
I wat a merry fule was he!
He's bought a bridle and a pair o' new spurs,
And pack'd them up in his breek thie.

Then Dickie's come on to Pudding-burn house,
E'en as fast as he might drie;
Then Dickie's come on to Pudding-burn,
Where there were thirty Armstrangs and three.

'O what's this come o' me now?' quo' Dickie;
'What mickle wae is this?' quo' he;
'For there is but ae innocent fule,
And there are thirty Armstrangs and three!'

Yet he has come up to the fair ha' board,
Sae weil he's become his courtesie!
'Weil may ye be, my gude Laird's Jock!
But the deil bless a' your cumpanie.

I'm come to plain o' your man, fair Johnie Armstrang,
And syne o' his billie Willie,' quo' he;
'How they've been in my house last night,
And they hae ta'en my three kye frae me.'

'Ha!' quo' fair Johnie Armstrang, 'we will him hang.'
'Na,' quo' Willie, 'we'll him slae.'
Then up and spak another young Armstrang,
'We'll gie him his batts, and let him gae.'

But up and spak the gude Laird's Jock,
The best falla in a' the cumpanie:
'Sit down thy ways a little while, Dickie,
And a piece o' thy ain cow's hough I'll gie ye.'

But Dickie's heart it grew sae grit,
That the ne'er a bit o't he dought to eat –
Then he was aware of an auld peat-house,
Where a' the night he thought for to sleep

Then Dickie was aware of an auld peat-house,
Where a' the night he thought for to lye –
And a' the prayers the pure fule prayed
Were, 'I wish I had amends for my gude three kye!'

It was then the use of Pudding-burn house,
And the house of Mangerton, all hail,
Them that cam na at the first ca',
Gat nae mair meat till the neist meal.

The lads, that hungry and weary were,
Abune the door-head they threw the key;
Dickie he took gude notice o' that,
Says – 'There will be a bootie for me.'

Then Dickie has in to the stable gane,
Where there stood thirty horses and three;
He has tied them a' wi' St Mary's knot,
A' these horses but barely three.

He has tied them a' wi' St Mary's knot,
A' these horses but barely three;
He's loupen on ane, ta'en another in hand,
And away as fast as he can hie.

But on the morn, when the day grew light,
The shouts and cries raise loud and hie –
'Ah! whae has done this?' quo' the gude Laird's Jock,
'Tell me the truth and the verity!

Whae has done this deed?' quo' the gude Laird's Jock;
'See that to me ye dinna lie!'
'Dickie has been in the stable last night,
And has ta'en my brother's horse and mine frae me.'

'Ye wad ne'er be tauld,' quo' the gude Laird's Jock;
'Have ye not found my tales fu' leil?
Ye ne'er wad out o' England bide,
Till crooked, and blind, and a' would steal.'

'But lend me thy bay,' fair Johnie can say;
'There's nae horse loose in the stable save he;
And I'll either fetch Dick o' the Cow again,
Or the day is come that he shall die.'

'To lend thee my bay!' the Laird's Jock can say,
'He's baith worth gowd and gude monie;
Dick o' the Cow has awa twa horse;
I wish na thou may make him three.'

He has ta'en the laird's jack on his back,
A twa-handed sword to hang by his thie;
He has ta'en a steil cap on his head,
And gallopped on to follow Dickie.

Dickie was na a mile frae aff the town,
I wat a mile but barely three,
When he was o'erta'en by fair Johnie Armstrang,
Hand for hand, on Cannobie lee.

'Abide, abide, thou traitour thief!
The day is come that thou maun die.'
Then Dickie look't owre his left shoulder,
Said – 'Johnie, hast thou nae mae in cumpanie?

There is a preacher in our chapell,
And a' the live lang day teaches he;
When day is gane and night is come,
There's ne'er ae word I mark but three.

The first and second is – Faith and Conscience;
The third – Ne'er let a traitour free:
But, Johnie, what faith and conscience was thine,
When thou took awa my three kye frae me?

And when thou had ta'en awa my three kye,
Thou thought in thy heart thou wast not weil sped,
Till thou sent thy billie Willie ower the know,
To tak three coverlets off my wife's bed!'

Then Johnie let a speir fa' laigh by his thie,
Thought weil to hae slain the innocent, I trow;
But the powers above were mair than he,
For he ran but the pure fule's jerkin through.

Together they ran, or ever they blan;
This was Dickie the fule and he!
Dickie could na win at him wi' the blade o' the sword,
But fell'd him wi' the plummet under the e'e.

Thus Dickie has fell'd fair Johnie Armstrang,
The prettiest man in the south country –
'Gramercy!' then can Dickie say,
'I had but twa horse, thou hast made me three.'

He's ta'en the steil jack aff Johnie's back,
The twa-handed sword that hang low by his thie;
He's ta'en the steil cap aff his head –
'Johnie, I'll tell my master I met wi' thee.'

When Johnie wakened out o' his dream,
I wat a dreirie man was he:
'And is thou gane? Now, Dickie, than
The shame and dule is left wi' me.

And is thou gane? Now, Dickie, than
The deil gae in thy cumpanie!
For if I should live these hundred years,
I ne'er shall fight wi' a fule after thee.'

Then Dickie's come hame to the gude Lord Scroope,
E'en as fast as he might hie;
'Now, Dickie, I'll neither eat not drink,
Till hie hanged thou shalt be.'

'The shame speed the liars, my lord!' quo' Dickie;
'This was na the promise ye made to me!
For I'd ne'er gane to Liddesdale to steal,
Had I not got my leave frae thee.'

'But what garr'd thee steal the Laird's Jock's horse?
And, limmer, what garr'd ye steal him?' quo' he;
'For lang thou mightst in Cumberland dwelt,
Ere the Laird's Jock had stown frae thee.'

'Indeed I wat ye lied, my lord!
And e'en sae loud as I hear ye lie!
I wan the horse frae fair Johnie Armstrang,
Hand to hand, on Cannobie lee.

'There is the jack was on his back;
This twa-handed sword hang laigh by his thie,
And there's the steil cap was on his head;
I brought a' these tokens to let thee see.'

'If that be true thou to me tells,
(And I think thou dares na tell a lie)
I'll gie thee fifteen punds for the horse,
Weil tald on thy cloak lap shall be.

'I'll gie thee ane o' my best milk kye,
To maintain thy wife and children three;
And that may be as gude, I think,
As ony twa o' thine wad be.'

'The shame speed the liars, my lord!' quo' Dickie;
'Trow ye aye to make a fule o' me?
I'll either hae twenty punds for the gude horse,
Or he's gae to Mortan fair wi' me.'

He's gien him twenty punds for the gude horse,
A' in goud and gude monie;
He's gien him ane o' his best milk kye,
To maintain his wife and children three.

Then Dickie's come down thro' Carlisle toun,
E'en as fast as he could drie;
The first o' men that he met wi'
Was my lord's brother, Bailiff Glozenburrie.

'Weil be ye met, my gude Ralph Scroope!'
'Welcome, my brother's fule!' quo' he:
'Where didst thou get fair Johnie Armstrang's horse?'
'Where did I get him? but steal him,' quo' he.

'But wilt thou sell me the bonny horse?
And, billie, wilt thou sell him to me?' quo' he:
'Aye; if thou'lt tell me the monie on my cloak lap,
For there's never ae penny I'll trust thee.'

'I'll gie thee ten punds for the gude horse,
Weil tald on thy cloak lap they shall be;
And I'll gie thee ane o' the best milk kye,
To maintain thy wife and children three.'

'The shame speed the liars, my lord!' quo' Dickie;
'Trow ye aye to mak a fule o' me!
I'll either hae twenty punds for the gude horse,
Or he's gae to Mortan fair wi' me.'

He's gien him twenty punds for the gude horse,
Baith in goud and gude monie;
He's gien him ane o' his best milk kye,
To maintain his wife and children three.

Then Dickie lap a loup fu' hie,
And I wat a loud laugh laughed he –
'I wish the neck o' the third horse were broken,
If ony of the twa were better than he!'

Then Dickie's come hame to his wife again;
'Judge ye how the poor fule had sped!'
He has gien her twa score English punds,
For the three auld coverlets ta'en aff her bed.

'And tak thee these twa as gude kye,
I trow, as a' thy three might be;
And yet here is a white-footed nagie,
I trow he'll carry baith thee and me.

But I may nae langer in Cumberland bide;
The Armstrangs they would hang me hie.'
So Dickie's ta'en leave at lord and master,
And at Burgh under Stanmuir there swells he.

Johnie Armstrang

Sum speikis of lords, sum speikis of lairds,
And sick lyke men of his hie degrie;
Of a gentleman I sing a sang,
Sum tyme called laird of Gilnockie.

The King he wrytes a luving letter,
With his ain hand dae tenderly,
And he hath sent it to Johnie Armstrang,
To cum and speik with him speedily.

The Eliots and Armstrangs did convene;
They were a gallnt cumpanie –
'We'll ride and meit our lawful King,
And bring him safe to Gilnockie.

Make kinnen and capon ready then,
And venison in great plentie;
We'll wellcum here our royal King;
I hope he'll dine at Gilnockie!'

They ran their horse on the Langhome howm,
And brak their speirs wi' mickle main;
The ladies lukit frae their loft windows –
'God bring our men weel back agen!'

When Johnie cam before the King,
Wi' a' his men sae brave tae see,
The King he movit his bonnet to him;
He ween'd he was a King as well as he.

'May I find grace, my sovereign leige,
Grace for my loyal men and me?
For my name it is Johnie Armstrang,
And a subject of yours, my liege,' said he.

'Away, away, thou traitor strang!
Out o' my sight soon may'st thou be!
I grantit niver a traitor's life,
And now I'll not begin wi' thee.'

'Grant me my life, my liege, my King!
And a bonny gift I'll gie to thee –
Full four and twenty milk-white steids,
Were a' foaled in ae year to me.

I'll gie thee a' these milk-white steids,
That prance and nicker at a speir;
And as mickle gude Inglish gilt,
As four o' their braid backs dow bear.'

'Away, away, thou traitor strang!
Out o' my sight soon may'st thou be!
I grantit niver a traitor's life,
And now I'll not begin wi' thee!'

'Grant me my life, my liege, my King!
And a bonny gift I'll gie to thee –
Gude four and twenty ganging mills,
That gang thro' a' the yeir to me.

These four and twenty mills complete,
Sall gang for thee thro' a' the yeir;
And as mickle of gude reid wheit,
As a' their happens dow to bear.'

'Away, away, thou traitor strang!
Out o' my sight soon may'st thou be!
I grantit niver a traitor's life,
And now I'll not begin wi' thee!'

'Grant me my life, my liege, my King!
And a great gift I'll gie to thee –
Bauld four-and-twenty sisters' sons,
Sall for thee fecht, tho' a' should flee!'

'Away, away, thou traitor strang!
Out o' my sight soon may'st thou be!
I grantit niver a traitor's life,
And now I'll not begin wi' thee!'

'Grant me my life, my liege, my King!
And a brave gift I'll gie to thee –
All between heir and Newcastle town
Sall pay their yearly rent to thee.'

'Away, away, thou traitor strang!
Out o' my sight soon may'st thou be!
I grantit niver a traitor's life,
And now I'll not begin wi' thee!'

'Ye lied, ye lied, now, King,' he says,
'Altho' a King and Prince ye be!
For I've luved naething in my life,
I weel dare say it, but honesty –

Save a fat horse, and a fair woman,
Twa bonny dogs to kill a deir;
But England suld have found me meal and mault,
Gif I had lived this hundred yeir!

Sche suld have found me meal and mault,
And beef and mutton in a' plentie;
But nevir a Scots wyfe could have said,
That e'er I skaith'd her a puir flee.

To seik het water beneith cauld ice,
Surely it is a greit folie –
I have asked grace at a graceless face,
But there is nane for my men and me!

But had I kenn'd ere I cam frae hame,
How thou unkind wadst been to me!
I wad have keepit the border side,
In spite of all thy force and thee.

Wist England's King that I was ta'en,
O gin a blythe man he wad be!
For anes I slew his sister's son,
And on his breist bane brak a trie.'

John wore a girdle about his middle,
Imbroidered ower wi' burning gold,
Bespangled wi' the same metal;
Maist beautiful was to behold.

There hang nine targats at Johnie's hat.
And ilk ane worth three hundred pound –
'What wants that knave that a King suld have,
But the sword of honour and the crown!'

'O whair got thou these targats, Johnie,
That blink sae brawly abune thy brie?'
'I gat them in the field fechting,
Where, cruel King, thou durst not be.

Had I my horse, and harness gude,
And riding as I wont to be,
It suld have been tald this hundred yeir,
This meeting of my King and me!

God be with thee, Kirsty, my brother!
Lang live thou laird of Mangertoun!
Lang may'st thou live on the border syde,
Ere thou see thy brother ride up and down!

And God be with thee, Kirsty, my son,
Where thou sits on thy nurse's knee!
But thou live this hundred yeir,
Thy father's better thou'lt nevir be.

Farewell! my bonny Gilnock hall,
Where on Esk side thou standest stout!
Gig I had lived but seven yeirs mair,
I wad hae gilt thee round about.'

John murdered was at Carlinrigg,
And all his gallant cumpanie;
But Scotland's heart was ne'er sae wae,
To see sae mony brave men die –

Because they saved their countrey deir,
Frae Englishmen! Nane were sae bauld
While Johnie lived on the border syde,
Nane of them durst cum neir his hauld.

Kinmont Willie

O have ye na heard o' the fause Sakelde?
O have ye na heard o' the keen Lord Scroope?
How they hae ta'en bauld Kinmont Willie,
On Haribee to hang him up?

Had Willie had but twenty men,
But twenty men as stout as he,
Fause Sakelde had never the Kinmont ta'en,
Wi' eight score in his cumpanie.

They band his legs beneath the steed,
They tied his hands behind his back;
They guarded him, fivesome on each side,
And they brought him ower the Liddel-rack.

They led him thro' the Liddel-rack,
And also thro' the Carlisle sands;
They brought him to Carlisle castell,
To be at my Lord Scroope's commands.

'My hands are tied, but my tongue is free,
And whae will dare this deed avow?
Or answer by the border law?
Or answer to the bauld Buccleuch!'

'Now baud thy tongue, thou rank reiver!
There's never a Scot shall set ye free:
Before ye cross my castle yate,
I trow ye shall take farewell o' me.'

'Fear na ye that, my lord,' quo' Willie:
'By the faith o' my body, Lord Scroope,' he said,
'I never yet lodged in a hostelrie,
But I paid my lawing before I gaed.'

Now word is gane to the bauld Keeper,
In Branksome Ha', where that he lay,
That Lord Scroope has ta'en the Kinmont Willie,
Between the hours of night and day.

He has ta'en the table wi' his hand,
He garr'd the red wine spring on hie –
'Now Christ's curse on my head,' he said,
'But avenged of Lord Scroope I'll be!

O is my basnet a widow's curch?
Or my lance a wand of the willow tree?
Or my arm a ladye's lilye hand,
That an English lord should lightly me!

And have they ta'en him, Kinmont Willie,
Against the truce of Border tide?
And forgotten that the bauld Buccleuch
Is Keeper here on the Scottish side?

And have they e'en ta'en him, Kinmont Willie,
Withouten either dread or fear?
And forgotten that the bauld Buccleuch
Can back a steed, or shake a spear?

O were there war between the lands,
As well I wot that there is none,
I would slight Carlisle castell high,
Tho' it were builded of marble stone.

I would set that castell in a low,
And sloken it with English blood!
There's nevir a man in Cumberland,
Should ken where Carlisle castell stood.

But since nae war's between the lands,
And there is peace, and peace should be;
I'll neither harm English lad or lass,
And yet the Kinmont freed shall be!'

He has call'd him forty marchmen bauld,
I trow they were of his ain name,
Except Sir Gilbert Elliot, call'd
The laird of Stobs, I mean the same.

He has call'd him forty marchmen bauld,
Were kinsmen to the bauld Buccleuch;
With spur on heel, and splent on spauld,
And gleuves of green, and feathers blue.

There were five and five before them a',
Wi' hunting horns and bugles bright;
And five and five came wi' Buccleuch,
Like warden's men, arrayed for fight:

And five and five, like a mason gang,
That carried the ladders lang and hie;
And five and five, like broken men;
And so they reached the Woodhouselee.

And as we cross'd the Bateable Land,
When to the English side we held,
The first o' men that we met wi',
Whae sould it be but fause Sakelde?

'Where be ye gaun, ye hunters keen?'
Quo' fause Sakelde; 'come tell to me!'
'We go to hunt an English stag,
Has trespassed on the Scots countrie.'

'Where be ye gaun, ye marshal men?'
Quo' fause Sakelde; 'come tell me true!'
'We go to catch a rank reiver,
Has broken faith wi' the bauld Buccleuch.'

'Where are ye gaun, ye mason lads,
Wi' a' your ladders, lang and hie?'
'We gang to herry a corbie's nest,
That wons not far frae Woodhouselee.'

'Where be ye gaun, ye broken men?'
Quo' fause Sakelde; 'come tell to me!'
Now Dickie of Dryhope led that band,
And the nevir a word o' lear had he.

'Why trespass ye on the English side,
Row-footed outlaws, stand!' quo' he;
The nevir a word had Dickie to say,
Sae he thrust the lance through his fause bodie.

Then on we held for Carlisle toun,
And at Staneshaw-bank the Eden we cross'd;
The water was great and meikle of spait,
But the nevir a horse nor man we lost.

And when we reached the Staneshaw-bank,
The wind was rising loud and hie;
And there the laird garr'd leave our steeds,
For fear that they should stamp and nie.

And when we left the Staneshaw-bank,
The wind began full loud to blaw;
But 'twas wind and weet, and fire and sleet,
When we came beneath the castle wa'.

We crept on knees, and held our breath,
Till we placed the ladders against the wa';
And sae ready was Buccleuch himsell
To mount the first, before us a'.

He has ta'en the watchman by the throat,
He flung him down upon the lead –
'Had there not been peace between our land,
Upon the other side thou hadst gaed!' –

'Now sound out, trumpets!' quo' Buccleuch;
'Let's waken Lord Scroope, right merrilie!'
Then loud the warden's trumpet blew –
'O *wha dare meddle wi' me?*'

Then speedilie to work we gaed,
And raised the slogan ane and a',
And cut a hole thro' a sheet of lead,
And so we wan to the castle ha'.

They thought King James and a' his men
Had won the house wi' bow and spear;
It was but twenty Scots and ten,
That put a thousand in sic a stear!

Wi' coulters, and wi' fore-hammers,
We garr'd the bars bang merrilie,
Until we cam to the inner prison,
Where Willie o' Kinmont he did lie.

And when we cam to the lower prison
Where Willie o' Kinmont he did lie –
'O sleep ye, wake ye, Kinmont Willie,
Upon the morn that thou's to die?'

'O I sleep saft, and I wake aft;
Its lang since sleeping was fleyed frae me!
Gie my service back to my wife and bairns,
And a' gude fellows that spier for me.

Then Red Rowan has hente him up,
The starkest man in Teviotdale –
'Abide, abide now, Red Rowan,
Till of my Lord Scroope I take farewell.

Farewell, farewell, my gude Lord Scroope!
My gude Lord Scroope, farewell!' he cried –
'I'll pay you for my lodging maill,
When first we meet on the Border side.'

Then shoulder high, with shout and cry,
We bore him down the ladder lang;
At every stride Red Rowan made,
I wot the Kinmont's airns played clang!

'O mony a time,' quo' Kinmont Willie,
I have ridden horse baith wild and wood;
But a rougher beast than Red Rowan, –
I ween my legs have ne'er bestrode.

And many a time,' quo' Kinmont Willie,
'I've pricked a horse out oure the furs;
But since the day I backed a steed,
I never wore sic cumbrous spurs!'

We scarce had won the Staneshaw-bank,
When a' the Carlisle bells were rung,
And a thousand men, in horse and foot,
Cam wi' the keen Lord Scroope along.

Buccleuch has turned to Eden water,
Even where it flowed frae bank to brim,
And he has plunged in wi' a' his band,
And safely swam them thro' the stream.

He turned him on the other side,
And at Lord Scroope his glove flung he –
'If ye like na my visit in merry England,
In fair Scotland come visit me!'

All sore astonished stood Lord Scroope,
He stood as still as rock of stane;
He scarcely dared to trew his eyes,
When thro' the water they had gane.

'He is either himself a devil frae hell,
Or else his mother a witch maun be;
I wad na have ridden that wan water,
For a' the gowd in Christentie.

The Raid of Reidswire

The seventh of July, the suith to say,
At the Reidswire the tryst was set;
Our wardens they affixed the day,
And, as they promised, so they met.
Alas! that day I'll ne'er forgen!
Was sure sae feard, and then sae faine-
They came theare justice for to gett
Will never green to come again.

Carmichael was our warden then,
He caused the country to conveen;
And the Laird's Wat, that worthie man,
Brought in that sirname weil beseen:
The Armestranges, that aye hae been
A hardie house, but not a hail,
The Elliot's honours to maintaine,
Brought down the lave o' Liddesdale.

Then Tividale came to wi' speid;
The sheriffe brought the Douglas down,
Wi' Cranstane, Gladstain, good at need
Baith Rewle water, and Hawick town.
Beanjeddart bauldly made him boun,
Wi' a' the Turnbills, stronge and stout;
The Rutherfoords, with grit renown,
Convoyed the town of Jedbrugh out.

Of other clans I cannot tell,
Because our warning was not wide –
Be this our folks hae taen the fell,
And planted down palliones there to bide.
We looked down the other side,
And saw come breasting ower the brae,
Wi' Sir John Forster for their guyde,
Full fifteen hundred men and mae.

It grieved him sair, that day, I trow,
Wi' Sir George Hearoune of Schipsydehouse:
Because we were not men enow,
They counted us not worth a louse.
Sir George was gentle, meek, and douse,
But *he* was hail and het as fire;
And yet, for all his cracking crouse,
He rewd the raid o' the Reidswire.

To deal with proud men is but pain;
For either must ye fight or flee,
Or else no answer make again,
But play the beast, and let them be.
It was na wonder he was hie,
Had Tindaill, Reedsdaill, at his hand,
Wi' Cukdaill, Gladsdaill on the lee,
And Hebsrime, and Northumberland

Yett was our meeting meek enough,
Begun wi' merriment and mowes,
And at the brae, aboon the heugh,
The clark sate down to call the rowes
And some for kyne, and some for ewes,
Called in of Dandrie, Hob, and Jock –
We saw, come marching ower the knows,
Five hundred Fennicks in a flock.

With jack and speir, and bows all bent,
And warlike weapons at their will:
Although we were na well content,
Yet be my trouth, we feard no ill.
Some gaed to drink, and some stude still,
And some to cards and dice them sped;
Till on ane Farnstein they fyled a bill,
And he was fugitive and fled.

Carmichael bade them speik out plainlie,
And cloke no cause for ill nor good;
The other, answering him as vainlie,
Began to reckon kin and blood:
He raise, and raxed him where he stood,
And bade him match him with his marrows,
Then Tindaill heard them reasun rude,
And they loot off a flight of arrows.

Then was there nought but bow and speir,
And every man pulled out a brand;
'A Schafton and a Fenwick' thare:
Gude Symington was slain frae hand.
The Scotsmen cried on other to stand,
Frae time they saw John Robson slain –
What should they cry? the King's command
Could cause no cowards turn again.

Up rose the laird to red the cumber,
Which would not be for all his boast
What could we doe with sic a number?
Fyve thousand men into a host.
Then Henry Purdie proved his cost,
And very narrowlie had mischiefed him,
And there we had our warden lost,
Wert not the grit God he relieved him.

Another throw the breiks him bair,
Whill flatlies to the ground he fell:
Than thought I weel we had lost him there,
Into my stomack it struck a knell!
Yet up he raise the treuth to tell ye,
And laid about him dints full dour;
His horsemen they raid sturdily,
And stude about him in the stoure.

Then raise the slogan with ane shout –
'Fy Tindaill to it! Jedbrugh's here!'
I trow he was not half sae stout,
But anis his stomach was asteir.
With gun and genzie, bow and speir,
Men might see mony a cracked crown!
But up amang the merchant geir,
They were as busy as we were down.

The swallow tail frae tackles flew,
Five hundreth flain into a flight,
But we had pestelets anow,
And shot among them as we might.
With help of God the game gaed right,
Frae time the foremost of them fell;
Then ower the know, without goodnight,
They ran with mony a shout and yell.

But after they had turned backs,
Yet Tindaill men they turned again;
And had not been the merchant packs,
There had been mae of Scotland slain.
But, Jesu! if the folks were fain
To put the bussing on their thies;
And so they fled, wi' a' their main,
Down ower the brae, like clogged bees.

Sir Francis Russell ta'en was there,
And hurt, as we hear men rehearse;
Proud Wallinton was wounded sair,
Albeit he be a Fennick fierce.
But if ye wald a souldier search,
Among them a' were ta'en that night,
Was nane sae wordie to put in verse,
As Collingwood, that courteous knight.

Young Henry Schafton, he is hurt;
A souldier shot him wi' a bow:
Scotland has cause to mak great sturt,
For laiming of the laird of Mow.
The Laird's Wat did weel, indeed;
His friends stood stoutlie by himsel',
With little Gladstain, gude in need,
For Gretein kend na gude be ill.

The Sheriffe wanted not gude will,
Howbeit he might not fight so fast;
Beanjeddart, Hundlie, and Hunthill,
Three, on they laid weel at the last.
Except the horsemen of the guard,
I could put men to availe,
None stoutlier stood out for their laird
Nor did the lads of Liddisdail.

But little harness had we there;
But auld Badreule had on a jack,
And did right weel, I you declare,
With all his Turrnbills at his back.
Gude Edderstane was not to lack,
Nor Kirktoun; Newton, noble men!
Thirs all the specials I of speake,
By others that I could not ken.

Who did invent that day of play,
We need not fear to find him soon;
For Sir John Forster, I dare well say,
Made us this noisome afternoon.
Not that I speak preceislie out,
That he supposed it would be perril;
But pride, and breaking out of feuid,
Garr'd Tindaill lads begin the quarrel.

Appendix 2

The Names

There were many reiver surnames, great and small. Some repeat endlessly down the decades, others are mentioned only once or twice. All of them are listed below. Alliances shifted and some families gave up land in one place (or were moved) to settle in another. Others were represented on both sides of the border. Here is an alphabetical list of all who were involved in the riding times and in brackets are the principal locations of the name.

Aglionby (North Cumbria)
Anderson (North Northumberland)
Armstrong (Liddesdale, Annandale, Eskdale and North Cumbria)
Beattie (also Batey, Bateson, Dumfriesshire)
Bell (Annandale, North Cumbria, North Northumberland)
Bromfield (Berwickshire)
Burn (also Bourne, Teviotdale)
Carleton (also Charlton, Tynedale and North Cumbria)
Carmichael (Dumfriesshire)
Carnaby (North Northumberland)
Carruthers (Dumfriesshire)
Collingwood (North Northumberland)
Cranston (Teviotdale and Berwickshire)
Craw (Berwickshire)
Crichton (Dumfriesshire)
Croser (also Crozier, Liddesdale and Teviotdale)
Curwen (North Cumbria)
Dacre (North Cumbria)
Dalgleish (Berwickshire)
Davison (also Davidson, Teviotdale)
Dickson (also Dixon, Roxburghshire and Berwickshire)

Dodd (Tynedale)
Douglas (Liddesdale and Dumfriesshire)
Dunne (North Northumberland)
Elliot (Liddesdale, Ewesdale, Teviotdale)
Fenwick (Tynedale, North Northumberland)
Forster (North Northumberland)
Gilchrist (Teviotdale)
Glendinning (Dumfriesshire)
Graham (North Cumbria and Dumfriesshire)
Gray (North Northumberland)
Hall (Liddesdale, Teviotdale, Redesdale)
Harden (North Cumbria)
Hedley (Redesdale)
Henderson (Liddesdale)
Heron (North Northumberland)
Hetherington (North Cumbria)
Hodgson (North Cumbria)
Hume (Berwickshire)
Hunter (Liddesdale)
Irvine (Annandale and Eskdale)
Jamieson (North Northumberland)
Jardine (Dumfriesshire)
Johnstone (Dumfriesshire)
Kerr (Roxburghshire)
Laidlaw (Liddesdale)
Lilburn (North Northumberland)
Lisle (Dumfriesshire)
Little (Dumfriesshire)
Lowther (North Cumbria)
Maxwell (Dumfriesshire)
Medford (North Northumberland)
Milburn (Tynedale)
Moffat (Dumfriesshire)
Musgrave (North Cumbria)
Nixon (Liddesdale, North Cumbria)
Noble (North Cumbria)
Ogle (North Northumberland)
Oliver (Teviotdale)
Percy (Northumberland)
Potts (North Northumberland)

Pringle (Roxburghshire)
Read (Redesdale)
Redpath (Berwickshire)
Ridley (North Northumberland)
Robson (Tynedale, Liddesdale, Teviotdale)
Routledge (North Cumbria)
Rutherford (Roxburghshire)
Salkeld (North Cumbria)
Scott (Teviotdale, Ewesdale)
Selby (North Northumberland)
Shafto (North Northumberland)
Stamper (North Northumberland)
Stapleton (Tynedale)
Stokoe (North Northumberland)
Storey (Eskdale, North Northumberland)
Tailor (North Cumbria)
Tait (Roxburghshire)
Thomson (Liddesdale, North Northumberland)
Trotter (Berwickshire)
Turnbull (Roxburghshire)
Turner (Liddesdale)
Wilkinson (North Northumberland)
Woodrington (North Northumberland)
Yarrow (Tynedale)
Young (Teviotdale)

Appendix 3

Kings and Queens

Even as late as the sixteenth century regnal years were often preferred to the modern system of AD dating. That is, 1510 was counted as the twenty-second year of the reign of James IV, rather than 1510. For that reason and the confusing fact that both the Stewarts and the Tudors were fond of repeating the same Christian names, here is a short but handy list of English and Scottish sovereigns in the sixteenth century:

English
Henry VII: 1485 to 1509
Henry VIII: 1513 to 1547
Edward VI: 1547 to 1553
Mary I: 1553 to 1558
Elizabeth I: 1558 to 1603
James VI and I: 1603 to 1625

Scottish
James IV: 1488 to 1513
James V: 1513 to 1542
Mary I: 1542 to 1567
James VI: 1567 to 1625

Appendix 4

How the Ferniehurst Kerrs Stopped Reiving and Became Part of the British Establishment

Sir Thomas Kerr of Ferniehurst remained a catholic until his death in 1585. His son, *Andrew*, became Provost of Jedburgh and was created the *first Lord Jedburgh* in 1621. Sir Thomas' cousin, *William Kerr of Ancrum*, really advanced the family's fortunes out of a local context when he sent his son to join the large band of Scotsmen on the make which followed James VI and I to London in 1603. *Robert Kerr of Ancrum* was elevated to the *earldom of Ancrum* and became *MP for Aylesbury* in 1625. After the Civil War he was exiled to Holland where he died in 1655. His son, *William*, managed the shifting politics of Cromwell's Commonwealth very adroitly. Supporting the Covenanting cause, he became the *third Earl of Lothian*. Promotion came for his successor, *Robert, the first Marquis of Lothian* in 1701. He also inherited the Ancrum title from his uncle and became Chief of the Name. Five *Williams* followed as Marquises. They lived at Newbattle Abbey near Edinburgh and managed always to choose the right political options. *William, the fourth Marquis*, brought his own regiment, Kerr's Horse (of course), to fight in the government army at Culloden in 1746. His grandson, also William, caused the monument on Penielheugh to be built. Visible from almost everywhere in the central Borders, it commemorates the Duke of Wellington's victory at Waterloo. In the nineteenth century Marquises of Lothian sat as MPs and also developed an impressive habit of winning double firsts at Oxford University. *Schomberg, ninth Marquis of Lothian*, not only sported a Christian name which would have baffled his reiving ancestors, he was also one of the first Secretaries of State for Scotland, in office from 1887 to 1892. Having established Monteviot House, near Jedburgh, as their principal residence, the Kerrs continued to be involved in politics with *Philip, the eleventh Marquis*, being appointed to the key post of Ambassador to the USA from 1939 to 1941. His son, Peter, became a minister in three Conservative administrations. And his son, known as *Michael Ancrum*, is also a prominent Conservative politician, and like the first Earl, sits for an English constituency. It is a very far cry from Ferniehurst, but a remarkable story of making and taking opportunities.

Appendix 5

The Common Riding Year

Since the timing of the Border Common Ridings follows ancient rubrics such as 'the first Friday after the second Monday in June', it is wise not to attach specific dates. Here is the time-honoured sequence:

June

* Hawick Common Riding
* Selkirk Common Riding
* Peebles Festival
* Melrose Festival
* Braw Lads Gathering at Galashiels

July

* Jethart Callants Festival
* Duns Reivers' Week
* Kelso Civic Week
* St Ronan's Festival Innerleithen
* Langholm Common Riding

August

* Coldstream Civic Week
* Lauder Common Riding

Bibliography

Most historians list vast bibliographies, almost like battle honours. I have spent years writing Border history but instead of showing off and noting everything I have read, here is a very select bibliography, something for those who really do want to read further:

Armstrong, P. *Otterburn 1388*, Ospey, Oxford 2006

Bates, Cadwallader J. *History of Northumberland London* 1895

Barr, N. *Flodden*, Tempus, Stroud 2003

Bogle, K.R. *Scotland's Common Ridings* Tempus, Stroud 2004

Burnett, J. *Riot, Revelry and Rout* Tuckwell Press, East Linton 2000

Davies, N. *Europe – A History* Oxford University Press, Oxford 1996

Douglas, Sir G. *Roxburgh, Selkirk and Peebles* 1894

Durham, K. and MacBride, A. *The Border Reivers* Osprey, Oxford 1995

Fraser, A.F. *The Native Horses of Scotland* John Donald, Edinburgh 1987

Fraser, G. MacDonald *The Steel Bonnets* Barrie and Jenkins, London 1971

Lynch, M. *Scotland – A New History* Century, London 1991

McCulloch, A. *Galloway* Birlinn, Edinburgh 2000

Macdonald, A. *Border Bloodshed* Tuckwell Press, East Linton 2000

MacIvor, I. *A Fortified Frontier* Tempus, Stroud 2001

Marsden. J. *The Illustrated Border Ballads* Macmillan, London 1990

Meikle, M.M. *A British Frontier?* Tuckwell Press, East Linton 2004

Miles, D. *The Tribes of Britain* Weidenfeld and Nicolson, London 2005

Moffat, A. *The Borders* Birlinn, Edinburgh 2007

Nicholson, R. *Scotland, the Later Middle Ages* Oliver & Boyd, Edinburgh 1974

Ridpath, G. *Border History* Berwick 1848

Robson M. *Ride with the Moonlight* Newcastleton 1987

Scott, S. and Duncan, C. *Return of the Black Death* Wiley, Chichester 2005

Sprott, G. *Farming* National Museums of Edinburgh, Edinburgh 1999

Tabraham, C. *Smailholm Tower* Historic Scotland, Edinburgh 1993

Tough D.L.W. *The Last Years of a Frontier* Oxford University Press, Oxford 1928

Watson, G. *The Border Reivers* Hale, London 1974

Winchester, A.J.L. *The Harvest of the Hills* Edinburgh University Press, Edinburgh 2000

Index

NOTE: References to families are placed before references to individuals carrying that surname. A page number followed by 'box' indicates that the item will be found in a box on the given page.

BIRLINN LTD (incorporating John Donald and Polygon) is one of Scotland's leading publishers with over four hundred titles in print. Should you wish to be put on our catalogue mailing list **contact**:

Catalogue Request
Birlinn Ltd
West Newington House
10 Newington Road
Edinburgh EH9 1QS
Scotland, UK

Tel: + 44 (0) 131 668 4371
Fax: + 44 (0) 131 668 4466
e-mail: info@birlinn.co.uk

Postage and packing is free within the UK. For overseas orders, postage and packing (airmail) will be charged at 30% of the total order value.

For more information, or to order online, visit our website at **www.birlinn.co.uk**

Birlinn Limited
IMPRINTS: JOHN DONALD · POLYGON